# THE NIGHT OF BROKEN GLASS

# THE NIGHT OF BROKEN GLASS

## EYEWITNESS ACCOUNTS
## OF KRISTALLNACHT

Edited by Uta Gerhardt and Thomas Karlauf

Translated by Robet Simmons and Nick Somers

polity

First published in German as *Nie mehr zurück in dieses Land* © Ullstein Buchverlage GmbH, Berlin. Published in 2009 by Propyläen Verlag

This English edition © Polity Press, 2012

The translation of this work was funded by Geisteswissenschaften International – Translation Funding for Humanities and Social Sciences from Germany, a joint initiative of the Fritz Thyssen Foundation, the German Federal Foreign Office, the collecting society VG WORT and the Börsenverein des Deutschen Buchhandels (German Publishers & Booksellers Association).

Polity Press
65 Bridge Street
Cambridge CB2 1UR, UK

Polity Press
350 Main Street
Malden, MA 02148, USA

ISBN-13: 978-0-7456-5084-5

A catalogue record for this book is available from the British Library.

Typeset in 10.5 on 12 pt Sabon
by Toppan Best-set Premedia Limited
Printed and bound in USA by Edwards Brothers, Inc.

For further information on Polity, visit our website: www.politybooks.com

# CONTENTS

# CONTENTS

# EDITORIAL NOTE AND ACKNOWLEDGEMENTS

In August 1939, Harvard University organized a prize competition with the title 'My Life in Germany Before and After 30 January 1933', for which more than 250 submissions were received from all over the world. The bundle of documents has been preserved since 1958 in the Houghton Library at Harvard in 25 boxes under the signature bMS Ger 91; the alphabetical list of the 263 authors can be viewed at http://oasis.lib.harvard.edu/oasis/deliver/~hou01275. In 1940, Edward Hartshorne, one of the three initiators of the competition, made a selection from the reports on the November pogroms to which he gave the title *Nazi Madness: November 1938*. This work was not published; the plan did not advance beyond editorial preliminaries. The bundle of documents was, however, preserved among Hartshorne's papers.

Of the 34 manuscripts that Hartshorne chose from this more limited group, the editors have selected 21. Not included are 13 shorter, purely descriptive, texts ranging from one to nine pages in length. These are extracts from the recollections of Elisabeth Braasch (Harvard file 35), Ernest Frank (66), Benno Kastan (104), Kurt Meissner (154), Mara Oppenheimer (171), Margarete Steiner (226) and Annemarie Wolfram (247; with 25 pages of the only longer text that was not included here); the authors of six other texts could not be identified, because the excerpts are not attached to names and Hartshorne used the original numbering of 1939–40. No concordance of the original and the Harvard numbering exists that would make a simple correlation possible.

The texts were edited in accordance with the copies Hartshorne had made and compared with the originals. In doing so, it turned out that the secretary, Mrs Wilson, was extremely reliable (misspellings

vii

such as *Xirkusgasse, Tuerkuscher Tempel,* or *Rathaus* instead of *Bethaus* were rare exceptions). Here the editors would like to express special thanks to Professor Dr Detlef Garz. He made available to us the microfilms in the Harvard holdings that were prepared in connection with a research project carried out by the Carl von Ossietzky University in Oldenburg in the second half of the 1990s; the project, led by Detlef Garz, which seeks to make a systematic evaluation of all the reports, has been pursued at the University of Mainz since 2002.

The passages regarding 9 November that Hartshorne chose are for the most part taken from longer reports (Carl Hecht's was the only report he planned to reproduce *in toto,* and even then with the exception of two introductory paragraphs); however, he made no cuts within the selected reports. The editors of this volume have followed the same policy. The Rosenthal manuscript represents an exception; its transcript is found complete in Hartshorne's papers; because its 128 pages would have exceeded this volume's limits, the editors have decided to include only pages 9–51. In the case of the Abraham manuscript, two introductory paragraphs were restored in order to make it easier for the reader to understand; two sentences at the end of the Schwabe and Rodeck manuscripts were omitted because in each case they opened a new subject.

As Hartshorne conceived it, the text would follow the chronology of events and be divided into three parts, each consisting of seven reports.

The name of Herschel Grynszpan (Grynspan, Grünspan, etc.) was standardized, as was that of the legation secretary vom Rath (often given in the manuscripts as *von* Roth) and that of the propaganda minister (often given as Göbbels); acronyms such as NSDAP, SS, SA, etc. were also adapted to the usual form (i.e., without full stops). On the other hand, stylistic peculiarities, including Austrianisms, were retained in the reports from Vienna, along with the occasional use of English expressions (e.g., 'concentration camp'). Excessive use of emphasis by means of the use of underlining, capital letters, and spaced-out words was reduced in the interest of legibility and replaced by italics. Subtitles were retained only when their meaning was made clear by the passages selected. Occasional additions by the editors appear between square brackets.

The numbers given at the beginning of each text correspond to the original 1939–40 numbering with which Hartshorne worked, while the numbers between parentheses refer to the current Harvard numbering. Information in the brief biographies preceding each text is taken from the cover sheets of the originals, from the accompanying letters, and the texts, as well as from the editors' own research. It often proved impossible to discover what happened to the contributors later on, or even their date of death. However, it can be broadly assumed that, with the exception of Siegfried Wolff, who emigrated to Holland and was murdered in Auschwitz in 1944, all the authors survived the war, since they had been able to leave the European continent in time.

The number of footnotes had to be kept to a minimum. Basic information regarding the events of 9 November will be found in the introduction; individual names and contexts are explained only on their first occurrence. The footnotes were produced by Thomas Karlauf. The editors thank the Buchenwald and Sachsenhausen Memorials for information on individual prisoners. The editors owe special thanks to Robin Hartshorne, who made the materials from his father's papers available to us and gave us access to many documents that were used in preparing the afterword. Finally, we would also like to thank Christian Seeger of Propyläen Verlag, who spontaneously supported the project and shepherded it into print with his usual care.

Uta Gerhardt and Thomas Karlauf
Heidelberg and Berlin, June 2009

# FOREWORD

The testimonies to the pogrom of 9 and 10 November 1938 and its sequels, assembled in this volume, describe what the authors deemed to be the height of Nazi barbarism. In reality, these events were but the faintest of preludes to what was about to happen to the Jews in Germany and in occupied Europe. Nonetheless, these reports carry a poignancy of their own that overwhelmingly evokes the suffocating and terror-filled atmosphere of Jewish everyday existence under the Reich during those November days and the immediate pre-war months.

These texts were written one or two years at most after the events and the countless details they relate, often vividly rendered, fit into the overall historical picture that we know so well today. Minor mistakes of interpretation in fact add to the sense of complete authenticity carried by each of these testimonies. They tell of the organized nature of these 'outbursts of popular anger', of the relentless and thuggish savagery of the SA, SS and Hitler Youth involved in the orgy of destruction and humiliation; they tell of the sheer perversity of the perpetrators and of their inventiveness: an old lady, for example, forced under SA supervision, hammer in hand, to herself destroy all the precious objects in her apartment; and much worse of course. But many of the witnesses also stress that Germans in different walks of life appeared embarrassed by the savagery of the regime and, at times, did not hesitate to express their empathy for the suffering of their Jewish neighbours. The voices of some of these German supporters (Marie Kahle and her family, among others) are included in the volume.

A few of the narratives offer lighter moments in the midst of the overall gloom. For instance, one cannot but be pleased in imagining the adventurous escape of Rudolf Bing and his wife from their house in Nuremberg as they slid down from their bedroom window on tied sheets while the mob was breaking down their front door. Generally, however, the narratives dwell on quite different scenes: the groups of Jews huddled in the waiting-room of the Berlin Bahnhof am Zoo, because these railway-station waiting-rooms remained some of the rare public places to which access was not yet forbidden to Jews; the endless queues of Jewish women in front of foreign consulates, as male Jews in their tens of thousands had been arrested and shipped off to camps – Buchenwald, Sachsenhausen and Dachau. Much has been written about camp existence, even during the pre-war period, yet the wave of sudden arrests of Jews, about 40,000 of them, created new and unexpected conditions in which the sadism of the SS guards found an ideal outlet. The constant beatings for every and any reason, the hours-long roll-calls in freezing weather, the repeated 'exercises', which on each occasion left a few of the old and sick inmates dead, the cramped barracks, the lack of food, the torturing thirst and the one constant fixation: How fast would getting a visa lead to release from the camp and allow quick departure from the country?

At times, a few inmates themselves drifted towards very problematic choices. Thus, Kurt Lederer, a Viennese physician, arrested and sent to Buchenwald before November 1938, improvised a small 'subcamp' in one of the buildings, in which, with the help of the camp authorities, he kept mentally ill inmates to avoid additional chaos among the prisoners; at one point, he was in charge of 150–60 people. As controlling the mentally ill without adequate medicine became increasingly difficult, one of the SS guards offered help: the physician could choose twenty of the most difficult cases and hand them over. He did. Ultimately, some thirty-five patients disappeared: they were 'killed in the bunker'. Did the physician foresee this outcome? Thus, even in these early testimonies, we at times approach that 'grey zone' which Primo Levi described many decades later when reflecting on human behaviour in the death camps.

In this volume, over and above the bare facts, readers will discover an extraordinary array of details about Jewish attitudes, perceptions, and reactions during these fateful months. They will grasp a wealth of aspects defining the atmosphere that suffused the world of central European Jewry in the penultimate phase of its existence, moments before its final doom.

Saul Friedländer

# INTRODUCTION: 'THUS ENDED MY LIFE IN GERMANY'[1]

## Thomas Karlauf

### 9 November 1938

At about 9.30 on the morning of 7 November 1938 Herschel Gryn-szpan, a 17-year-old Polish Jew, entered the Hôtel de Beauharnais at 78 rue de Lille, which had since 1814 been the site of the Prussian, later the German, embassy in Paris. The porter's wife was the first person he met in the courtyard. He said he had an important document to deliver and wanted to speak to an embassy secretary. Frau Mathes directed him to the corresponding door. Grynszpan rang and repeated his business to the aide who opened the door. After he had sat for a short time in the waiting room, he was shown into the office of the legation secretary, Ernst vom Rath.

A few minutes later the aide heard loud cries. He raced back and found the legation secretary lying wounded in the corridor. While two of his colleagues saw to the wounded man, the aide led away the assassin, who had put down his revolver and put up no resistance, and handed him over to the police officer posted in front of the embassy. The severely injured vom Rath was taken to the nearby Alma Clinic, where he was immediately operated on.

Herschel Grynszpan's parents had emigrated from western Russia to Germany in 1911 and settled in Hanover. After the reconstitution of Poland at the end of the First World War, they acquired Polish citizenship, but remained in Hanover, where his father first worked as a tailor and later eked out a living selling junk. In the summer of 1936, when he was fifteen years old, Herschel fled these impoverished conditions and travelled through Belgium to Paris, where he was taken in by one of his father's brothers.

In late October 1938, Grynszpan received terrible news. On 31 March, the Polish government had announced that all Poles who had lived abroad for more than five years would lose their Polish citizenship. New passport regulations were issued to that effect on 30 October. This measure was aimed above all at Polish Jews living in Germany and would have left them stranded there. The Reich Foreign Office sought to prevent this from happening by expelling Polish Jews before the deadline. On 27 and 28 October, the police and the SS arrested about 16,000 Jews throughout the Reich, transported them to a point on the Berlin–Poznan railway line just short of Zbąszyń, and then herded them over the Obra River. The Polish authorities denied them the right to cross the border, so they wandered about for days in the no-man's land between Germany and Poland, in pouring rain and without food or a roof over their heads. Grynszpan's parents were among these deportees.

'My heart bleeds when I think about our tragedy,' Herschel said in a note he left for his uncle on the morning of the assassination. 'I have to protest in such a way that the whole world hears my protest, and that is what I intend to do.'[2] Then he bought a revolver in a gun shop and took the metro to the German embassy. The rumours suggesting that Grynszpan's attack might have had a private motive, since both he and vom Rath frequented homosexual milieus, have no foundation in fact.[3] It was pure chance that Grynszpan was sent to the office of vom Rath, who just happened to be on duty on Mondays.

The following morning, Professor Georg Magnus, the director of the University Surgical Clinic II and his chief physician, Dr Brandt, arrived in Paris. The two doctors, sent as an 'expression of the Führer's sympathy, made a visible impression on Herr vom Rath', wrote the German ambassador, Graf Welczek, in the report that he prepared for the Foreign Office that evening.[4] Vom Rath's condition, which Magnus and Brandt had described in their first bulletin as promising, deteriorated rapidly in the course of the day. Hitler, who by sending his personal physician had shown his unfailing instinct for the explosiveness of a situation, immediately promoted the young diplomat to the rank of Gesandtschaftsrat I. Klasse (legation councillor first-class), two floors up, even though he had only recently been appointed a legation secretary.

Grynszpan's desperate act immediately reminded people of the Gustloff case which had occurred only a few years earlier. On 4 February 1936, David Frankfurter, a medical student, had fired five revolver shots at the Nazi party's regional group leader, Wilhelm Gustloff, in his apartment in Davos, killing him as a protest against Germany's policy regarding Jews. Gustloff's body was transported with great ceremony from Switzerland to Schwerin, where Hitler attended the burial. In his speech, the Führer blamed international Jewry for the crime and described Gustloff as a 'holy martyr' and 'the first genuine martyr for National Socialism abroad'.[5] However, because the Winter Olympic Games were to begin in Garmisch-Partenkirchen two days after Gustloff's assassination, no anti-Jewish reprisals were taken at that time.

In November 1938, there were neither Olympic Games nor foreign powers whose reactions had to be taken into account. On the contrary, after the Munich Agreement, in which the western powers had only five weeks earlier caved in and accepted the transfer of the Sudetenland to the German Reich, the National Socialist regime was more powerful than ever. Many people in Germany were awaiting the opportunity finally to strike and initiate a great, nationwide action against the Jews.

On the basis of the first reports from Paris, the Propaganda Ministry had advised the press to give the assassination 'the greatest attention' and to emphasize that this act 'was certain to have the most serious consequences for Jews in Germany'. On 8 November, the tension was ratcheted up another notch, and the next day the German News Bureau announced that vom Rath was expected to die.[6] In Berlin, 'an oppressive anxiety like that felt before a storm' prevailed that morning, as the journalist Ruth Andreas-Friedrich noted in her diary. When she asked Heinrich Mühsam, a colleague who had been dismissed and whom she had stopped to see on her way to work, whether vom Rath was likely to die, he replied: 'Of course he will die. Otherwise the whole thing would make no sense ... Don't you know that political incidents usually occur only when everything has been prepared down to the last detail?'[7]

When at about 4.30 p.m. on 9 November vom Rath finally succumbed to his injuries, practically the entire state and party leadership had assembled in Munich. On the preceding evening, Hitler had inaugurated the annual commemoration of the failed putsch of 1923 by giving a speech in the Bürgerbräukeller. The programme for 9 November included an 'informal gathering of the NSDAP leadership' at the City Hall, whose concluding high point was to be the swearing-in of new SS units in front of the Feldherrnhalle at midnight. Just how the news of the death of vom Rath – who was now referred to only as an envoy or party member – reached Munich by telephone between 5 p.m. and 6 p.m. is not absolutely clear. What is clear is that at the party leadership's dinner in the Rathaus, Hitler had an intense conversation with Goebbels, who was seated next to him.[8] Immediately afterwards, Hitler surprised the other guests by leaving and having himself driven to his apartment on the Prinzregentenplatz, where he prepared for the midnight ceremony. He obviously considered it more prudent not to be directly connected with the speech that Goebbels was about to deliver.[9] He could count on his propaganda minister. Hitler's preference for blanket verbal authorization, leaving precise intentions open to interpretation, was 'typical of the unstructured and non-formalized style of reaching decisions in the Third Reich'.[10]

At this time Goebbels was on top form. On 10 November, when Ernst vom Rath's life still hung by a thread, Goebbels wrote 'If only we could release the wrath of the people right now', as if he couldn't wait for the diplomat to die.[11] Did the cynical Goebbels really believe in the wrath of the people? Didn't he see it instead as an instrument that had only to be correctly manipulated? An SD memo of January 1937 concerning the situation of Jews in Germany had stated that 'the wrath of the people is the most effective means of depriving Jews of their sense of security. . . . This is all the more comprehensible from a psychological point of view because Jews have learned a great deal from the pogroms of recent centuries and fear nothing more than a hostile mood that can turn against them at any time.'[12] In November 1938, 'the wrath of the people' (*Volkszorn*) was one of Goebbels's favourite expressions. When the right moment comes, he noted on the day after the riots, it would be necessary to 'let things take their course'.[13]

Goebbels knew that by instigating a pogrom he could score points with Hitler. A large-scale action against the Jews would help him, put him once again at the centre of things and strengthen his position (which had been weakened by his affair with the actress Lida Baarova) in the delicate power mechanism of the Third Reich. Among all the Nazi paladins, Goebbels certainly had the keenest ear for Hitler's obsession with driving Jews out of Germany by any means. As they sat cosily with the old guard in Hitler's favourite café the previous evening, discussing 'all possible questions' until 3 a.m., the two of them had probably already arrived at an agreement on their options with regard to the attack in Paris.

In the particular situation of 9 November, Goebbels sensed a unique opportunity to steal a march on his greatest rival, Hermann Göring, who had taken over one office after another and since 1936 had enjoyed enormous power as plenipotentiary for the Four-Year Plan. Göring had recently proven his ruthlessness in the Blomberg–Fritsch affair and in the annexation of Austria; but during the Sudeten crisis of late September, he had for the first time been among those who hesitated and urged caution. Since then his star had been on the decline. Göring had repeatedly spoken out against anti-Jewish demonstrations because they only further aggravated the Reich's economic difficulties, particularly with regard to the currency problem. 'Gentlemen, I have had enough of these demonstrations,' he said indignantly and with his characteristic theatricality during the extraordinary meeting he called two days after the pogroms. 'They do not harm the Jews, but rather me, because as the final authority I am responsible for the entire economy.'[14]

Four years earlier, in the run-up to the Nuremberg party rally where the 'race laws' were promulgated, there had already been conflict between authorities regarding the 'Jewish question'. Under the motto 'This city must become free of Jews (judenfrei)', almost every German community had come up with its own perversities, and the attacks on Jews had been threatening to get out of hand. On 20 August 1935, Hjalmar Schacht, then the Reich's Minister of Economic Affairs, had called a meeting of leaders at which he complained about the 'serious damage to the German economy being done by the exaggerations and excesses of anti-Semitic propaganda'.[15] Consequently, interior minister Wilhelm Frick issued a statement informing regional governments that 'individual actions against Jews . . . must absolutely stop.'[16] However, the head of the Gestapo, Reinhard Heydrich, had already decreed that 'in order to collect information regarding Jews in Germany . . . a Jewish registry should be drawn up.'[17] In the regulations issued in August 1935, three basic tendencies of the November pogroms are already clearly foreshadowed: the centralization of state intervention, the prevention of spontaneous actions and the protection of German economic interests.

All the steps taken served one and the same goal, about which there was general agreement: the Jews had to be expelled. 'Jews have to be expelled from Germany, indeed from Europe as a whole,' Goebbels wrote after a long conversation with Hitler at the end of November 1937. 'It will take a while, but it will and must happen. The Führer has made up his mind on this point.'[18] The question was only in what way this goal could best be achieved without inflicting too much damage on Germans. Moreover, the state and party leadership were confident that in implementing the necessary measures they could count on the support of the population.

At the previously mentioned meeting with the minister for economic affairs in August 1935, Adolf Wagner, the Gauleiter of Munich-Upper Bavaria, acting as the Führer's representative, put on record his view that 80 per cent of the population called for 'a solution to the Jewish question in line with the party's programme; the Reich government has to respond to this demand, otherwise it will suffer a loss of authority.' To reassure other participants in the meeting who were less inclined to take immediate action, he added that 'this need not happen all at once.'[19]

With the annexation of Austria in March 1938, the 'Jewish question' acquired a new dynamic, and suddenly everything had to move very fast. Of the approximately 520,000 Jews who had been living in Germany in 1933, only about 360,000 were still in the country; now there were in addition some 190,000 Austrian Jews (of whom about 170,000 lived in Vienna). The Germans immediately increased the pressure. In a very short time, they not only implemented in Austria all the laws and regulations that had for the past five years made life increasingly difficult for Jews in the Old Reich, but also introduced numerous new rules to coerce the Jews to hand over all their possessions and then leave the country. In the spring of 1938, there were further, even more violent, riots and, in the context of the so-called 'June action', 1,500 Jews were sent to concentration camps. When at the international conference on refugees organized by the United States in Evian in July, all of the thirty-two participating states declared more or less openly that they could not increase their immigration quotas, the German press commented scornfully on the conference's failure and let it be known that, since no other country would accept the Jews, no meddling in the question of how Germans dealt with the 'Jewish problem' would be tolerated. In August, the first Central Office for Jewish Emigration was set up under the direction of Adolf Eichmann.

It was against the background of the stepping-up of anti-Jewish measures in Austria and the successful expulsion of the 16,000 Polish Jews at the end of October, the prestige won in Munich, the inaction by the international community, and also the growing pressure among party members, especially in the ranks of the SA and the Hitler Youth, to finally get rid of the Jews that, on the evening of 9 November, Hitler unleashed his propaganda minister. The fanatical thirty-minute hate speech that Goebbels delivered (and of which no verbatim record has been preserved) before the party bigwigs who had gathered in the great hall of the Munich Rathaus was received, as Goebbels himself noted in his diary, with thunderous applause: 'They all immediately dashed to the telephones. Now the people will act.'[20]

In his speech, Goebbels had made it clear that the Nazi party would have to 'organize and implement' everything, but should not 'outwardly appear to be the instigator of the demonstrations'.[21] The

6

district and local group leaders and SA leaders throughout the Reich were instructed to set the corresponding actions in motion – and these instructions were understood to mean also that 'Jewish blood should flow.'[22] In the meantime, Hitler received the national leader of the SS and the head of the German police in his apartment on Prinzregentenplatz. Himmler was obviously surprised. Although he had himself given an inflammatory anti-Jewish speech to the SS Standarte 'Deutschland' the preceding evening – 'We will force them out with unparalleled ruthlessness'[23] – he found it annoying that Goebbels had been quicker to seize the opportunity and had been able to use the Paris attack to further his own interests. In this awkward situation, Himmler fell back on his position as supreme protector of order: a clever tactic that led to the SS – and in particular the head of the secret police and the SD, Reinhard Heydrich – emerging from the events of November as the great winners. When Heydrich, who had been awakened in his hotel room around 11.30 p.m. so that he could examine reports from the Munich Gestapo, asked how the police and the SS should respond, Hitler told him – on Himmler's advice, according to Ian Kershaw[24] – that the SS should keep out of it, but that the police should ensure that the pogrom was carried out in an orderly way.

Heydrich did not have much time to transform his orders into specific actions. His telegraph to all police chiefs, which went out around 1.20 a.m. – 'Flash, urgent, pass on immediately!' – was completely unambiguous. The police forces received orders not to hinder the 'demonstrations' likely to occur throughout the Reich, and to intervene only if German property was endangered. 'Businesses and apartments belonging to Jews are only to be destroyed, not plundered.' The police actions were to be led by the local state police departments or by security police inspectors, who were also expected to see to it that 'as soon as the events of this night allow the use of the regular officials', as many Jews as 'could be accommodated in the available holding cells' were immediately arrested. At first, only male Jews who were healthy, not too old, and if possible, wealthy, were to be arrested and transported to the concentration camps concerned after consultation with camp officials.[25] Barely 64 hours had passed since the shooting in Paris.

On the morning of 10 November, synagogues all over Germany were put to the torch. The fire brigade was allowed to intervene only if the fires threatened to spread to neighbouring buildings. Thousands of apartments were demolished during that night, and thousands of Jewish businesses were smashed to bits in the course of the following day. The broken glass that piled up in the streets gave the night the ironically euphemistic name of *Kristallnacht*, 'the night of broken glass'. It is estimated that 400 people were murdered or driven to suicide. About 40,000 Jews were arrested, and 30,000 of them were sent to Dachau, Buchenwald or Sachsenhausen,[26] where they were subjected to the cruellest harassment. Those who were lucky enough to be able to prove that they had the necessary visas and were about to emigrate were released; the number of Jews who died in concentration camps as a result of the 'November action' is estimated to be about 1,000. Whereas in the first half of 1938 only about 14,000 Jews had emigrated from Germany, the number of emigrants now rose dramatically. By the end of 1939, about 100,000 Jews had left Germany, and another 100,000 had left Austria. Most of those who remained were poor or old.

During lunch in the Osteria in the Schwabing area of Munich, Goebbels gave the Führer a report. 'He approves of everything. His views are very radical and aggressive.'[27] Others were less enthusiastic; Göring, who had travelled back from Berlin the previous night and had not been informed, telephoned Hitler to complain about the enormous economic damage that had been incurred. While Goebbels was busy winding down the actions before 'mob rule took over'[28] and instructing the press to play down the events – 'no big headlines on page one, no pictures for the time being'[29] – Göring was preparing for the Saturday morning meeting, at which the next steps to be taken against the Jews were to be coordinated with account taken of economic considerations. The declared goal of the 12 November meeting, which lasted several hours and in which representatives of all the departments concerned participated – over a hundred persons from the interior, finance, economic affairs and justice ministries, from the Foreign Office, the Reichsbank, and so on – was the complete exclusion of Jews from German economic life. The idea of the new measures was to isolate them and put them under pressure so they would be forced to leave Germany rapidly and in large numbers. Heydrich had had Eichmann specially brought in from Vienna in order to report on his experiences there.

The decisions made on 12 November can once again be traced in essence back to Hitler himself. In 1936, in his memo on the Four-Year Plan, he had already demanded that 'the whole of Jewry be held responsible for all the damage individual examples of this criminality have done to the German economy and thus to the German people'.[30] As retribution for Gustloff's murder, he suggested that Jews be subjected to collective punishment, but at the time this plan was not realized because of bureaucratic reservations expressed by the ministries, and especially because of Göring's concerns. Now Göring took up the idea and on 12 November issued an order to the effect that the Jews, as 'atonement' for their hostile attitude toward the German people, should pay a fine of one billion Reichsmarks. The no less obscene idea that the Jews themselves not only had to see to it that the damage was repaired but also that all monies proceeding from insurance claims were to be confiscated by the Reich was also Hitler's; it occurred to him while he was lunching with Goebbels at the Osteria. Göring implemented this proposal in his own 'Order on the restoration of the appearance of the streets by Jewish businesses'.

Whereas the two speakers at the 12 November meeting, Göring and Goebbels, sought to outdo each other in outlining perverse means of harassment – should Jews continue to be able to walk in German forests? What restrictions should be put on their use of railway sleeping cars? – Heydrich reminded them of the question they were there to discuss. He asked whether, in view of the fact that it would probably be eight or ten years before the last Jews left Germany, it wouldn't make sense to provide them with a special badge. Göring ridiculed this suggestion – 'A uniform!' – and recommended for his part the construction of ghettos, which Heydrich rejected, however, pointing to the impoverishment and criminality to which that would lead. This went on, back and forth, for hours: in its brutality, cynicism and bureaucratic laziness in conceiving regulations whose sole goal was to destroy the lives of hundreds of thousands of people, the record of the meeting on 12 November 1938 was every bit the equal of the Wannsee conference in January 1942.[31]

In the early afternoon, as the meeting was about to end, Göring indulged in a grim prediction of what German Jews could expect: 'If within any foreseeable future the German Reich is involved in some conflict with another nation, it goes without saying that here in Germany we will think first of all of settling accounts with the Jews.' Two and a half months later Hitler, in his notorious, often-cited speech delivered on 30 January 1939, which he later liked to claim was given on the day war broke out, said almost the same thing, but with significantly more aggressiveness and the crucial difference that he then immediately named 'world Jewry' as the instigator of a possible war: 'If international Jewish financiers inside and outside Europe should succeed in plunging nations once again into a world war, then the result will be not the bolshevization of the world and thus the victory of Jewry but rather the annihilation of the Jewish race in Europe.'[32] It was this poisonous symbiosis of madness and calculation that made it possible for the death of a legation secretary to become the pretext for the greatest organized pogrom in modern history.

'I am reminded of what an Aryan in a Düsseldorf cinema experienced,' we read at the end of the memoirs of Harry Kaufman, a young man who was able to emigrate in late 1938. 'It was in 1937, when people were not yet so firmly convinced that Jews were to blame for everything. An insurance company was showing a promotional film about the consequences of a traffic accident. After the accident took place, on the screen there appeared in large letters the question: "And who is to blame for this?" A joker in the cinema shouted: "The Jews!" People laughed so hard that for several minutes you couldn't hear a word.'[33] The mirth in the cinema gives us a good idea of the country's mood on the eve of the pogroms: most people didn't know what to make of anti-Semitic agitation. It probably wouldn't do any harm to reduce somewhat the influence of Jews in economic life, as the government had already been successfully doing for years, and maybe it would actually be best for the Jews to leave Germany, sooner or later. But why this fervour, this strident rabble-rousing? After all, the Nazis' conspiracy theories were sometimes positively ludicrous. The joker in the cinema had put it in a nutshell.

How the November pogroms were received by the German people and to what extent they approved of them is still a subject of controversy. Can the indifference that according to sources characterized the great majority of the population already be seen as an indication of 'passive complicity' (Kulka/Rodrigue), or does the awkward silence point instead to an 'embarrassed distance' (Frank Bajohr)?[34] In endeavouring to arrive at a balanced judgement it should not be forgotten – as Peter Longerich recently emphasized again – that in the Third Reich there was no such thing as public opinion built on the free expression of personal views. Under National Socialism, 'public opinion' always meant 'the public opinion staged, controlled and manipulated by the regime'. In this area, 'in which the guiding principles and interpretive models were reproduced', it was very dangerous to confide one's views to another person unless one was sure that this other person shared them.[35]

As a result, there are few documents that provide reliable answers to the question as to what most Germans thought in November 1938. The government-commissioned reports on the situation and public opinion, including reports made by local offices regarding the success of the measures taken, are sources that have to be evaluated critically, as are the 'Deutschland-Berichte der SOPADE' produced by the lead-

10

ership of the Social Democratic Party in exile in Prague. Although the idealists in exile tended, for understandable reasons, to greatly overestimate Germans' covert resistance to Hitler, we nonetheless have to agree with their general conclusion that 'the riots were strongly condemned by the great majority of the German people.'[36] But this condemnation was nowhere expressed in open protests.

The collection of materials published last year by the Wiener Library made a significant contribution to our understanding of the initial impression from the point of view of the victims.[37] Immediately after the outbreak of the pogroms, the Jewish Central Information Office in Amsterdam had begun to collect all the information it could get its hands on in order to find out exactly what had happened and which Jewish communities were affected in what way by the catastrophe. The exchange of personal communications, names and dates was intended to help put an end to uncertainty concerning the survival of relatives and friends.

At its outset, the present book also reaches back seventy years, but has an entirely different background. On 7 August 1939, nine months after the pogroms, the *New York Times* reported, under the headline 'Prize for Nazi Stories', that scholars at Harvard University were seeking eyewitness accounts of life in Germany before and after 1933 and to this end had organized a competition with prizes totalling one thousand dollars. Anyone who could report, on the basis of his own experiences, on how everyday life had changed after Hitler's seizure of power, was eligible to enter the contest. These reports could be presented anonymously or under a pseudonym, and were to be handled with strict confidentiality – 'but they must be authentic'.

'My Life in Germany Before and After 30 January 1933' – that was the name given the prize competition, and the detailed invitation, written in German, to submit entries which was subsequently distributed all over the world by Jewish information offices and aid associations outlined the project very exactly. The life stories should be about eighty pages long, '*as simple as possible, direct, complete, and vividly recounted*'. Only 'real occurrences' should be described, and therefore anyone who had 'a good memory, a gift for sharp observation and a knowledge of people' could take part, even if he had never written anything before. 'Quotations from *letters, notebooks*, and *other personal writings* give your description the desired *credibility* and *completeness*.' Those who did not win a prize could also be sure that their 'work could be very useful for the study of the new Germany and National Socialism'. The deadline for submissions was 1 April 1940.

11

# PRIZE FOR NAZI STORIES

## Harvard Faculty Men Seek Personal Histories of Experiences

CAMBRIDGE, Mass., Aug. 6.—A $1,000 prize competition for the best unpublished personal life histories of persons who have experienced the effects of National Socialism in Germany was announced today by three members of the Harvard University faculty.

The purpose of the competition, which is open to "all persons who have known Germany well before and since Hitler," is to collect materials which will be used in a study of the social and psychological effects of National Socialism on German society and on the German people.

The Harvard faculty members who are personally sponsoring the competition and who will serve as judges are Dr. Gordon W. Allport, associate professor of psychology, chairman of the Harvard Department of Psychology; Dr. Sidney B. Fay, Professor of History and an authority on German history, and Dr. Edward Y. Hartshorne, instructor in sociology.

The competition awards will be a first prize of $500, second prize of $250, third prize $100, fourth prize $50 and five fifth prizes of $20 each. Manuscripts may be submitted under a pseudonym or anonymously, but they must be authentic, and all papers submitted will be treated as strictly confidential.

Figure 1: Prize advertisement

12

More than 250 manuscripts from all over the world were received in Cambridge. Of these, 155 came from the United States, 96 of them from New York alone; 31 authors gave return addresses in Great Britain, and 20 sent their contributions from Palestine. Six manuscripts were mailed in from Shanghai, the only territory in the world where no visa was required and where a Jewish enclave had therefore rapidly grown up. Moreover, not only Jews who had emigrated from Germany responded to the call. For example, a Silesian confectioner who had been hired as a cook by the merchant navy and who was now confined in a British camp as an 'enemy alien' expressed his enthusiasm for the new Germany, as did an au-pair girl from Berlin who happened to be in America when war broke out – but these texts were exceptions. The great majority of those who submitted reports were Jews who had left Germany and Austria after the pogroms of November 1938.

Most of them had lived in large cities; 61 came from Berlin and 39 from Vienna. The liberal professions, lawyers and doctors, university lecturers and members of the writing community were over-represented; however, in addition to representatives of the wealthy bourgeoisie, salesmen and people who had eked out a living with occasional jobs also wrote contributions. About a quarter of the accounts came from women.

The participants' motives varied as much as the social milieus from which they came. With the first-place prize of 500 dollars, an emigrant could survive for several months in most countries, and more than one participant described winning a prize as his 'last hope'. Others had literary ambitions; even though it was expressly mentioned that this was not a literary contest and that the judges had 'no interest in philosophical considerations', a few complete novel manuscripts were submitted. The organizers helped some of these authors by putting them in contact with publishers and editors; some participants, disappointed that their contributions neither received a prize nor were published, demanded that their work be returned to them. In individual cases, the researchers at Harvard also tried to do something for those who had been interned by the British and transferred to camps in Australia or Canada.

The chief motive of most of the participants was, as the Berlin publicist Wolf Citron put it, 'to say farewell to Germany by working through and recapitulating what was experienced'. No one did so as radically as Moritz Berger, 21, who gave his account the title 'Revenge' and 'dreamed of being a bomber pilot and reducing his home city to ruins'.[38] However, all the accounts agreed that the unrestrained

# $1,000 *Preisausschreiben*

★

## *AN ALLE*

*die Deutschland vor und nach Hitler gut kennen!*

★

Zum Zweck rein wissenschaftlicher Materialsammlung, die für eine Untersuchung der *gesellschaftlichen und seelischen Wirkungen des Nationalsozialismus auf die deutsche Gesellschaft und das deutsche Volk* verwendet werden soll, stellen wir eintausend Dollar als Preis für die *besten unveröffentlichten Lebensbeschreibungen (Autobiographieen)* mit dem folgenden Thema zur Verfügung—

"MEIN LEBEN IN DEUTSCHLAND VOR UND NACH DEM 30. JANUAR 1933"

Das Preisausschreiben steht unter der persönlichen Leitung der folgenden Mitglieder des Lehrkörpers der Universität Harvard, die auch das Preisrichterkollegium bilden werden. Sie tragen die alleinige Verantwortung für die Beurteilung der eingereichten Manuskripte und für die Preisverteilung:

| | |
|---|---|
| GORDON WILLARD ALLPORT | *Psychologe* |
| SIDNEY BRADSHAW FAY | *Historiker* |
| EDWARD YARNALL HARTSHORNE | *Soziologe* |

Die folgenden Preise werden ausgesetzt:

ERSTER PREIS $500     ZWEITER PREIS $250     DRITTER PREIS $100

VIERTER PREIS $50     5 FÜNFTE PREISE JE $20

Manuskripte können unter *einem angenommen Namen oder ohne Namensnennung* eingereicht werden; sie müssen aber *wahrheitsgetreu sein.*

Die Manuskripte können *Deutsch oder Englisch* geschrieben sein: die Wahl der Sprache hat keinen Einfluss auf die Beurteilung. Die Arbeiten können *beliebig lang* sein, sollen aber ein Minimum von 20,000 Worte betragen. ≠ *80 Tippt.*

Das Preisausschreiben schliesst am 1. April 1940. (Manuskripte müssen den Poststempel spätestens dieses Datums tragen.)

Die Arbeiten werden *streng vertraulich* behandelt werden.

## *BESONDERE RICHTLINIEN:*

Manuskripte werden nur angenommen, wenn auf der ersten Seite klar die folgenden Angaben gemacht werden: ALTER (ungefähr) und GESCHLECHT des Verfassers; die GEGEND Deutschlands, in der der Verfasser lebte, und die EINWOHNER-ZAHL SEINES WOHNORTS; die RELIGION des Verfassers, sowie weitere wesentliche Angaben über die GESELLSCHAFT-LICHE STELLUNG des Verfassers in Deutschland (z.B. verheiratet oder ledig, Kinder, ungefähres Einkommen, Ausbildung, usw.) (Ihre gesellschaftliche Stellung als solche hat keinen Einfluss auf Ihre Gewinnaussichten.)

Ihre Lebensbeschreibung sollte möglichst *einfach, unmittelbar, vollständig und anschaulich* gehalten sein. Bitte BESCHREIBEN Sie wirkliche Vorkommnisse, die WORTE und TATEN DER MENSCHEN, soweit erinnerlich. Die Preisrichter haben kein Interesse an philosophischen Erwägungen über die Vergangenheit, sondern vor allem an einem Bericht persönlicher Erlebnisse. Zitate aus *Briefen, Tagebüchern, Notizbüchern,* und *sonstigen persönlichen Schriftstücken* geben Ihrer Schilderung die erwünschte *Glaubwürdigkeit* und *Vollständigkeit.* Dies soll kein literarisches Preisausschreiben sein. Sie sollten sich daran wagen, selbst wenn Sie nie vorher geschrieben haben, wenn Sie nur ein gutes Gedächtnis, scharfe Beobachtungsgabe, und Menschenkenntnis besitzen. Selbst wenn Sie keinen Preis bekommen, kann Ihre Arbeit als Quelle für das Studium des neuen Deutschlands und des Nationalsozialismus sehr wertvoll sein.

*Anschriften erbeten an:*

S. B. FAY, 776 WIDENER LIBRARY, CAMBRIDGE, MASSACHUSETTS, U. S. A.

*Weitere Exemplare dieser Ankündigung* stehen auf Ansuchen gern zur Verfügung.

Figure 2: Competition guidelines

14

brutality of National Socialism on the night of 9 November 1938 represented the greatest breach of civilization in western history, and that it was, for a German Jew, simply unthinkable ever to live in that country again. 'Nie mehr zurück in dieses Land' ('Never back to that country'), wrote the Berlin doctor Hertha Nathorff one week after the pogrom, 'once we have left it alive.' Several authors concluded their memoirs by adopting the prize competition's title, summarizing the irreversibility of the events in the sentence: 'So endete mein Leben in Deutschland' ('So ended my life in Germany').

Most of the contributors had complied with the guidelines and submitted typescripts of 50–100 pages; some sent only 3–5 pages, others thick bundles of several hundred pages. About 12 per cent of the contributions were written in English, and a few were handwritten. The evaluation of the total of more than 10,000 pages was at first very promising. The texts were assessed by research assistants according to a specially designed 19-page schema, and at the same time so-called 'thumbnail summaries' were made. But after the prizes had been awarded, the process came to a halt. This had to do not only with global political developments – on 10 May 1940, five weeks after the submission deadline, the Germans began the war on the western front – but also with the fact that the three initiators of the project – the psychologist Gordon Allport, the historian Sidney Fay and the sociologist Edward Hartshorne – had differing interests.[39]

Hartshorne, the youngest of the three and at the same time the soul of the whole project, was the only one who followed through on it beyond the final report. In August 1941, he sent his publisher, John Farrar, a manuscript that was intended to wake up American readers and bore the working title, 'Nazi Madness: November 1938'. The core of Hartshorne's book was to be a selection of especially impressive descriptions excerpted from the more than 250 autobiographies submitted to the Harvard competition, which he had read through. He was particularly interested in accounts on *Reichskristallnacht* ('The Night of Broken Glass') and the recollections of persons who, in the wake of the riots, had been interned in Buchenwald, Dachau or Sachsenhausen. The example of 9 November, he believed, was particularly well-suited to document the regime's mendacity because it was not, as Goebbels had tried to persuade the world, a 'boiling over of the people's soul', but rather a well-prepared action centrally directed by the Nazi party and the SS.

When Hartshorne entered the American Secret Service (the later OSS) on 1 September 1941, the project came to an end. Through various postings within the American army, Hartshorne came in May

1945 to Marburg as an officer of the occupying forces. On the evening of 28 August 1946, he was the victim of an assassination attack and died from his injuries two days later.

In 1948, Sidney Fay gave the collection of autobiographies that had been submitted in the prize competition in 1939–40 to Harvard's Houghton Library, where they were classified in alphabetical order and numbered 1 to 263; sixteen accounts from this collection have since been published.[40] However, all traces of the book that Hartshorne had prepared for publication in the summer of 1941 were lost. He had studied the text over a period of many weeks and repeatedly rearranged the excerpted passages in an effort to give them the greatest possible impact. In a provisional final version, 'Nazi Madness: November 1938' was to consist of about 500 pages of excerpts from 34 autobiographies. But where was the manuscript?

For over half a century, 'Nazi Madness' lay unnoticed in a cardboard box that grew ever dustier over time and finally ended up in Berkeley, California. In her research on Hartshorne's biography, Uta Gerhardt heard of this bundle of papers in the 1990s; in the summer of 2008, the editors saw it for the first time and prepared it for publication.[41] They are convinced that, on the one hand, the density and authenticity of the carefully elaborated memoirs, and on the other hand, the singular history of their genesis make this collection a document of the greatest importance for modern history.

There is no such thing as non-judgemental memory. The judges in the Harvard competition set the necessary standards and demanded precision and vividness from the authors. It is evident from the texts how difficult it must have been for many writers to describe, objectively and with a steady hand, the atrocious events that had taken place only a year earlier and that had destroyed their material existence and identity as German Jews. But it is not only the immediate proximity of the events that takes our breath away in many passages. Underlying all the accounts is the certainty that Jewish life in Germany came to an end on 9 November 1938. As we now know – and this is the uncanny thing about the texts – this day was in reality a kind of dress rehearsal for the murder of millions of Jews in all parts of German-occupied Europe. These accounts document, as it were, the end *before* the end – and stop for just a moment the turning wheel of history.

# — Part I —

## The Terror

# HUGO MOSES

## Manuscript 39 (159)

*Born in the Rhineland in 1894; employed since 1920 by the Oppen-heim Bank; married, two children; emigrated to the USA in 1939.*

Exactly one year later, the greatest organized pogrom the world has ever seen occurred in Germany. The 1905 pogroms in Russia, the pogroms in Romania and in all the other countries of the world pale in comparison. The latter were only outflows of public opinion and their products, but this one was planned, organized and encouraged by the government. The preceding sufferings, privations, humiliations and horrors cannot be compared with what happened on this single night.

It was the harrowing night of 10 November 1938, when in Germany, in accordance with a very precisely elaborated plan, the homes and shops of Jews were senselessly vandalized, plundered, destroyed and put to the torch. On that night, synagogues and thousands of prayer halls and schools were set on fire at precisely the same time, and fire brigades and police all over Germany were not allowed to leave their quarters unless an express command to that effect had been given. In a single hour on that night, a horde of drunken animals in uniform wrecked the possessions, the past and the future of thousands of people, while bloodthirsty, savage, brutal creatures, decked out in and protected by the brown and black uniforms of the ruling party, slaughtered poor, tormented people in the thousands and sadistically abused thousands of wretched people.

I am going to describe one more time the events of that night, even if some of the details are already known, and even if hundreds of my poor fellow Jews may have suffered still more. I am going to describe them because the memory has still not grown fainter – although in

19

the meantime a year and a half has gone by – and because they were the worst thing that the human mind could have imagined and carried out.

At the beginning of March 1938, all of the Jews in Germany had their passports confiscated. On 27 April 1938, we Jews in Germany who had more than 5,000 marks had to declare our possessions in cash, real estate, jewellery and so on.

In mid-October 1938, I met with a man from Berlin with whom I had had many business dealings, and who I knew had very good connections at the highest levels of the party and the government. Here is exactly what he said to me on that evening: 'If you knew what was going to happen to you, and if you can justify it to your family and your company, get out of Germany as fast as you can. If not with a passport, then try to sneak across the border somewhere. In Berlin, they are preparing to do dreadful things to the Jews.' When I explained to him that I had as yet made no preparations to emigrate and in any case would not leave my family in the lurch, he was astonished and said: 'Soon there won't be a single Jew left here who can or would want to emigrate.'

When I asked him what was actually going on, and he saw my frightened face, he said: 'Give me your word not to say anything to anyone; it could cost me my life. Soon Jews will have to make enormous financial payments; they are going to be housed in ghettos, and Jews up to the age of sixty are going to be put in concentration camps to do forced labour. Barracks for this purpose are being built everywhere. In addition, all the synagogues are to be closed.' I emphasize that I was told this around the middle of October 1938, and the assassination of Herr vom Rath, which the German government claimed was what triggered the Jewish pogroms in November 1938, did not take place until the early days of November 1938. I was very depressed and at home I could not conceal my feelings. My wife, to whom I have always told my joys and concerns, and who shared everything with me in true companionship, saw that I was depressed, and I told her what I knew. So my wife is the living witness to the truth of what I have said.

The abominable and damnable act in Paris had taken place: the Jew Grynszpan had shot the German vom Rath, and the external and probably very welcome excuse for carrying out and stepping up the planned measures against Jews described above had been provided. Everyone in Germany knew and felt that all Jews would have to pay a dreadful price for this act of an irresponsible young man. The occasion for the attack in Paris was the expulsion of all Polish Jews from

Germany. May it also be said here that, since Grynszpan's parents were also affected by this expulsion, the true and perhaps sole reason for his act is to be found in the regime's order.

On a Monday morning in October 1938,[1] the Gestapo suddenly appeared at the homes of all Jews of Polish ancestry in every city in Germany and told them to vacate their apartments within five hours, taking all their moveable goods with them. The unfortunate people packed up the most indispensable of their meagre possessions and gathered, weeping and lamenting, at their assembly points. In the city where I was employed, the poor gathered on the busiest square in the middle of the city. The children had been taken out of school and picked up by officials; hungry, frightened and crying loudly, they ran to their parents. The cordoning officials had great difficulty holding back the excited and shouting people who had gathered around the square. A few Aryan men and women who had expressed their criticisms too loudly were led away. An Aryan doctor took out of the crowd a Polish woman who was about to give birth and accompanied her to the hospital. Two days later the child was born.

The others were led away to the railway station and there loaded onto cattle wagons, and we Jewish men used lorries and cars to help them load their few possessions until our hands were bleeding in the freezing air. A girlfriend of my daughter's later wrote to her from a camp on the Polish border: 'Had the train run off the rails and killed us all, we would have been better off.'

On the evening of 9 November 1938, the SA brown-shirts and the SS black-shirts met in bars to celebrate the fifteenth anniversary of the day of the failed putsch in Munich. Around eleven o'clock in the evening, I came home from a Jewish aid organization meeting and I can testify that most of the 'German people' who a day later the government said were responsible for what happened that night lay peacefully in bed that evening. Everywhere lights had been put out, and nothing suggested that in the following hours such terrible events would take place.

Even the uniformed party members were not in on the plan; the order to destroy Jewish property came shortly before they moved from the bars to the Jewish houses. (I have this information from the brother of an SS man who took an active part in the pogroms.)

At 3 a.m. sharp, someone insistently rang at the door to my apartment. I went to the window and saw that the streetlights had been turned off. Nonetheless, I could make out a transport vehicle out of which emerged about twenty uniformed men. I recognized only one of them, a man who served as the leader; the rest came from other localities and cities and were distributed over the district in accordance with marching orders. I called out to my wife: 'Don't be afraid, they are party men; please keep calm.' Then I went to the door in my pyjamas and opened it.

A wave of alcohol hit me, and the mob forced its way into the house. A leader pushed by me and yanked the telephone off the wall. A leader of the SS men, green-faced with drunkenness, cocked his revolver as I watched and then held it to my forehead and slurred: 'Do you know why we've come here, you swine?' I replied, 'No,' and he went on, 'Because of the outrageous act committed in Paris, for which you are also to blame. If you even try to move, I'll shoot you like a pig.' I kept quiet and stood, my hands behind my back, in the ice-cold draught coming in the open door. An SA man, who must have had a little human feeling, whispered to me: 'Keep still. Don't move.' During all this time and for another twenty minutes, the drunken SS leader fumbled threateningly with his revolver near my forehead. An inadvertent movement on my part or a clumsy one on his and my life would have been over. And if I live to be a hundred, I will never forget that brutish face and those dreadful minutes.

In the meantime, about ten uniformed men had invaded my house. I heard my wife cry: 'What do you want with my children? You'll touch the children over my dead body!' Then I heard only the crashing of overturned furniture, the breaking of glass and the trampling of heavy boots. Weeks later, I was still waking from restless sleep, still hearing that crashing, hammering and striking. We will never forget that night. After about half an hour, which seemed to me an eternity, the brutish drunks left our apartment, shouting and bellowing. The leader blew a whistle and, as his subordinates stumbled past him, fired his revolver close to my head, two shots into the ceiling. I thought my eardrums had burst but I stood there like a wall. (A few hours later I showed a police officer the two bullet holes.) The last SA man who left the building hit me on the head so hard with the walking stick he had used to destroy my pictures that a fortnight later the swelling was still perceptible. As he went out, he shouted at me: 'There you are, you Jewish pig. Have fun.'

My poor wife and the children, trembling with fear, sat weeping on the floor. We no longer had chairs or beds. Luckily, the burning stove was undamaged – otherwise our house would have gone up in flames, as did many others.

Towards dawn, a police officer appeared in order to determine whether there was any damage visible from the outside, such as broken window glass or furniture thrown out into the street. Shaking his head, he said to us, as I showed him the bullet holes from the preceding night: 'It's a disgrace to see all this. It wouldn't have happened if we hadn't had to stay in our barracks.' As he left, the officer said: 'I hope it's the last time this will happen to you.'

The next evening people were afraid that the same thing might happen again. But on that night, the police continually patrolled the streets, especially in the area where there were Jewish houses. A police officer, who was a friend of mine, later told me: 'On the second night, every policeman carried two revolvers. It's too bad that the gang didn't come back.'

Two hours later, another police officer appeared and told me exactly this: 'I'm sorry but I have to arrest you.' I said to him, 'I have never broken the law; tell me why you are arresting me.' The officer: 'I have been ordered to arrest all Jewish men. Don't make it so hard for me, just follow me.' My wife accompanied me to the police station. In front of the door to my house, the officer said to us: 'Please go on ahead, I will follow you at a distance. We don't need to make a spectacle of this.'

At the police station, the officers were almost all nice to us. Only one officer told my wife: 'Go home. You may see your husband again after a few years of forced labour in the concentration camp, if he's still alive.' Another officer, who had been at school with me, said to his comrade: 'Man, don't talk such nonsense.' To my wife he said: 'Just go home now, you'll soon have your husband back.' A few hours later my little boy came to see me again. The experiences of that terrible night and my arrest were too much for the little soul, and he kept weeping and looking at me as if I were about to be shot. The police officer I knew well took the child by the hand and said to me: 'I'll take the child to my office until you are taken away. If the boy saw that, he'd never forget it for the rest of his life.' A last kiss, a last look. When and where will I see my wife, my children and my 75-year-old mother again? What do they want now from us poor, beleaguered, tormented people?

The transportation to the prison in the nearby city took place in the bitter cold in an open car. When we arrived, there were ten of us men, and we were put in a huge cell in which about sixty men were already waiting for us. The air was heavy with the smell of wet clothing and cold, stale food. The first person to greet me was an ophthalmologist whom I knew, along with his son, a small, pale boy who had turned sixteen a week before. Both were wearing pyjamas; they'd been taken out of bed and had not been allowed to get dressed or to say farewell to the wife and mother. Four days later, the child was

23

taken away from the father and transferred, still in his pyjamas and slippers, to the concentration camp in Dachau. The father's pain was hardly bearable. Immediately after I was released, I used all my energy and connections to make it possible for the young man to emigrate, and in that way to save him from the concentration camp, that hell. Four weeks later, the poor parents were able to hold their child in their arms again, and one day later he was in England. The parents are still in Germany . . .

We were in the big cell for three hours as the daylight slowly faded and it grew dark. As if by magic, a light bulb on the ceiling lit up. Then the door opened and a guard led us into the prison courtyard. High walls all around, and high up small, poorly lit and barred windows. Yesterday evening still at home, in the peaceful family circle: this evening everything senselessly destroyed and annihilated and scattered. The women and children amid the ruins and devastation, the men in prison. And nowhere a gleam of salvation, nowhere a ray of hope. Moreover, this was Friday evening, the beginning of the Sabbath . . .

Ten minutes later the high lattice gates closed behind us; we were incarcerated. The next morning the newspaper report said that Jewish men had had to be taken into protective custody 'in order to protect them from the people's wrath'.

Three men were put in each individual cell; we could hardly move. Laughing, the prison guard explained to us: 'We were not expecting such a crowd.' Then there was a dark broth, probably supposed to be coffee, a few slices of bread and a little jam, and the cell door closed again. The first night in prison. Suddenly the light went out and we sat there in the dark. We spread our overcoats on the floor and tried to rest. Sleep was impossible. The hard ground prevented my body from relaxing, my head was tired from brooding and thinking, and my thoughts were at home with my wife and children and my old mother. My heart was agitated by the events of the last twenty-four hours, my thoughts constantly turned around the questions 'Why are you here, how long will it last, what is going to happen to you?'

Every quarter of an hour, the clock in the nearby church tower chimed. If I stood on the table, I could look out over part of the city, which I knew well. A part of the city in which I had worked; good friends of mine used to live not far from the prison. Why, oh God, do you chastise your people? Why must we of all people suffer so much for the name of justice? What have we done wrong?

At six in the morning, the light came back on, as if lit by spectral hands, and a new day began. We had to get up immediately, clean

24

the floor and wash ourselves in a tin basin. We had to relieve ourselves in a tin pail and were very ashamed. At seven o'clock, we had to wash out our vessels in the prison corridor, and then there was coffee. The days were endlessly boring. Smoking and playing cards, if we had cards and something to smoke, were allowed. There were endless conversations about the meaning of everything on earth and about the meaning of everything eternal; never has there been so much philosophizing as among Jewish men in German prisons during these days.

Monday, 14 November 1938, four in the afternoon. A never-ending, dull, rainy day was slowly coming to a close. Then the door opened and we were once again led down to the courtyard. We saw each other for the first time since our arrest. Unrecognizable, these pale, tired, emaciated faces, framed by beards. Big, black eyes that bore within them the suffering of generations, of centuries of torments endured. Eight hundred men in a small prison courtyard, eight hundred innocent men, husbands, sons, fathers and grand-children ... A few Gestapo officers were waiting for us, big fat faces. Importantly, carrying portfolios, they went up and down the front line, well rested, well fed, and in the mood to commit new infamies.

After an hour in the drizzling rain, our clothes stuck to our bodies, we were exhausted, our nerves ready to break. Then we were called up one by one before a row of young Nazi party doctors wearing riding boots and carrying riding whips who glanced fleetingly at our haggard, weary bodies. When it was my turn, I saw an elderly foren-sic doctor I knew, who waved to me and called: 'You will be exam-ined by me.' The young party doctors let me pass, and the elderly doctor examined me very carefully. After a minute, I knew my fate. 'Physically not sufficiently developed for use in the work service.' My knees almost gave way; God had clearly put his hand over me to protect me from worse, for I had escaped the concentration camp by the skin of my teeth. I was hardly able to give the old doctor a grate-ful glance, because it was the turn of the next fellow-sufferer. My two cellmates, both men over sixty, drew the same lot. In this night we slept a little for the first time, although our bodies and our nerves were stretched to the limit.

The days dragged on. Every day consisted of thirteen endless hours from the time the light was turned on to the time it was turned off. Thirteen hours filled with idleness, brooding and reflection, with meaningless talk, with eating and drinking, insofar as we could digest the prison food, with nothing, nothing at all. We heard the noise of the street outside, children playing, the sounds of the large barred building, the doorbell, people going up and down iron stairways, the convicts marching in the prison courtyard, the guards shouting orders, always the same, always the same . . . Great God, how much longer still and why all this, why? From one quarter-hour to the next on the nearby church tower, another day, another evening. How many more days, how many evenings, how many months, how many years?

Wednesday, 16 November 1938, the Day of Prayer and Repentance in Germany. Suddenly, at five in the morning, the light went on, and we got up, thinking our watches were running an hour late. Somehow we vaguely felt that this was a special day. At 5.30, the coffee was handed out before the cells were cleaned. At 6.00, cell doors on the corridor were opened, names were read. The door to our cell remained closed, nobody was paying any attention to us. At 6.15, all the Jews whose names were read appeared in the dark prison courtyard. Jews in overcoats, without overcoats, in pyjamas and slippers. Names were read out by lamplight, names of friends, acquaintances, people, brothers, fellow believers, names, names . . . Then, like a thunderbolt, the truth struck us: they were going to the concentration camp, to the hell from which there is no escape. There is only work and hunger, disease and the sadism of the guards; there is only DEATH, DEATH, DEATH . . .

Under our cell window, those doomed to die were handed over to the police. The names were read once again, then came a command that I will hear until the end of my life: 'Guards on the outside, Jews in the middle. Break step!' Tears rolled down our faces, we did not wipe them away, farewell, you brothers, farewell, you friends, God be with you, you Jewish men, God protect your wives, your children, your mothers, your fiancées, your grandparents. Farewell! Their steps faded slowly away in the gloom of a grey, foggy morning; then again a police officer shouted, and in the distance they were already departing. Slowly the gates of the prison closed again . . .

That is what happened on the morning of Prayer and Repentance Day in all the prisons of Germany, in the year 1938!

Two days later, when I had been ordered to go down the prison corridor to get food, someone put a packet of cigarettes in my hand. A voice whispered: 'From Frau I.' I looked round, but couldn't see anything in the darkness. A hand took me by the shoulder and shoved me onward, and I didn't know where the gift came from. My brain worked feverishly. Then I understood. Frau I. was the wife of a good Aryan acquaintance whom I knew to have connections with the Gestapo. My cellmates regarded the packet of cigarettes like children in front of a Christmas tree. I opened the packet, and out fell a note, written on a typewriter: 'You will be released on Saturday at eleven o'clock. We are all working to get you released. I.'

My head was spinning; I had to sit down. My cellmates saw to me and mopped my face with cold water; my heart was racing. I had to lie down on the straw mattress. Another eighteen hours to go, seventeen, sixteen. The light went out, my cellmates gave me the straw mattress and they bedded down on their overcoats, even though they were twenty years older than I. I lay there and thought, from one quarter-hourly stroke of the clock tower bell to the next. Was it really my last night in prison, the last night away from my wife, children and mother? Did they know that the hour of liberation was approaching? Seven hours more, six hours, dawn broke slowly, the light went on. Got up, cleaned the cell, got coffee, drank coffee, the light went out. A grey, rainy day appeared on the horizon, the sounds in the street began, bells rang in the great, grey building, the lockstep of marching convicts, commands. Three hours to go, two hours . . .

Saturday, 19 November 1938, 10.45 in the morning. Nothing, nothing at all. 10.50, everything was just as it was on other days. I sat spellbound on the prison stool and listened to the sounds in the prison corridor. 10.55, nothing – nothing at all. Was this another sadistic act on the part of a Gestapo officer who knew something about a connection between me and the I. family? My cellmates were looking at me with concern; my face must have been ghostly white.

Eleven o'clock. The door opened, the guard came in and said: 'Hand over your things, order from the Gestapo; you are to be released immediately.' The blood roared in my ears. I could hardly stand up. The officer: 'Move, we still have more to do.' A quick farewell to my cellmates, greetings to their families, the cell door closed behind me. I was in the corridor with the guard. Down the iron stairway to the discharging officer. With a smile on his face he said: 'Go home, now, we don't want you. Not you or the others, either.' The last iron door closed behind me, I was free again.

First to my office. The women co-workers came towards me, tears streaming down their faces, and even the men's eyes were moist. Everybody talking, relating and listening to the stories. Torrents of words. Among other things, I heard that men of the Jewish race who had hidden on 10 and 11 November had not been arrested.

During the train ride home it was obvious that passions were still high about the events of the pogrom night. One man talked about his neighbour, and said: 'Never have I laughed so much as on that night when the Jews danced around their houses. For the first time,

27

I saw the Jewish whores working, when they had to use their slender fingers to pick up the shards of window glass in the street. They bled like pigs.' A second man replied: 'The best came the next morning when the teachers took the schoolchildren to see the Jewish temple and the Jews' homes. We've cleaned them out once again. They showed that our Führer can rely on his boys.' Here the two men got out of the train. I had tears in my eyes and my heart pained me. Oh Germany, Oh fatherland – it was precisely the date on which I had returned, twenty years earlier, from the Great War. Once again I was coming home, but this time from prison, innocent, and again I was a weary, defeated man.

When I had returned home on this day twenty years earlier, my late father had picked me up at the railway station. His joy that his only son had returned uninjured from adversity and death had shown in his face. Relatives and friends were waiting for me, and it was a festive, blessed day. Although at that time I was inwardly upset by the fate of the German people, over the defeat of the German army, in my young heart trust and belief in the future lived on, and I knew that even the severest test and the most difficult time of suffering would some day come to an end.

Today I returned home, my heart full of sadness and despair, full of concern about my family and our future. I felt that, from now on, all was lost, that after these events we could no longer stay in Germany, and that we would have to share the fate of our ancestors: take up our staffs and roam, roam . . .

At home, the damage that could be seen from outside the house had been cleaned up as much as possible. Christian neighbours had lent us a few pieces of furniture so that we could at least eat and sleep. The people in my home town were for the most part very disheartened by what had happened. My wife told me that during the first days a few Aryan women, particularly workers' wives for whom she had earlier done many favours, had come to see her. One woman had wept loudly and said: 'That is now the thanks you get for your love and generosity: it's enough to make one despair of humanity.' Another woman said: 'This is worse than in Russia. The swine who ordered this destruction ought to have their necks wrung.' Under cover of darkness, one of my acquaintances said to me: 'This time it was your temples, the next time it will be our Catholic churches.' (People no longer dared speak with us in broad daylight.)

At Christmas 1938, I received a card and a gift package from a decent old friend who was a Christian. On the card he had written: 'And no matter how long winter endures, spring must come again.'[2]

After 10 November, my children were forbidden to attend secondary school. Since 1933, my daughter had been in a convent school and was treated very well by the Catholic nuns there. When this school was shut down at Easter in 1938 and the large building transformed into a factory, she moved to a high school in the nearby city. Since Easter 1938, my son had been attending the grammar school in another city. Before he was accepted, I visited the headmaster of the school to ask whether he thought it would be wise for me to send my son to his school. This was his answer: 'I am a good Catholic and have been doing this job for more than thirty years. In my school, only ability and knowledge count; the party does not yet control things here. Don't worry, you can send your son here.'

My son, who was then nine years old, was from the outset placed by his teacher on a bench all by himself, while the other children sat two-by-two on their benches. Once, he dropped a pencil on the floor and a classmate tried to pick it up. The teacher shouted: 'Let the Jew pick up his own pencil!' Another time the teacher wanted change for a coin. When it turned out that my son was the only pupil in the class who could give him change, the teacher said scornfully, 'No, I don't touch Jewish money.' My child was not allowed to swim with the others during swimming class, and the teacher said to him in front of the other pupils: 'Go into the Jordan with your flat feet. You are not allowed to contaminate German water.' In class, he was not called upon a single time and his written work was not corrected. Only once, when the class was to write an essay on the theme 'Adolf Hitler, saviour of the German people from the worldwide Jewish plague' did the teacher call to my boy: 'Now let's hear what you've written.' When my son said, correctly, that his father had forbidden him to write this essay, the teacher wanted to have nothing more to do with him. Because of this gem of a teacher, the boy no longer existed in the world. On the other hand, the other teachers were good to him.

When this tormenting of an innocent child became unbearable, I had to make the difficult trip to see the headmaster and tell him what was going on. He said to me: 'This is all news to me and hard to understand. When I inspected the classes a few days ago, the teacher asked your son a question and got a satisfactory answer.' My son confirmed what the director said, and the whole thing bears eloquent testimony to the baseness of the German teacher. The headmaster also said: 'Unfortunately, I cannot take action against the teacher concerned. He is the chairman of the teachers' association, and a protest would cost me my position.'

When Jewish children were forbidden to pursue higher education, my son, who was then ten years old, said to me: 'Father, if you had forced me to continue going to school just a little longer, I would have thrown myself under a train.'[3] My hair stood on end with horror, and a shiver ran down my back. What must have happened in the mind of this boy, how must educators in the new Germany have tormented him that such resolutions could be formed in the heart of an innocent 10-year-old?

In late January 1939, my beloved old mother had a stroke brought on by the distress of the preceding weeks. For three days she lay unconscious before she was fortunate enough to be taken from this world. During these three days, just after it got dark, Aryan men and women visited us in order to enquire about her condition. A Christian woman whom my mother had always supported and whose children she had helped to bring up was with her day and night. This woman said over and over: 'Never did I love my own mother as much as this true and good mother who now lies there so helpless. She was always ready to help me and my family in word and deed, and now we cannot help her. When she dies, I will lose my mother a second time.'

One of this woman's sons, a soldier, came in the evening, in full uniform, even though in Germany soldiers were strictly forbidden to enter Jewish houses, to see how my mother was doing. Tears rolled down his face when he said goodbye to her. 'Never have I so much respected a Jewish woman as I do your mother,' he said. In the evenings, neighbours sent coffee and fruit, even though these treats were by now very rare in Germany, and wished her a prompt recovery. The whole town knew that the old woman lay dying. And yet school-boys leaving school at noon stood in front of the house and sang:

> Now the Jew is
> Finally finished.

Sad German youth . . .

To us mourners, my mother's burial seemed like a dog's burial. The hearse took her to the cemetery. Some twenty Jewish men and women followed at a distance on the pavement, to avoid attracting attention. Aryan acquaintances and neighbours had sent messages saying things like: 'We mourn with you' or 'Our thoughts are with you' or 'We will never forget her.' Within an hour, we were home again, alone with our heavy hearts and thoughts.

When I was in prison after the pogrom night in November, my wife telegrammed her old American uncle in connection with an affidavit.

To tell the truth, up to that point I would have found it very difficult to leave the old homeland and my parents' house, where I had dreamed my youthful dreams and where my two children had grown up. But when I stood in my pyjamas with that drunken vandal holding his revolver to my head on that cold, dreadful night, while other inebriated thugs in brown and black uniforms were destroying my house, I made up my mind. I was going to get out of this country of infamy and disgrace, where people who had never in their lives done anything bad could no longer live and breathe, merely because they were born Jews. Where Jewish children were beaten by others their age, where they were insulted and had stones thrown at them, because they were Jewish children. The poison of persecution, cast like a terrible seed into children's hearts and souls, will inevitably yield a hundredfold harvest that in the end will turn against those who spread this poison. In this country, there can no longer be any place for members of such a people whose first and most noble article of belief is: 'Love thy neighbour as thyself.'

So we prepared to emigrate. The few possessions that we were left with after 10 November were quickly packed. When we had to go to the American consulate in Stuttgart, we found in that city no restaurant or café that did not bear the inscription: 'Jews not welcome here.' Unfortunately, the few places where Jews could find lodging, to which I had first turned, were also full. Late at night, we were lucky enough to find beds in a small inn. When we told the friendly innkeeper we were Jews, she said: 'I don't care. I have not put up the signs. Any decent person who pays for his room and meal can stay in my inn.' When we got our visas the next day, there was no one in that whole city happier than we were.

I spent the last days in Germany saying farewell to the old homeland. With my children I walked in the spring weather the old familiar paths that I had walked so often in the course of four decades, the paths through woods and fields that I had first trodden holding my parents' hands, every tree and house evoking a memory. Never in my life was I to walk those paths again, for we had to rip out of our hearts the memory of almost half a century of our lives.

And this, because a man appeared, the leader of a nation of eighty million people, who declared that a Jew can have no homeland, that Jews are nomadic peoples who belong to Asiatic desert tribes and who must always wander and leave behind them a devastated world . . .

Back to the cemetery, in which four generations of my ancestors rest. The gravestones, overturned four times by the Hitler Youth, had been put more or less straight again. There was the grave of an elderly

31

couple from the neighbouring town, who were well known to us, and who had been murdered by the Nazis on the night of 10 November, bound together with wire and thrown into the river; their bodies had surfaced a few days later. We were assigned to bury the dead, 'but no burial mound must be visible.' We waited at the cemetery for the dead, who were brought there in a cart. We buried both of the old people in the same grave, and we did not make a burial mound.

So rest in peace, beloved ancestors, and may your blessing accompany us in our wanderings. Wherever we are, our thoughts will always be with you, and you will always be with us. We are not leaving your graves behind willingly; we are being driven away. So we put your last resting place in the hand of our God.

A last glance backwards, and then that, too, was past, over.

My children, most of whose lives had been lived in the shadow of these difficult and terrible events, were delighted by the prospect of a sea voyage. Their thoughts were taken up entirely by the ship that was to take them to the new, unknown land, and by the land itself. Their hearts easily embraced the new future; nothing bound them to the land of repression and persecution. In contrast, we adults were leaving the graves of our ancestors, our youth and our childhood behind us. For what had we lived, fought, suffered and striven for almost half a century? For what?

To be sure, we have to forget, we must forget, what lies behind us. But can one just wave away the experiences of half a century of life? May my children, for whose sake we had to leave our homeland behind, succeed in building a new future in the new land. May God bless the country that has welcomed with open arms us poor, stricken people. And yet, I know that the shadows of the past will creep into my dreams. The homeland that I have had to leave in order to escape the death threats of the Nazi gangs, in order to find a new and final homeland, will live on in my memories and dreams, the old paths, the buildings, the mountains, forests and fields. What does the earth of our homeland know about the monstrous products of these hellish fantasies of a savage regime that took from hundreds of thousands of people their freedom, their honour and their lives?

Earth is earth and people remain people.

Our Aryan friends commiserated with us as we made our preparations to leave. They brought us gifts, flowers and good wishes. A few of them said to me: 'Take me with you. Here we're headed for war, and we have no desire to play war again.' Others said: 'You're lucky, we envy you. You're going towards freedom; we're staying here under the rule of violence.'

32

Two Aryan friends accompanied us to the railway station, even though we were leaving at noon. With tears in his eyes, one of them said on the platform: 'Some day we will pick you up here again in triumph.' As the train pulled out, tears were rolling down his cheeks, and for a long time we looked back at them, waving their handkerchiefs. Germany lay behind us.

But not yet; there was still the border to cross. In our compartment sat a Dutch businessman who was returning from the Orient, and a Dutch woman who was coming from South Africa to visit her aged mother in Holland. Half an hour before the border, the door of the compartment opened and an SS man bellowed: 'Any Jews in here?' I identified myself, and there followed an excruciating interrogation regarding the purpose of our trip, an interrogation so nasty that even the foreigners blushed. Among other things, the SS man said: 'If only all you swine had left Germany in 1932.' That was our final farewell from Germany, the last words we heard spoken by a German. The two foreigners had understood every word, and, as the train finally rolled over the border, the Dutch woman said: 'Now be glad: nowhere else in the whole world will you ever hear such words again.'

Some Dutch friends who had often been our guests in Germany met us at the station. They invited us into their home and slowly we overcame our anxiety about appearing in public, our dread at walking down a busy street and saying anything. They showed us pictures of Jewish houses and synagogues that had been burned in Germany, which they had themselves taken in border towns.

The night we left on the spotlessly clean Dutch ship was dark and rainy, and it was hard for us to say goodbye to our friends. A final expression of good wishes, a tearful glance, and we were alone. Two days later we had a last view of the English coast in the brilliant sunshine. Farewell, Europe, adieu, Old World . . .

We passed by the Statue of Liberty in New York harbour on a sunny summer morning. We had found our way to our new home in the land of humanity, in the land of freedom. Like a bad dream, the time of subjugation and deprivation of rights lay behind us. We felt that this country, which welcomed us with open arms, should and must become a new homeland for us poor refugees. We wanted to do everything we could to become good and respected citizens; we wanted and had to forget all the tribulations behind us.

In conclusion, I want to emphasize that every word in my account is the simple truth. Hatred has not guided my pen, only the truth and the courage to tell it. Everything that I had in the way of notes and letters was destroyed or taken away by unfettered beasts on that terrible night. My desk was smashed and senselessly ransacked, and I destroyed the rest so as not to compromise anyone. If I constantly emphasize that with few exceptions my earlier Aryan friends and acquaintances were good and generous to us right up until our departure, that means that in their hearts a large part of the German people did not approve or participate in the anti-Semitic pogrom. Were it otherwise, I could not write these lines today on my way to the land of freedom without concern for the lives of those dear to me. Then those unfortunate fellow Jews who are now still having to maintain their miserable existence in Germany would certainly no longer be alive.

If the majority of the more mature German people had even a fraction of the regime's anti-Semitism, if the pogrom mood into which the German people is whipped up from time to time did not scare off the more rational part of the population, the last Jew would have left Germany long ago. The government agitates and stirs up the people until bloody violence takes place somewhere, and then sanctimoniously declares that this is the 'voice of the people' and that the government has never told anyone to kill even one Jew. This tactic has long since been seen through by everyone. An employee of my tax office who wears the party insignia told me, when this subject came up as I was consulting him about my taxes: 'All this has the mark not of the devil's cloven hoof but of Goebbel's clubfoot!'

On the other hand, the young people are contaminated from the outset. The poison systematically injected into them leads them to become liars, thieves and murderers. The youths who were sent into Jewish synagogues and homes on 11 November 1938 to finish off the destruction started by their fathers and brothers are called by Adolf Hitler 'Germany's pride and hope'.

## New York, October 1939

Germany has now long been engaged in war; six years of a mad dictatorship have isolated the country from all the world's civilized nations. Just as on 10 November 1938 Jews sat in the dark with their dead among the ruins of their homes, millions of their tormentors now sit in the darkness of their cities and wait anxiously for the bad news from all over the world. The stocks of food and clothing that had been foolishly destroyed a year earlier are now desperately needed by the famished and freezing people. God's judgement has struck this country, and the angels of law and justice have turned away in horror from this country that six short and yet infinitely long years have cast back into the darkest time of the Middle Ages. God's punishment will be severe, but just . . .

(These lines are in the form of a diary begun on the sea voyage to the USA. My intention was to provide a true and accurate description of the events and experiences for my children. I do not intend to publish these pages from my diary.)

Should these lines nonetheless some day be published, then it should be under the pseudonym 'Spectator'. I expressly ask this because I know that every word of the truth that is published abroad will necessarily have terrible consequences for my Jewish brothers in Germany. And so I ask that my [American] place of residence not be mentioned, for I am sure that even here there are countless informers.

# SIEGFRIED MERECKI

## Manuscript 166 (156)

*Born in Galicia in 1887; moved to Vienna in 1914; lawyer, married, three children; emigrated to the USA in 1938.*

Towards the end of September 1938, a movement began to destroy Jewish places of worship. There was such a place in the courtyard of the apartment building where I live. I was therefore able to observe what happened.

It must have been on Friday, 28 September[1] that during the night I heard a noise coming from the courtyard. I went to the window where, hidden behind the curtain, I saw that a group of men was destroying the synagogue. It was illuminated, and I could gather that everything inside was being smashed. Suddenly, there was a short circuit in the electrical lighting. It was destroyed. After a time, the men disappeared.

The impression that this event made on the people who, not knowing what had happened, came the next day to the synagogue was shattering. As soon as they saw the destruction, they quickly took to their heels, without looking around or asking what had actually happened.

Scarcely three weeks later, I was woken again by a loud noise coming from the ruined synagogue. I saw about twenty people going in and out, and all of them were carrying off heavy packages and a few objects. This time there were also women. The synagogue was being robbed. Then I watched them all slink away in the dark courtyard.

Two hours later I heard another noise. Again, I saw packages being carried away, this time towards the front, towards the street. I ran to a front window to see what was happening. Shadowy figures were moving towards the bridge over the Danube. Then I understood. The Torah rolls were being taken to the bridge and thrown into the river. I watched and counted six and heard hideous laughter.

The final demolition of this synagogue took place on 10 November 1938. It was the most terrible day of the Nazi regime. We were supposed to pay the price for the murder of vom Rath. I, too, was among the victims. There can be no doubt that everything took place in accordance with a plan worked out long before and that they were only waiting for a suitable opportunity.

The 'work' began in the early hours. Arrests, abuse, plundering. In my building the confectioner was badly beaten, taken away and robbed, his apartment demolished.

From the balcony of my apartment, I saw individuals and whole groups of arrested men being taken to vehicles standing ready on the bridge. The drivers were policemen or men in civilian clothing wearing swastika armbands.

About eight o'clock in the morning, I heard a noise coming from the courtyard. Once again, it came from the synagogue. It was already completely destroyed. No one looked after it any more. What business do the people who are inflicting the punishment for Rath have there now, I wondered? But there was a thirst for destruction and a labour of destruction that can only be believed by someone who saw it. The window and door frames were torn out of the walls and thrown to the ground with such violence that they shattered into tiny splinters. Every little thing that was still inside was taken out and smashed to pieces. The floor was torn up. The people seemed to have superhuman strength; their faces were distorted.

During that morning, an Aryan man from the provinces came to visit me. He had ridden fast on his motorcycle and had not noticed what was going on in the street. He asked why I was so upset. Without a word I led him to the window and had him look down at the courtyard. My nerves failed, and I broke into tears. The man stood there, speechless.

Again and again, terrible news came in. I learned that all the Jewish temples had been set on fire, and these reports were confirmed when I saw plumes of smoke rising from the corresponding locations.

I sent my two eldest children to be cared for by a single woman who was a friend of mine on the assumption that they would be safer there. But there too a committee appeared and started searching houses. They [the children] came back home immediately.

In the late afternoon, things seemed to have calmed down a little. Strangely enough, all day long I had not thought that I myself might be in any danger. But about 5.30, I heard heavy steps in the corridor. Through the spy-hole in the door, I saw several men wearing arm-bands, along with an SA man, leading up the stairs a man named Korein who lived in the same building, and who was quite upset – it seems that 7,000 schillings were confiscated from his apartment. I heard him ask the group why they didn't go into my apartment. But they didn't, and instead carried on up, as far as I could gather, to a family named Kohn who lived on the floor above.

The clattering and banging that these people made could be heard for some time coming from Kohn's apartment. Curiously, I still didn't feel that danger was imminent, and also had not thought about whether and where I might hide. But I stood at the door listening, as if nailed to the floor. Finally the men came downstairs again, and this time they took away both the Kohn family's sons, a doctor and a businessman. This led me to believe that my calmness was indeed not unfounded because they passed my apartment door, walked along the corridor, and went down to the floor below. But suddenly they turned around and came back, whether at the instigation of Korein, I was not able to learn.

They knocked, and I opened the door. And that was it. They left me under guard in the vestibule, along with the other people who had been arrested, and began working over my apartment. I saw nothing, but I heard the threats made by these people, who were demanding money and jewels, and the lamenting and weeping of my wife and children. Finally, they all came back to the vestibule. My wife told me that they had taken her gold watch. They also brought out the typewriter to make off with it but finally changed their minds. They let me take my personal documents with me but emptied my wallet – the SA man stuck the money in his pocket – and then we were all taken away. I have never forgotten the heart-rending wailing of my family and especially of my little one.

We – that is, the two Kohns, Korein, myself and two other men who were arrested for reasons unknown to me – were led to the nearby Taborstrasse and put into a completely unfurnished but par-ticularly brightly lit apartment that had apparently been taken away from a Jewish family not long before. At the door an old man stood watch, without a coat, but with a large belly and a very long mous-tache; he was carrying a submachine gun. I recognized him as the janitor in a neighbouring building. We were led into an empty room and had to wait there for a long time. Then we were called one after the other into another room. When it was my turn, they made me take off my winter coat and wait. Soon a man came back with my coat. Both arms had been half cut away. I brought this coat with me to America, and am ready to show it to anyone.

After this petty work of destruction had been completed, I was taken into another room, where my fellow sufferers were lined up. They had all had their sliced-up coats put on inside out, so that the lining was on the outside. The same was done to me. Before we were led away, one of these brave men spied my almost new, wide-brimmed felt hat. Saying that he would make it still more beautiful, he took scissors and cut the brim to pieces and made large holes in it. I also brought this hat to America for anyone interested in seeing it.

Then we were made to march down the street in rank and file and with our inside-out coats. I noticed that other prisoners' trousers had been cut short and their coat-tails cut away. I had gone completely numb. The few people on the street hardly noticed us, probably because on that day it was not at all unusual.

We were taken to the police station in the Grosse Mohrengasse, where a large crowd shouted threats. In the guardroom, there were about fifty other fellow sufferers, several guards and a few SA men. When one of the guards saw our strange get-ups, he asked what kind of farce we were playing and ordered us to put our coats back on in the usual way.

We waited for a fairly long time. Our names were written down, and none of us dared to speak.

Suddenly one of the SA men there waved me into another room where there was no one. He ordered me to clean his boots. They were very clean, and I gathered that I was not the first to have this honour. I was ordered to clean them with the tail of my overcoat and then with the silk lining. I rubbed as hard as I could. Finally, he let me go unharmed.

After a time we were all ordered to move out. Outside stood an exceptionally high, open lorry. We had to get in quickly and the SA men who were there shoved and pushed us. I noticed an elderly, very fat SA man who wore a uniform that constantly threatened to split open and who cursed and hit us more than the others. How I managed for the first time in my life to climb into such a high lorry from the side by stepping on the wheels, and with only one or at most two tries, I cannot explain.

During the trip, I stood fairly far back in the lorry, with SA men behind me who struck us from time to time. We were not allowed to hold on or to look to the side. We drove past the Praterstern, which I then saw for the last time, to the Prater police station. How courteously I had always been treated there and how different it was to be now. The storm troopers who were accompanying us said to one another that anyone who didn't jump out of the lorry at a single bound was to be beaten. I don't know how I managed it, but the lorry had hardly stopped before I was down. Many people who tried to do the same thing fell heavily to the ground. All the rest were beaten and hounded out of the lorry.

We were herded into the building like wild animals. Soon I found myself in a small cell in the basement. The prisoners with me barely filled half the room. Immediately afterwards we heard a hellish shouting, and in a moment the rest of the room was filled with people whose fearful, scratched faces and downcast eyes gave us an idea of what awaited us.

I learned that these people had been arrested early in the morning and that they had spent the whole day without food in the cellar near a furnace and had been repeatedly mistreated.

Soon the little room was so full that we could hardly breathe. Everyone held his arms up in the air in order to gain space.

SA men appeared and ordered us to do squats. Because it was impossible to move, everyone just bent their knees a little.

The terrible atmosphere in this room made us long for the moment when we would get out of this hell.

This soon happened, but the change was not good. We were pushed into a larger room that was only half-full. There some of the people were picked out and dreadfully beaten by jeering SA men. Suddenly one of the SA men saw a stocky man in his fifties whom I did not know and called loudly to him: 'Aha, the building surveyor!' This man was immediately punched and kicked so much that he was left covered in blood and apparently unconscious.

Then the SA men repeatedly chose two prisoners and told them to box with each other. Since the prisoners did not want to hurt each other and therefore avoided hitting too hard, the men shouted: 'That's not real boxing. We'll show you how it's done.' And then they knocked the unfortunate victims' teeth out and left them with cuts on their faces. However, a young, athletic-looking man struck a real blow against his Nazi opponent. Shouting 'This Jewish riffraff dares to strike a German man!', the heroic swastika-wearing thugs fell on him and beat him so badly that he fell to the floor. Then they worked him over with their boots. During the whole rest of our detention, I observed this young man. His face was swollen and covered with crusted blood.

Successive boxing matches were then carried out, even between the prisoners, without pity. They preferred to hit each other hard rather than let it come to a boxing match with the heroic armed thugs. I myself was not forced to box.

Finally, we were allowed to leave this room, but it was not yet over. We were once again driven into a room that was already almost full of people who were standing in such a way that each put his deeply bowed head between the shoulders of the two men in front of him. I had to do the same and immediately realized why this was happening. Behind us SA men were running up and down and hitting everyone on the neck. Fortunately, this did not last long because soon a second and third row of new prisoners was formed, and the earlier rows could no longer be reached.

From this cell, we went to the offices upstairs. Everyone had to wait a long time before it was his turn to have his details taken down. In addition to the usual questions about personal data and party membership, the officials wanted to know whether we had a relationship with an Aryan woman or had helped to perform an abortion.

The officials who were taking down this information knew me personally and spoke with me, but they were not able to tell me what was to happen to us afterwards.

After the information had been recorded, we were taken into the courtyard between two rows of SA men who were hitting people on all sides. It was very dark, and I could make out that the courtyard was very large and surrounded by high walls. All around I could see prisoners arranged in dense rows along the walls. I too was put in such a row. On the ground lay large numbers of hats that earlier companions in suffering had left behind in their haste. We had to stand on the hats.

Despite my certainly not-very-rosy mood, this reminded me of a story I'd heard earlier.

I knew a Herr Lustig who used to be a bank official, but after the bank crash he took over his father's butcher shop and ran it. In May 1938, he too was sent to Dachau. He had married a very pretty young Aryan woman. In the shop, his wife now said, 'You see, I'm not worried about my husband. He is used to work and will be able to stand Dachau. But the poor man had debated for months about whether he should buy a new hat, whether his finances would allow it. And now they've taken him away with his new hat!'

We all stood in the courtyard for quite a long time. I heard the clock in the tower strike twelve and one. From time to time, we also heard moaning or shouting. The SA men were going from one group to another and mistreating the unfortunates.

41

Finally, large vehicles of various kinds appeared and the prisoners started to be taken away. It was a long time before it was my turn. This time no one was harassed. Not during the trip, either.

We were unloaded in a large courtyard, and I realized that it was the courtyard of the Vienna mounted police riding school. There were already thirty to forty groups of prisoners there, standing in rank and file. The new arrivals were called out by name and put in line. New prisoners were constantly being brought in. The courtyard was not lit, but we could see because light was coming out of the arena through the open door. We stood in the courtyard for about two hours and I had an opportunity to see how many acquaintances shared my fate. What was going on in the arena I still did not know.

Finally, my group was led into the arena. It was a very large, well-lit arena with a clay floor. The riding school. I estimated that it was about thirty metres long and twenty metres wide. It was already more than half full of people who were standing in rank and file. The heat was unbearable, the thirst terrible.

It must have already been getting light when the influx of new arrivals ended. The arena was so full that we could only stand. There was nothing to sit on anyway, not even anything to lean against. We were intentionally kept standing in rank and file, so that everyone could get in.

It was already broad daylight when we were finally allowed to move freely. But all of us had to move together slowly. There was no room for individual movement. It was a dense mass of people moving around. Nonetheless, we could talk to each other. I learned that at some collection points, people had been treated better, but in some even worse than we had been at the Prater police station. Most people had bruises to show for it; no one had received medical treatment.

So many people moving about in an enclosed space – it was said there were five thousand – had made dust rise from the clay floor, and soon reddish layers of dust lay on people's clothes, faces and hair. Our tongues were also dry and dusty.

A few people tried to lie down on the floor in order to rest a bit. Then others did the same. That made the space so tight that we could hardly breathe. I noticed that there was a group of people standing in line along the wall. Because in a riding school there are no privies, a shallow latrine trench had been made in the courtyard for that purpose. In order to prevent too great a crush, access to the trench had to be regulated. So people had to queue a long time for their turn. There were people who, having just returned from the courtyard, immediately got back in line in order to have their turn again in case they needed to.

Many young men were acting as stewards to maintain order. When someone had an especially urgent need to go, after speaking with a steward he could be allowed to do so out of turn.

Providing water for so many people was a very serious problem. Until ten o'clock on Friday morning, there was no opportunity to quench our thirst. Only then did two young men appear, each carrying a bucket that was used to water horses; each had a glass and brought water. That was supposed to slake the thirst of five thousand people. Heart-rending scenes ensued. Five to ten people shared one glass of water. We were happy to get a single swallow.

Not until Friday afternoon did the situation improve in this regard. More drinking glasses were brought in and more buckets of water were passed around. People could slake their thirst.

The first chance to get something to eat came only in the afternoon. Then a man came in with a basket of bread rolls which was soon sold out. He returned again and again. But few people seemed to feel hungry, and I, too, was not thinking about food.

In the meantime, people's fatigue had reached undreamt-of levels. Just think of my own case. Since six on Thursday evening, I had not had an opportunity to rest for one moment, not to sit down nor even lean against something. And in addition there was my frame of mind, which made it even more depressing.

Here in the arena, the guards who were on duty were not Nazis. Thus there was no beating, no cursing and no terror. On the contrary, the guards wanted to help us, and we could see that they were angry that so many people had been crowded into the arena. But they could only console us by saying that they were certain that we would soon be released. I believed it, because I couldn't imagine that they would want to hold so many people in a single space – without any way to rest, even on the floor – much longer.

By Friday night, many people could no longer stand up and they collapsed. Soon, part of the arena was covered with people lying on the floor. The others had hardly enough place to stand. A few complained to the guard in command. He tried to issue an order forbidding people to lie on the floor. But when he came to the area where people were lying and saw the wretched creatures burrowed into the clay, he left without saying a word.

Late on Friday night, we were ordered to line up. It took almost an hour before we were ready. We were told that Dr Langer, the Gestapo official under whose authority these arrests had taken place, would come. It was said that he would release us all, late at night, so that no more attention would be drawn to us. Dr Langer came around 2 a.m. A small space among the lined-up groups had been left open, where he himself could stride in. He made his entrance followed by a whole entourage, put on a dictatorial expression, looked us all up and down as if we were soldiers, and finally disappeared without having spoken a single syllable.

Everything went on as before, another great disappointment.

Soon thereafter I suddenly felt a terrible fatigue, and the idea that there was nothing I could do about it so overwhelmed me that I almost thought of committing suicide. I could feel my toes going numb.

After a short time, the guard gave the order that no one was allowed to lie on the floor for more than half an hour, so that everyone could rest a little. Supervision was left to the stewards. Around five o'clock in the morning it was my turn. For the first time in thirty-five hours I had the right to lie down on the clay floor among many other bodies lying close to one another. But before I could even find a place, the time was up, and I was more tired than ever.

A guard had announced that those who could prove that they had passage on a ship should report to an official who was to carry out his duties in a room on the courtyard. I was the fortunate possessor of a confirmation that I held a ticket on the Hamburg-America line. But on Friday I had not been able to make my way to this official. So I spoke to a steward, and at seven in the morning on Saturday he took me into the courtyard, so that I could wait for the official in front of his office.

Thus it happened that on Saturday morning I left the arena and never entered it again. Since the official in question was not supposed to come until nine o'clock, I waited all alone in the courtyard. It was very cold and I had not washed, but I did not want to put on my winter coat, in order to avoid questions about the cut-off sleeves. In any case, it was better than being in there, in that hell. I now had plenty of opportunity to witness many sad scenes.

I saw the uninterrupted stream of people going up to the latrine trench, and I saw how the stewards kept a sharp eye on each of them, so that he did not stay there too long. I saw two people help and comfort a third man who had broken down. At first, all three men were allowed to pass through the gate together. Later, the two helpers were stopped at the gate and the stewards took care of the ill person. Around eleven in the morning, a doctor and his assistant appeared who treated the ill and then sent them back into the arena.

Each time I asked for the official, I was told that I still had to wait. From time to time I was also asked by a steward what I was doing out there. My explanation, that because of my boat ticket I was waiting for the official concerned – the commandant, as he was called – seemed to satisfy him.

In the courtyard, I saw an elderly man with a strikingly pale face who repeatedly went up to a guard standing in the courtyard, said something to him, was turned away, and then came back again. This happened so often that not only the guard seemed to be getting nervous, but even I was becoming impatient. The man looked like he was mentally ill. Finally, during a moment when no one was watching, I spoke to him and said that the guard might become angry and harm him. He replied, in a voice that suggested how desperate he was: 'Can't you see what I'm trying to do?' And I understood. The man was pretending to be mentally ill.

So many things I saw there in that courtyard. Unwashed and unshaven men whose faces were distorted with fear. People lying unconscious on the ground who were treated by the doctor. People who went to the latrine and who were immediately pushed back. From time to time, the gate opened, a mounted guard came in, rode around the arena and disappeared into the back part of the arena. And then came a wagon into which the rubbish lying in the courtyard was loaded. Among the rubbish, I saw Jewish scriptures and phylacteries.

The commandant still hadn't come. In fact, he was there, but had me told that he had to go away, and that I should wait until he came back. Around noon, a few people came out of the arena and stood in front of me. Others came and pushed me out of the place where I had been waiting up to that point. I learned that in the arena someone had shouted that all people whose names began with the letters A to F and who had a boat ticket should wait in front of the commandant's office.

Protesting against being pushed out of the place I had held since early in the morning was of no help. When it became known that my name did not even begin with the letters A to F, I was pushed even further back.

Then suddenly the main gate opened and a few military supply lorries, loaded with bread and tea, drove in. This was the first food delivery and was prepared, as we later learned, by the Jewish religious community. A great rush followed, and no one was interested any longer in waiting in front of the commandant's office. All the prisoners stormed out of the arena and were directed to the food lorries where they got bread and tea.

I was very downhearted because I realized that it would probably no longer be possible to make my way to the commandant, and my hope that I would soon be released was dashed for the time being.

After things calmed down a little, we all stood again in front of the commandant's office and waited.

Shortly afterward, an official told us that our papers would be examined not here, but in the police headquarters at Rossauer Lände. He announced that we would be immediately transferred there.

The gate was soon opened, and two lorries were commandeered, carrying thirty men apiece under strict guard. I was happy to finally be able to sit down after 44 hours, even if it was in a police van. I also hoped to be released before long, as soon as my papers had been checked.

Outside, in front of the riding school, many women were waiting. I saw no one from my family.

It should be noted that during the internment in Pramergasse no one[2] had a hair on his head touched. It was only that we were forced to stand up the whole time and had no opportunity to rest. My feet were all swollen. I could no longer feel my toes, a condition that improved only after I had been in America for a number of months.

However, we had hardly got into the lorry before the storm troopers took command, and the blows and insults began before the lorry had even started to move.

It didn't last long because now came a terrible disappointment. We had been told that we would be taken to the police headquarters at Rossauer Lände, so that our potential emigration could be checked by presenting our boat tickets. But the lorry did not stop in front of the police headquarters. At first, I thought it was going to the rear entrance. But when it did not do so, I told myself that we would be taken to the municipal prison in Hahngasse. But the lorry didn't stop there, either, and we drove along the Ring and turned into Westbahnstrasse, and then there was no longer any doubt: we were going to the Westbahnhof, the place that all Viennese dreaded, as it was the railway station from which the trains left for Dachau. I didn't doubt for a moment any more that we were headed for Dachau.

The lorry finally stopped in front of a building that I did not know. We were all forced to run up to the second floor. I assumed that it was the rear wing of the Westbahnhof.

We were given no time to examine the room we entered. It was also dark. On the floor, 30–40 figures lay on their fronts, their heads in the centre, like the spokes of a wheel. We did the same. We were forbidden from looking up, on pain of punishment. I heard other people constantly coming in. A soldier marched up and down the room and stated various rules of behaviour that were appropriate for Dachau. All this strongly confirmed my belief that we were on our way to Dachau.

After lying on the floor for about two hours, we were allowed to stand up. There were already more than a hundred people in the room. I also saw that we were not in the Westbahnhof. It was clearly a schoolroom, since there were tables and a few stools, and so we were finally able to sit down. When I went to the window, I was able to see where we were. It was the school in Kenyongasse. I met a few acquaintances, and we were able to exchange ideas.

The SS man finally left the room and appointed a prisoner room commander. We began to prepare for the night. In the room there was also a tap and we were able to drink. The commander received seven loaves of bread, which he cut into little pieces and distributed to us. He warned us to eat sparingly in order to be prepared for all eventualities.

Then we were allotted sleeping places on the floor. It was not easy because there was not enough space for so many people. I was happy finally to be able to stretch out and take off my shoes. I saw how badly my feet had suffered.

Late in the night, a new batch of people came into the room. To make room for them, we were forced to crowd together even more. The tables had to be used as well. I learned that the riding school in Pramergasse was being entirely cleared out.

People were so tired that they all slept.

Sunday, 13 November, was a very hard day for us. SS men repeatedly appeared and forced us to do very difficult exercises. At first it was bearable, but the horrors we had been through and our sleepless nights very quickly made us exhausted. Other SS men repeatedly came in and the game began all over again. The whole day went this way. Exercises and then more exercises. I could tell from the way my acquaintances looked what they had all gone through. From time to time, SS men came in and mistreated and insulted the prisoners. Once, an SS man demanded that the room commander give him the daily report. The commander said: 'Respectfully report that 137 men are here.' Then he was slapped in the face, so he then repeated what he had said, and the answer came: 'There are not 137 men here, but rather 137 Jewish swine.' The next time a soldier came in, our commander had learned his lesson: 'Respectfully report that there are 137

Jews here.' For this report he really got hit, because this SS man thought he was joking.

In the room there was also a prisoner who was immediately recognizable as an Orthodox rabbi. He wore the usual caftan and a little cap on his head. He constantly mumbled prayers. One could see that his beard had already been cut short by the SS men. We all felt very sorry for this man, because he seemed to be suffering a great deal. This environment must after all have had the most terrible effect on this otherwise very retiring person.

The day went by with great suffering. We could hardly stand up any more. Exercises again and again. It seemed that even our tormentors were getting tired. Then a gymnastics teacher who had been arrested along with us was called forward and assigned to take over command. He knew in what shape we were, and chose exercises that put less stress on us. This did not please the soldiers, and the teacher was sent back and the merciless persecution and tormenting began again.

In the afternoon, an SS man came in and said it would be advisable to take a collection to buy medical supplies in case someone should need them. More than RM 50 was contributed. Then he took out a package of cotton wool and a little iodine. Value: half a mark; the rest of the money went into his pocket. Another man did the same thing and pocketed RM 40.

Once an SS man asked why this was all happening to us. No one answered. But when he became insistent, a doctor by the name of Kohn, a former schoolmate of mine, said slowly and with emphasis in a stentorian voice: 'Because a German was murdered by a Jew.' The SS man nodded his head in agreement and added: 'Because all must atone for one.' Later on, this question was often repeated, and Dr Kohn always gave the same answer.

In the early evening, bread and tea were brought in. This time, a large quantity. Each man got a cup of tea. Afterwards, one of the guards came in and demanded that all prisoners who were 60 years old step forward. Since there were none, he called out 59-, 58- and 57-year-olds. We thought they would be released. To the general amusement, it was then declared that there were about 25 cups of tea left in the teapot that these elderly men might now drink.

Thus we waited impatiently for night, which would finally give us some peace. We had no reason to assume that it would be different from the preceding night. We all lay down on the floor to sleep, and this time different uniformed men kept looking into the room, which had not been the case the preceding night.

About 2 a.m., we were woken by shrill commands. Men shouted: up, down, up, down. Although we were all sleepy and dead-tired, we were on our feet in a moment and we jumped up and down rapidly. The four or five uniformed men who had come in insisted that we do everything precisely, that every time we were commanded to get 'down' we lay fully on the floor, and every time we were commanded to get 'up' we stood straight. It is a wonder to me today that I was able to do all this with the others. In any case, I stood at the back and cheated a lot.

After two hours of this, the men went away; for a while, we heard the commands being shouted in the other rooms but went back to sleep.

I do not know how long it was before we were woken again by the deafening commands 'up and down'. The old routine started all over again. Suddenly the SS men noticed the Orthodox rabbi I mentioned earlier. In an instant, he was brought to the podium and made to sing Jewish songs. Just imagine the situation: below a crowd of tormented, terrified and sleepy men, and before them a singing rabbi surrounded by laughing SS thugs.

They came up to the man and, while he had to go on singing, one after another they cut off the remnants of his beard. Whenever he got so tired that he stopped singing, he was struck in the face and on the head and had to continue. He sang his monotone melody over and over without interruption, except that from time to time he let his voice grow softer and then began to sing loudly again. The SS men demanded a new song, but he continued to sing the same one. The men kept on saying that he would soon be executed.

Then they began a conversation with him. And it turned out that this unfortunate man was not only intelligent but courageous. We were astonished how soberly he answered the questions addressed to him, as if he had before him not men who were torturing him to death but rather men who had engaged in a learned debate with him. In particular, he answered the question regarding the reason for the arrests and abuse not as Dr Kohn had answered it, but said instead that it was ridiculous to hold responsible for the act of a young, inexperienced foreigner people who had nothing to do with him. He himself seemed aware of the impression that his answers made on the SS men and on us, and even the SS men became somewhat more subdued. They tried to make fun of his name, as was usually done, but when he explained that his name was Rosenberg, and stuck to it when the men pretended to hear 'Rosenthal' or 'Rosenduft', they also had to give up this effort, since the name Rosenberg is, after all, that of a well-known Nazi bigwig.

Finally, the men said: 'We're going to have you shot now, and not just you, but a few others as well.' They then grabbed a young, good-looking man, let the pair of them take everything they had with them and led them away. We never saw them again. Shortly afterwards we heard a shouted command outside and then a salvo of gunshots, but we were not at the time worried by this. We thought that it was only a trick to alarm us. And I never heard subsequently that anyone had been shot at that time. We listened again for a while to the shouted orders and the singing of Jewish melodies coming from other rooms, but then it grew quiet, and this dreadful night was not interrupted again.

The next morning, we had hardly awakened before an official appeared and ordered all those who had boat tickets to go and stand in the corridor. I was one of the first. Behind me was a crowd of other prisoners who did not have any such papers but who wanted to take advantage of the opportunity to get out of this terrible hell.

We were led into the main corridor, where hundreds of people were already waiting, all of them with their faces turned to the wall. Only a very few of these people could have already had boat tickets. I got in line as well. So did the many people who were constantly joining us. Finally, I was taken into a room where a great many officials sat at typewriters. The same information was recorded as in the district police station on Thursday evening, but in addition many file cards were also filled out.

We waited for a while longer and were finally led to the police van, and set off for the police headquarters at Rossauer Lände. Finally, a prospect of being set free!

Once we had arrived at Rossauer Lände, we had another huge disappointment. Even before we were unloaded, I heard the director of the prison say that we had to go back, because too many prisoners had already been brought there and these had to be processed first. The prison was indeed overflowing.

Immediately thereafter we drove back to Kenyongasse, whence we had come. I was desperate. So close to being saved and now back to this hellhole. I felt that I could not survive another such night.

This time we were not taken to the same room where we had been earlier, but to another, where there were only fellow sufferers who had been brought back there by the police. I was told that a high official was supposed to have said that we would all be taken back to police headquarters that same day, possibly late at night.

In this room there was also much exercising, beating and cursing. On one occasion, a very young SS man came in and engaged us all in conversation. The commander of this room was a young lawyer, an intelligent and spirited fellow. This young SS man spoke with him in a very affable way. He talked about Italy, Tyrol and many other things. When he was finished, he gave this lawyer with whom he had had such a good conversation a staggering box on the ear.

That afternoon, one of the guards said he was willing to get sausages for us. Two hundred Reichsmarks were collected and handed over to him for this purpose. Afterwards, he told us that he had been given permission to buy only one sausage for each person. That would have cost 70 marks at most. The rest of the money disappeared.

As evening drew on, an official in civilian clothes entered and told us to come with him. I was happy not to have to spend another night in that place. It all happened so fast that the sausages had to be distributed in the corridor. I was so happy that I gave mine to another prisoner because I could not eat.

We waited again in the corridor and again we were taken to the same offices. The official I approached told me that the information taken down in the morning had been mislaid, and that therefore he would have to fill out the same forms all over again. When he heard that I was a lawyer, he was particularly friendly, talked to me about my approaching voyage to America and even took the trouble to go to the director about my request, to ask whether I might count on being released the same day.

I waited again until midnight and then was put into a vehicle filled with 24 other prisoners. Once more, we went to the police headquarters at Rossauer Lände.

There the corridors were still full of prisoners waiting for their cases to be dealt with. We were shoved into a prison cell. In comparison to what we had had up to that point, it was paradise. There were benches, straw mattresses, water and a man even offered to buy things for us.

Though I had often had professional business at Rossauer Lände, I had never seen a cell or even a police van from the inside. Now, shortly before my emigration, I was to have that great privilege!

Everyone got ready to go to sleep. I thought it would be advisable to stay awake, since we were soon to be picked up. The others thought differently and so I was also persuaded to lie down between two other men. Soon everyone was sound asleep. But after perhaps an hour we were woken and very forcefully ordered to follow. I hardly found time to tie my shoes.

We were led into a very large room where many other people were already standing facing the wall. They let us wait. Then the guards left, and SS men came back in. Naturally, the mistreatment began at once, and then we were ordered to do exercises. I no longer know what this exercise was called, but it consisted in standing on tiptoe with our arms held high and we had to clench and unclench our fists. This seemed to me a particularly easy exercise, and I no longer worried about it, especially since I expected soon to be at the end of my sufferings. But after ten to fifteen minutes I was so exhausted that I could no longer lift my arms. An SS man noticed that I was not obeying and made me step forward. I insisted that I could no longer lift my arms and asked him to allow me to take off my winter coat; perhaps then it would be possible. He gave me a short telling-off and then let me go.

Soon thereafter it was my turn to go into room 49. How often I had had business in this room. I knew its every nook and cranny.

A young official entirely unknown to me was in charge there; he had been assigned to decide what was to happen next to the prisoners. Perhaps fifteen prisoners stood in front of me. We were asked whether any of us was ill. Even before the answer came, an official shouted ironically: 'Of course, you all are!' But only one person had said he was ill; he was examined then and there, and in fact he had several physical infirmities.

From the way in which my predecessors were dealt with, I gathered that when 'E' was called, 'release' [entlassen] was meant. 'Z' meant 'back to the cell' [wieder zürück in die Zelle], and 'Aunt Dora' meant that the person concerned was to be sent to Dachau. My turn came, and I showed my boat ticket and my letter to the American Consul General, and pointed out that I was even sailing on a German ship. I saw the official write a large 'E' on my card with a red pencil.

Another statement in duplicate was laid before me for my signature; in it I declared that I had been well-treated while detained and undertook, on pain of punishment, to say nothing about anything that had happened during my detention.

I was then led through several corridors, keeping my face turned to the wall, as ordered, saw the unfortunate people who were being sent to Dachau hurrying down the corridors and, after filling out more forms, was finally released.

I think I can safely say that I am not breaking my word when I now relate what happened in prison because that was not a voluntary but a coerced declaration. Had I not made it, I would not have been released. I was told that one man who had merely asked why he had to sign twice was for that reason alone beaten to a pulp. In addition, now that I am abroad, I am not bound by any threatened punishment in my former country, regarding which I had to declare, contrary to Austrian and international law, never to return.

Around 2.30 a.m., I finally left police headquarters in the company of a man previously unknown to me, who had shared my lot and who, like me, was headed for the police headquarters. The first persons who approached me were a woman and a young girl who asked about their husband and father. Unfortunately, I was unable to give them any information as I didn't know the man. On the way home I saw in front of the Hotel Metropole[3] a line of people that stretched far down Franz-Josefs-Kai. These were women who had been waiting all night in front of the Gestapo in order to inquire about their husbands when morning came.

The news that I was home again spread quickly, and many women came to see me in order to learn what had happened to their husbands. I did what I could to console them.

In the course of the following days, quite a large number of victims of the November events came home. But very many also went to Dachau. Since after my release I had a great deal to do to prepare for my departure and was therefore on the streets more than usual, I often saw vehicles transporting prisoners from Kenyongasse to police headquarters. I imagined vividly what was going to happen to each of the inmates.

After 10 November 1938, Jews were avoided even by Aryans who had not previously done so. We were rejected everywhere. All public places without exception now put up signs: 'Jews forbidden to enter.' Sometimes also: 'Jews unwanted.' There were no longer any Jewish shops. Jews could only still buy things in a very small number of Aryan shops.

Jewish pupils had already been excluded from state schools. In Jewish areas, a few primary schools were reserved for Jewish children. There was a Hebrew high school in Vienna, the Chajesgymnasium. This school was allowed to remain open and was supposed to accept all Jewish middle-school pupils. But since it had room for only 500 children, it was decided that only those who had up to that point made exceptional progress would be accepted. So few pupils applied that the above number was not reached. They had all emigrated or intended to do so, and the administration had asked that only those who could stay for the whole academic year apply.

I was told that soon thereafter the Chajesgymnasium was forced to close its doors. Aryan boys were always hanging around in front of the school to beat up the Jewish children as they left. Most of the teachers had emigrated or been taken to Dachau. So here too things came to an end.

In Vienna, there were several soup kitchens where poor and impoverished Jews used to get meals every day. Although the Jewish community bore the cost, there had always been many non-Jews among the thousands of people who waited there for their meals. On 10 November, these soup kitchens were completely destroyed; even the crockery was smashed. These kitchens were later started up again.

After 10 November 1938, there was no longer anywhere that a Jew could say his prayers. All the temples were destroyed, even the main temple in Seitenstättengasse. I myself saw the remains of its pews being carted away. The magnificent temple in Tempelgasse was also destroyed. There the head cantor Marolies had had his private residence. He told me that he had not been able to save even his clothes and linens. When I was being transported as a prisoner to the police station in Kleine Mohrengasse, I saw the Turkish temple in Zirkusgasse ablaze.

A few years earlier, the Jewish religious community had opened a ceremonial hall in Vienna's Central Cemetery that was said to be the most beautiful and sumptuous in Europe. When I visited the graves of my parents before my departure, I had to go in through a small side door. The windows of the ceremonial hall were boarded up and the cupola was completely destroyed.

On 10 November 1938, not only were the last remaining Jewish shops closed, but the apartments of the small shopkeepers were also sealed up. My daughter had been having several dresses made by her seamstress. This seamstress's apartment was now sealed up, and she was therefore forced to live with acquaintances. She was not even allowed to get a coat or shoes from her apartment. She wore galoshes that someone had given her. When we left Vienna, her apartment was still sealed. My children's clothes had to remain behind. Only months later could they be sent on.

The winter coat that I had ordered for myself because the other one had been cut up suffered the same fate. It was to be made by the famous tailors Nadeler and Goldenberg. They were forbidden to practise their trade, but they had important connections and received permission around 25 November to open the shop and complete the articles already in production. Thus I was able to have an overcoat for my trip.

How the fine for the vom Rath affair was collected I no longer remember. The fact is that, although I left behind me no debts of any kind and in particular no tax obligations, I had been informed by the Post Office Savings Bank and my bank that any funds that came into my accounts there after my departure would be confiscated. I did not ask, but I presume that this was also for the atonement.

# RUDOLF BING

## Manuscript 252a (28)

*Born in Nuremberg in 1876; lawyer, married, two daughters; emigrated to Palestine in 1939, died there in 1963.*

Now I come to the high point of Hitler's Jewish policy, namely the events of 9 November and the following days, when a secretary at the German embassy in Paris, vom Rath, died of his wounds after being shot by the Polish Jew Grynszpan. It was not as though this event had really upset the German people. When the news broke, the situation on the streets did not alter in any way.

But in Nuremberg the whole SA was ordered to appear on the main market square in full uniform at midnight. Individual units were then dispersed over the whole city. Every single street was to be covered and each unit was given its own particular area under a designated leader. Everything was planned beforehand; no non-uniformed civilian was involved when the units marched into their areas.

We lived on the first floor of a large apartment building that was owned by my family[1] and that had a very large, empty courtyard with outbuildings and storehouses. About three o'clock in the morning, my wife and I were woken. We heard a dreadful bellowing by the front door and in the dark I saw a great many people standing in front of the building. All the doorbells were being rung and voices were shouting: 'Open up, open up immediately!' I immediately called police headquarters and, after giving my name, said: 'a mob is trying to break into my building.'

'Are you Aryan?' asked a female voice. 'No,' I answered. She hung up without saying anything further.

In the meantime, the people in front of the building had broken through the door panels. They had brought the necessary tools such

56

as axes and the like with them. They stormed up the stairs to the upper floors. We were alone in the apartment: because of well-known difficulties that Jews had in finding servants, we had long had to manage for ourselves without help. Words cannot express what I owe to the presence of mind and clarity of my beloved wife, who, even though she was suffering, did not lose her head for one moment during these critical minutes.

We heard plaintive cries from the stairway; apparently a Jewish neighbour – we recognized his voice – was being beaten. 'We want to avoid falling into their hands at any price.' It was my wife who first made this decision. In the past, we had, half in jest, thought about how we could escape from our apartment in the event that we were in danger of being arrested. We now acted accordingly. We locked the door to the apartment and then the doors to our bedroom with the adjoining dressing room, tied the linen bed sheets together and attached them to the window frame. I expressed my concern as to whether it would hold our weight. We could already hear the door to our apartment being broken down.

The window of the dressing room looked out onto a narrow street opposite a hops storehouse. In front of it, opposite the window, was a porch roof that was somewhat lower; this roof was two and a half metres from our window. Making a quick decision, I threw a mattress onto the porch roof and leapt across the street onto it, then threw the mattress to the ground and jumped down. Above me, the people were forcing their way into our apartment. My wife didn't believe that the window frame and bed sheets would hold. Suddenly, she was hanging by her fingertips from the window sill; then she let go. Fortunately, she landed in my arms, since I was standing immediately underneath her on the mattress I had thrown down. Naturally, I fell over with my burden, but the mattress cushioned our fall. We were saved. The height from which my wife let herself fall was that of a normal first floor. I estimated it to be about ten metres. Everything happened in a few seconds.

We were, of course, only scantily clothed. Luckily, it was a mild night. While upstairs in our apartment and in all the other Jewish apartments we could hear the terrible crashing of falling furniture and breaking glass, we ran across the big courtyard in the shadow of the storage sheds behind the back building where a few poorer people lived, broke pickets from a fence, slipped through and ended up in an open shed where Christmas trees were stored, under which we hid, shivering. The clamour and crashing in the front building went on for hours. As dawn approached, we knocked on the door of a Christian family who lived in the back building and on whose loyalty we could rely. We learned that the mob had left our apartment; then we returned to our home.

It was an indescribable sight. In the rooms, we literally waded through ruins and shards. The mirrors and all the crockery were shattered. All the cupboards had been overturned and smashed with chair legs and axes. My pictures, including valuable oils of which I was proud, had been slashed. The stuffing from the ripped-open upholstered furniture was strewn around the whole apartment. Not a single chair or table was still intact. The radio had obviously been trampled on with boots. My wife had already outfitted herself for our emigration. Sixteen of her dresses, almost all of them new, had been cut to pieces. However, a few pieces of jewellery that she had left behind in the bedroom we found under the rubble. Nothing had been stolen.

In the course of the day, I found that my office[2] had been wrecked in the same way; all the typewriters as well as other furnishings had been completely destroyed. Files had been scattered through all the rooms or ripped up.

Most of the Jewish apartments in the city looked the same, and all the shops had been completely destroyed. Soon, however, we heard much sadder news. The preceding afternoon my wife had seen three of her girlhood friends at our apartment, where she regularly met them once a month. The husband of one of her friends had been beaten to death that night in front of his wife, and she herself lay in the hospital with severe injuries to her face. The husband of her second friend had been injured in the face and head and remained in a critical condition for months; as a consequence, one of his arms was permanently paralysed and he suffered from significant speech difficulties. The husband of the third friend had been taken from their apartment and was on his way to the concentration camp in Dachau.

If I tried to describe the consequences of that night for my immediate circle of acquaintances, I would have to write a whole book about them. A woman friend of ours lived alone with her 3-year-old daughter. The barbarians forced their way even into her daughter's room and smashed her dolls and toys before the weeping child's eyes and with mocking words. Then they told her mother: 'you can drown your brat in the Jordan.' Another lady in our circle of friends was alone in her apartment. After the gang had finished its work there, the leader walked up to her, hit her in the face and said: 'There you have the revenge for Paris.' Another acquaintance, still under the effects of anaesthetic and bandaged after a hernia operation that was in itself not dangerous, lay in the Jewish hospital in Fürth. Police officers came to transport him to Dachau. They ordered him to get up. He had to obey and after a few minutes he fell dead of a heart attack.

In the street alone where my wife's friend's husband was killed, three other men had been beaten to death. Everywhere, we heard of people who had committed suicide in despair. Two widows who chose this way out are known to me by name, and I have already mentioned the suicide of the two privy counsellors named Frankenburger.

On the same night, more than 300 Jewish men were arrested, and almost as many in Fürth. All of those who were under 58 years old were sent to Dachau, and the others, including the 78-year-old chairman of the religious community, remained in the Nuremberg penitentiary for about a week. The fate of those who were sent to Dachau, where they met fellow sufferers from all over southern Germany, was as you would imagine. Large barracks and prisoners' clothing with the Star of David had been prepared for them, a proof that this action had been planned long in advance and would have taken place even without the murder of Herr vom Rath.

Those interned in Dachau only returned months later.

When the morning after this abominable night people who had not taken part in it as police or as SA men awoke and saw the destruction that had been wrought, something happened that the instigators had not expected. A deep feeling of depression and shame clearly gripped the public. For the first time, some of the population dared to show sympathy with us. One heard people saying: 'I am ashamed to be a German.' I know of one teacher in a state institution of higher education who, having seen the destruction of apartments in his building, informed his superior that he was ill and put in a request for his pension because he no longer wanted to serve such a government. In particular, the working population was indignant. What did the party and the SA do? The latter sent their spies into the bars in the working-class suburbs, where they engaged the guests in conversations about the events in order to provoke them into making careless statements and then inform on them. I was reliably informed of this by an elderly worker. But on the day after that terrible night, Herr Streicher organized a kind of victory celebration in the main market square, and in his speech castigated a few women who had wept on seeing the destroyed Jewish shops, telling them that they lacked a sense of the magnitude of these events.[3]

Demolitions, mistreatment and huge transportations of people to concentration camps took place throughout Germany. What I describe in the following is characteristic of what happened in Nuremberg, and of Streicher in particular. They wanted to take advantage of the situation to destroy Jewish property, especially real estate.

The officials responsible for Aryanization in Nuremberg and Fürth are the so-called district economic advisors, of whom there are four. It is typical that of these four, three had declared bankruptcy before the beginning of the Third Reich while the fourth was a fairly unscrupulous real estate broker. I should add that my close personal experience had led to my being very well informed about one of the three bankrupt men when I defended his former Jewish attorney before the Court of Honour, against whom he had made the defamatory charge that he had extorted a high honorarium from him by threatening otherwise to report to the party his connection with him as a Jew. This claim turned out to be utter slander, and the public prosecutor himself had described the man as a chronic liar. All this had happened hardly a year ago.

As a defence attorney, I had at that time access to trial documents from which it emerged that this man was demanding high damages because of his impotence resulting from a traffic accident, but according to expert witnesses he had been impotent before the accident. I mention this to show how justified the judgement made by the British Consul General in Frankfurt was in the White Book[4] when he attributed some aspects of the behaviour of Nazi leaders to sexual abnormality. The district economic advisors were all active as brokers while carrying out Aryanization and took large kickbacks from their victims.

Immediately after the 'Night of the People's Indignation' [*Nacht der Volksempörung*], as 9 November was officially called, Jewish landowners and also mortgage creditors of all ages and sexes were taken to party buildings. They were held in dark cellars; in some cases they were made to strip naked and were photographed, allegedly for the purposes of racial science. They were made to wait for hours. When the waiting room was entered by an Aryan, even if it was a very young SA man, all the Jews had to spring up and stand to attention in a military manner. They were made to do exercises like recruits – not just the men, but women too. I also know one elderly man who experienced this. The people waiting were made to shout insults in unison against the Jewish race.

When they were duly exhausted, they were taken to the district economic advisor who was directing the whole thing. They were forced to sell their land or mortgages, usually for one tenth of its value, to the National Socialist party or to one of its organizations, and for the most part to bear all the costs, including the district economic advisor's commission. If they refused, they remained in detention, and their bad treatment continued. Then they were taken to a notary in the same building so that everything could be made binding, and they also had to grant the district economic advisor full power of attorney. A few notaries had enough moral fibre to refuse to collaborate.

In addition, other Aryanizations that were thought to have long since been completed were gone over again. For example, I know of a case in which an elderly man who had sold his shop in exchange for a life annuity was forced to sacrifice half of his income, a sacrifice that certainly did not benefit his buyer but rather some party authority. This was doubtless also considered to be the confiscation of profits from Aryanization.

But I want to continue my account of my personal experience.

Since we were unable to stay in our own home, we spent the night following St Bartholomew's Night at the home of my brother-in-law, who lived across the street from Streicher's palace and whose apartment had been spared in order to preserve appearances in the neighbourhood.

We wanted to stay there the following night as well. But the next afternoon a whole contingent of Gestapo agents appeared at the home of my brother-in-law, who had a serious heart problem. They told him that he had to move out of his apartment immediately and for good and leave Nuremberg because no Jews were to be allowed in to the neighbourhood of Streicher. They stayed in the apartment while a removal van and removers were immediately called in, and within three hours the apartment was cleaned out under constant supervision and coercion of the Gestapo agents. The removal company took care of my ill brother-in-law so he was able at least to ride in the remover's own car as far as Erlangen, where he spent the night in a hotel before going on to stay in Fürth. Only after some weeks did he receive permission to return to a different apartment in Nuremberg. Other Jews in the neighbourhood suffered a similar fate. My brother-in-law died of a heart attack a few weeks after this turmoil.

As a result of these events and with repeated news of further arrests and arraignments, my wife pressed for our departure. With her usual foresight, she had somehow set aside a small sum out of her housekeeping money that was enough for us to live on for a few days. We hurried to the train station with little luggage and took the express train at random to Stuttgart. At the Reichsbahn hotel in the railway station, the concierge immediately recognized us as refugees and, no

61

doubt taking advantage of the situation, gave us the most expensive room. During that night, Jews were arrested in many hotels in Stuttgart and taken to Dachau. I presume that the concierge was decent enough not to reveal our Jewish identity to the authorities.

We stayed in Baden-Baden until the situation in Nuremberg had calmed down somewhat. In Baden-Baden as well, Jewish shops had been demolished and Jewish men interned, but the apartments were undamaged. The people clearly condemned the violent acts. Here, too, as all over Germany, the synagogue had been burned down, and the fire brigade had only been called out to protect the neighbouring buildings from the flames.

After my return to Nuremberg, I took over the leadership of the Palestine office, and also collaborated, as far as my preparations for emigration allowed me to do so, in the administration of the community. It was astonishing how in general the Jews in Nuremberg, despite all the hard knocks they had been dealt by fate, did not languish submissively but instead actively took matters in hand in their shrunken community, helped those who needed help, tried to keep the school and worship going and in particular, with everyone's support, made it possible for young people to emigrate.

Here I'd like to mention in particular our 78-year-old community chairman who, after he was released from prison, immediately resumed his work with unusual energy. Under his leadership, an organization was at once created in order to help the many people who had been driven out of their homes.

The Aryanization taken on by the four district economic advisors and their accomplices had an unexpected sequel. It can be assumed that in Central Headquarters no one had been upset about this violation. But it caused great confusion in the fiscal situation of all those concerned and, as a result of the real estate cessions, the tax offices saw their tax levies and securities threatened. There were also some party members from other cliques who envied their profits. First, a law was enacted that was supposed to make the validity of all these forced transactions subject to special government authorizations. The district leadership got wind of the fact that this law was to go into effect on a certain day and was to apply to all real estate transactions that had not yet been entered into the land register before that date. The day in question was a Monday. On the preceding Sunday, the officials of the Nuremberg deed registry office, judges and secretaries were dragged out of bed, and party officials and district advisors who held the coerced powers of attorney for Jewish property worked feverishly with the notaries. All this in order to finish entering all these transactions into the registry of deeds on Sunday, before the deadline. Independent judges and notaries had to take part in these shenanigans.

However, after a few days, a Gestapo commission arrived from Berlin. Not only the district advisors but also countless others who had been involved in the forced Aryanizations were arrested. Many Jews were interrogated, and a few optimists already glimpsed a return to the rule of law. Then things suddenly went quiet again. The people arrested were released, and the Jews who had been deprived of their rights did not receive even the tenth part of the value of their land and mortgages that they had been promised. That at least was the situation when I left Nuremberg in the middle of May 1939.

Government agencies obtained the pickings from the night of 9 November, which Goebbels and his propaganda dared to represent abroad as a spontaneous popular movement.

To fill his coffers, Göring demanded the now well-known contribution of a billion Reichsmarks from the Jewish people as a whole. Within six months, the Jews had to deliver, in four payments, one fifth of their assets. The basis for this was the declaration of assets that they had been forced to make the preceding year. The losses occasioned by the compulsory cessions of real estate after 9 November were not taken into account. For example, I had to pay 8,000 marks on my share of a piece of land that had belonged to my family for fifty years which was worth about 40,000 marks, even though all that I got in exchange was a claim on the National Socialist party to the sum of RM 4,000, which I never received, and probably never will receive.

In addition, I had to pay a *Reichsfluchtsteuer* [Reich Emigration Tax] of one-quarter of my current assets and also one-quarter of what I had given my daughters in 1933 and 1934 to enable them to emigrate to Palestine.

Then all jewellery and all silver items had to be handed over to the municipal pawn shop, but my wife and I were allowed to take two silver knives, forks and spoons each with us. I could wait no longer to receive payment of the estimated value of a few thousand marks that I had a right to claim for these items. All my moveable assets had been destroyed. I had to pay a large sum of money for new purchases and repairs in preparation for leaving. Had I been insured against damages resulting from disturbances and riots, it would not have been of any help to me because the government also appropriated for the Reich any insurance pay-outs without offsetting them in any way.

And if that wasn't enough, I also had to pay an indemnity of almost 10,000 marks for the property we were taking with us, which had an estimated value of about 4,000 marks and consisted of necessities.

In addition, there were back taxes to pay, following an extensive audit carried out by the tax office, based on the fact that the closure of my law office had naturally produced income that would otherwise have been distributed over several years.

I recount all these facts only because they are typical of how the German authorities dealt with all Jewish emigrants as a means of robbing them of their possessions!

# TONI LESSLER

## Manuscript 81 (133)

*Born Toni Heine in Bückeburg in 1874; teacher; founded the first private school in Berlin in 1912; emigrated to the USA in 1939; died in New York in 1952.*

It was generally recognized that the situation was coming to a head, but what happened in November was worse than we ever imagined.

The shooting of the legation secretary vom Rath in the German embassy in Paris gave the German authorities the pretext they had been looking for to take extreme retaliatory measures against German Jews. When the news that a Polish Jew had murdered vom Rath reached Germany, the government announced that the Jews would be subject to the harshest punishment and that the nature of this punishment, which could never be harsh enough, would be made known in a few days. No one imagined in what form the already severely tried German Jews would be further tormented. People spent the first days of November in fear and apprehension. The heavy fine – a billion marks were supposed to be raised for the Reich – was already an excessive hardship; but people had resigned themselves to this punishment.

Nonetheless, the events that took place simultaneously in all parts of Germany on 10 November 1938 went beyond our worst expectations.

A grey, cloudy November morning was dawning; out in Grunewald, people had as yet no idea of the tragic events that were going on in the city, indeed all over Germany. The first electric tram bringing about sixty children from the Kurfürstendamm area to school[1] arrived. Trembling, so upset they could hardly speak, the children

65

whispered as they entered the school, 'The synagogue in Fasanen-strasse is burning.' 'Quiet,' I warned them, 'don't say that again until my friends who live in Fasanenstrasse have confirmed it by telephone.' Then the second tram arrived, bringing the children from the Bavarian quarter. The same shocked and terrified look was on the faces of these pupils: 'The synagogue in Prinzregentenstrasse is burning,' they said. Finally, the children from Grunewald arrived at school on foot. They confirmed that our dear little temple in Grune-wald was ablaze and that the firemen were standing there doing nothing. The older pupils said they had heard them say: 'Usually we would put it out, but today we're not allowed to.' I no longer needed to get confirmation by telephone; children were coming in from all parts of Berlin and reporting that the temples in their areas had been set on fire.

After thinking for a moment, I sent the children, each group accom-panied by a teacher, back to the various parts of the city so that the parents would at least have their children with them. No one knew what would happen next. And it was a good thing that I had imme-diately sent the children home. The Jewish schools had to remain closed for ten days until the 'excitement' among the population had died down. People constantly spoke about the 'people's wrath' that had led to the destruction of the houses of worship, but everyone was well aware of how this 'wrath' had been stirred up.

After a ten-day interruption, we resumed classes, but many chil-dren were missing. Anyone who could, by any means, still get out with his family had done so. I noted that 92 of the fathers of our pupils were in concentration camps. The treatment must have been dreadful in these camps; without exception the men had been housed in unheated rooms and the cold November and December days had exacted many a victim. Those who were not already suffering from the cold or from the terrible illnesses of the concentration camps were mentally and physically exhausted. Naturally, the tone and the treat-ment in the various camps differed. It was particularly harsh in Dachau near Munich, where several of my acquaintances 'suddenly' died. A beloved relative was beaten to death there. With these sad events the year 1938 ended, and we could hardly wait to finally be able to leave our 'fatherland' for ever. In the meantime, many things had changed in my own affairs.

Fortunately, by 1 November I had already given up my house, packed up the furniture that I intended to take with me to the USA ready for the shipping crate and put it all in a storehouse. The super-fluous school benches, tables and chairs, which I could not even give away, were picked up by the junkmen, who chopped them up for firewood.

Luckily, I had already let my housekeeper go. My cook had served me faithfully for twelve years. Since 1933, I had repeatedly urged her to give up her position with me and find one in an Aryan household. But each time she refused, saying that she would remain with me because there was no man living in my house. The first thing the Nuremberg laws had demanded was in fact that only servants over 45 years old could remain in Jewish households where men were present. 'You have always been just like a mother to me. I'll stay with you as long as I can, and I'm not looking for another position.' That was how it stayed from 1933 to 1935.

On May Day 1936, I had given all the maids the whole day off, as I did every year. Late that evening, they returned full of enthusiasm, especially the cook, who had earlier seemed immune to Nazi influences and who now told me excitedly that she had seen Hitler and that he had greeted her, yes, her, and smiled at her. From that day on, a transformation began in her. Beforehand, when she came back from her holidays in Pomerania she had always said: 'People in the countryside are so stupid; they tell me to give up my position in your house; otherwise I'll never be able to be in service in an Aryan household.'

However, such advice eventually fell on fertile ground. Unfortunately, she could not find a suitable position and asked me repeatedly to be allowed to stay. I granted her all kinds of privileges because as a Jew I was not allowed to dismiss her, and yet I was more than happy when I was able to tell her on 1 October 1938 that I was going to dissolve my private household on 1 November and would have to dismiss all my staff. Beside herself with rage, she threw a fit and wailed: 'That's what I get; I'll never find another position in an Aryan house because I have served Jews so long.' However, through the efforts of my Aryan friends, I was able to find places for all my employees in good Aryan families and, as we said farewell, I said to her mainly out of politeness: 'Anna, once I'm over there in America, I'll send you a couple of nice picture postcards for your album in which you've been keeping all the beautiful cards I've sent you from my travels.'

'Oh, no, you mustn't write to me at all any more, now I'm in an Aryan house.'

This didn't bother me so much, but even this little statement was characteristic of the success of the party propaganda. After I had vacated the house on Roseneck, it was immediately transformed into an office for the Nazi party. With my sister, I rented two small furnished rooms across the street and had my hands full getting on with the increasingly arduous preparations for emigration. The last Christmas holidays that I was to spend in Germany passed without any major disturbances. The teaching staff, of whom only a few – in all, only eight women – had succeeded in taking steps towards emigration, were still causing me all kinds of problems, but I could no longer get upset over anything. I promised to leave the school, such as it was, to them: they could and should resign themselves to the facts, and I left the full amount of the operating capital in the school, not least because after all the levies I could no longer transfer any money.

Shortly before the end of the year, my jewellery and valuables were audited. The tax assessor was surprised by the many valuables that came in part from family mementos and in part from Russian princelings from the year 1918. They were all carefully assessed, registered, packed in an approved box and sealed. 'I doubt whether you will be able to take everything with you, because there are so many beautiful things, but as yet no prohibition has been put on taking jewellery out of the country.' Three days later this prohibition was decreed. Thus I had to obey a summons to go to the state pawn shop, where I was forced to hand over all my precious things at a price that did not correspond to even one fiftieth of their value.

So in the end I had to leave everything behind but I was still able to provide a good wardrobe of clothes and a pleasant voyage on the *Queen Mary* for myself and my sister. The time until emigration now went very quickly. Despite all the difficulties and upsets of recent months, I couldn't think about saying goodbye and I had decided that I would disappear as quietly as possible from my circle of friends.

When I was visiting old friends about six weeks before my departure, I remarked: 'It's really hard to go away!' With tears in his eyes, the old man replied: 'Staying here is even harder!' Then I realized that it would probably be better not to say farewell to anyone.

We had scheduled our departure for the beginning of March, because we had booked our passage on the *Queen Mary* for 4 March from Southampton. Beforehand, we still wanted to visit our close relatives in the Rhineland and Westphalia, who had been more than friends and relatives during these difficult years. Though we did not want to bid anyone farewell, we could not avoid saying goodbye to those closest to us. On the evening before our departure, we met with our two best women friends in the third-class waiting room at Bahnhof Zoo. We could no longer receive anyone in our cramped, tiny room, which was packed full of suitcases. No café, no pastry shop such as those in which we used to like to drink a cup of coffee in the evening, was now available to us. Jews were not allowed to enter any such place. And the few Jewish restaurants that still existed and that would have been delighted had we sought them out were so far away from our different apartments that for months the waiting rooms at the major railway stations had been the only meeting places for Jewish circles. Since the beginning of November and the fateful day when the synagogues were destroyed, it had no longer been possible for Jews to take even the slightest refreshment in any bar or restaurant. This was twice as disagreeable for us when we had to spend hours in the city in various offices running the last errands before emigrating.

Because we worked at school during the week, we couldn't go into the city before five o'clock, and so we had to do all our errands on Saturday. We set out at 9 a.m. and seldom came home before four or five in the afternoon. The only place where we could sometimes rest for an hour and get some light refreshment was, as I mentioned earlier, the restaurants in the railway stations. Above all, we frequented the waiting rooms on Alexanderplatz, in Friedrichstrasse, and at Bahnhof Zoo, because there was a lot of coming and going in them because of the international traffic, and no one paid any attention to the few quiet Jewish visitors.

Just as difficult as getting food in restaurants was procuring the necessary supplies for larger enterprises such as our school. Up to that point, when feasible, I had given preference to Jewish firms; since I bought everything in bulk and needed a great deal, everyone was glad to supply me. Since November, the Jewish firms had either closed down or, in the case of the larger ones, passed into Aryan hands. In September 1938, when I asked for the new price list, a large grocery firm from which I had purchased vegetables, fruit and canned goods by the hundredweight over more than ten years sent me a card with the following message: 'To the Waldschule Grunewald. Before we send you the new price list, as we do every year, we ask you to inform us whether your school is an Aryan institution.' Since I was well aware that if I gave the real answer, the firm would not send me anything, I immediately wrote back: 'I hereby inform you that I direct a Jewish school that you have supplied for many years. I have transferred my annual order to a Jewish firm.' I must also mention that this Jewish firm was still able to deliver everything on time until 10 November, when it too passed into Aryan hands.

I now come back to the meeting with our friends at Bahnhof Zoo. We were all in the saddest state of mind; each tried not to make saying farewell still harder for the others. When we looked around the room on our way out, we saw at least twenty tables with groups similar to ours: friends and relatives who were saying goodbye to each other, none of whom could find any other meeting place than this dreary railway station waiting room – a station that was being rebuilt – that offered the most uncomfortable possible place to meet. How many tears were shed on that evening I could not say. The waiter who served us was so sympathetic that he said as we left: 'I don't understand why the Jewish customers all sit and cry because they have to go away. They should be happy to be getting out of this lousy country. I'd be happy if I could leave with you; I've had it up to here', holding his hand under his chin. Naturally, we gave no outward sign that we had heard this remark but instead went silently on our way, and on the way home none of us could say a word.

At seven o'clock the next morning, our faithful house seamstress appeared; she was the only one of our Aryan employees who had remained true to us. She packed up our last things, stuck a bouquet of violets in our jackets, walked with us to the car and said: 'I cannot accompany you ladies to the railway station, because I would only make saying goodbye harder for you by weeping. But I ask one thing of you, don't forget me, and always remember that I and many of your Aryan friends think just as highly of you as they used to. My whole circle speaks of you with such respect and love, and if I now give you pleasure with this little bouquet of violets, remember that these little flowers represent the number of your Aryan supporters, who will miss you very much and who will think of you with devotion and fidelity.' Then she closed the car door, and we drove to Anhalter railway station, where we met two more related families, to whom we also quickly said goodbye.

We had to cut short our farewells; only someone who has experienced it himself can know what 'emigration' means. We travelled as far as Aachen, where we spent a few peaceful days in the house of dear relatives; on 1 March, we left Germany and, after a three-hour journey, arrived in Emmerich on the German–Dutch border. Of the many passengers, we were the only ones who had to get out and open our hand baggage – the heavy baggage had gone through Hamburg by ship to Southampton – at the customs office.

The German customs officials spent a whole hour examining our things. They were interested particularly in our worthless jewellery; we had already had to hand over our valuable things to the pawn shop and had the written proof of this with us. But for a long time we sought in vain to make it clear to the official that the gold-plated silver chains that the Berlin authorities had let us take with us were not gold, and when I repeatedly asked him to accept that what I said was true, he drew my attention to the 800 stamp. For him, that was a proof that it was gold! My sister was wearing a real gold necklace that was the only valuable piece of jewellery she had been allowed to take along, even though it was not an especially fine piece of work, but it was ignored by the officials with the comment: 'That's not gold.' When I asked that a superior official be brought in, the latter finally came to us, examined our valuables and of course immediately let them pass.

In the meantime, the direct train to Rotterdam had already left and we had sat for three hours, in our sorrow at leaving home, in the shabby border station. Finally, the time passed, and we got on the train that would now take us over the German border into Holland. It was a modern, international carriage in which we found two places, and we had hardly settled ourselves wearily into the upholstered seats when a Dutch waiter asked us if we wouldn't like a cup of coffee to refresh ourselves. How glad we would have been to do so, but he did not take German money. Without my having noticed it, a very nice elderly gentleman went up to him and ordered two cups of coffee for us, along with the best cake to be had. When he brought it, this gentleman let us know that he had wanted to give us this little treat. When we had enjoyed the refreshments, he sat down beside us and said: 'For months I have been travelling this route to Rotterdam. I see immediately when emigrants are on the train and I have under- taken to give these people their first pleasure on Dutch soil by having some little refreshment brought to them that they can't procure for themselves despite the low price because they don't have Dutch money.' We began to talk and soon forgot our sadness at leaving Germany.

This experience was our first on foreign soil; the Dutchman, a high official, spoke to us in the most benevolent, friendly way, and with tears in my eyes I could only compare his words with those of the German officials who had given us so much trouble at the border. It should be borne in mind that we were leaving our fatherland. Not a single kind look, not a single understanding word for we women travelling alone, who at that moment would probably have aroused sympathy in even the hardest and cruellest person, showed that the people at the German border had any sympathy for emigrating Jews. But they had to follow their instructions and they carried out their orders so crassly and strictly that we could only breathe a sigh of relief when we finally escaped their domain and crossed the border.

# SOFONI HERZ

## Manuscript 24 (96)

*Born in 1905, Herz became an educator in the Jewish orphanage in Dinslaken in November 1937; emigrated in July 1939; interned in Northern Ireland as an 'enemy alien' after war broke out and was subsequently transferred to a camp in Australia.*

In early September, I returned to D[inslaken] to resume my work there. Since the director of the home was at that time starting out on a long trip abroad,[1] the board entrusted me with the overall administration of the orphanage. Every day, I noticed that the political situation was becoming more and more critical. Then I received a telephone call from the border city W[esel] requesting me to accept immediately a few Jewish children whose parents (Austrians) were trying to cross the Dutch border illegally. Residents of D., who had been called up for temporary military service because of the Czech crisis, told me when they returned that they were very glad that it had not ended in a war, but that the battle against the 'internal enemy' was certain to increase in the coming weeks.

One evening not long afterwards, all our Polish children who were over 15 years of age were arrested by police officers for deportation to Poland the following day. The orphanage was thrown into enormous turmoil. The deportees could take with them only the most important items of clothing. The following morning, I saw these unfortunate people in front of the town hall stuffing their last possessions into a little lorry.

By late October 1938, it was clear to me that the situation for us Jews was becoming untenable. To avoid problems, I ordered that, so far as possible, no residents of the orphanage were to be on the streets after eight in the evening. On the evening of 9 November, I tried to

72

visit another Jewish family. The demolished garden fence, the smashed window panes and other damage showed that acts of revenge for the assassination in Paris were already being staged here. The family was no longer there.

## 10 November!!!

Morning, 5.45. The insistent ringing of the doorbell in the early morning hours quickly woke me up. I threw on an overcoat and, suspecting the worst, opened the door to the building. Three men (two Gestapo agents and a police officer) came in and immediately declared that they had to undertake a search for weapons in the orphanage, as in all Jewish homes. The officials immediately went about their task, but searched only the ground-floor rooms, in particular the small office and the children's study room. In the office, the telephone line was cut, boxes and books checked and cash searched for. In a moment when he was not being observed, the Gestapo officer Schn. whispered in my ear: 'All the Jewish men in the city were arrested last night. Don't worry. Nothing will happen to you!' After searching for about twenty minutes without finding anything at all, the Gestapo officers left, telling me: 'No one must leave the building before ten o'clock this morning. All the blinds on the street side must remain closed. After ten, it will all (!) be over.'

About an hour later, around seven o'clock, the morning prayer service was supposed to begin in the orphanage's synagogue. A few men from the city usually also took part, but this time they were almost all absent. Only the town's Jewish teacher and two Jews of Polish nationality (who had not been caught during the preceding operation against Poles) turned up. Then, somewhat later, a man I did not know told me, with the greatest trepidation, that he had spent the past night in the waiting room of the main railway station in G. (Rhineland). He wanted to take refuge in the orphanage, just for a few days. Everywhere – so he had heard on the train – terrible anti-Semitic riots had broken out.

Despite this very upsetting news, I remained calm in order to prevent panic. But since I wanted to keep the children and trainees from being caught entirely unprepared by the approaching catastrophe, I called them all together at 7.30 in the orphanage's refectory – 46 persons, including 32 children aged from six to sixteen. I told them this, in a short, simple speech:

'As you all know, last evening Herr vom Rath, a member of the German legation in Paris, died from injuries he received in an attack. People are making us Jews responsible for this. The high political tension in Germany has now taken on a distinctly anti-Semitic tone, and over the coming hours it will probably result in anti-Semitic violence in our city as well. I suspect that not since the Middle Ages have we Jews in Germany had to tread a path as hard as the one we now have to take. Stay strong! Trust God! We will survive this hard time as well! From now on, no one will go into the upper rooms in the building! The door to the street will be opened only by me! Everyone will now obey only my instructions!'

After eating breakfast together, all the pupils were sent to the study and the teacher tried to find something for all of them to do.

9.30 a.m.! Loud ringing at the door to the building. I opened it and a group of about fifty men – many with the collars of their overcoats or jackets turned up – immediately stormed into the house and went to the refectory, which was fortunately empty, in order to begin destroying things with an almost scientific thoroughness. The children's terrible cries of fear echoed throughout the building. I shouted in a very loud voice: 'All children go with me into the street!' (This command was, of course, contrary to the Gestapo's order. But I thought the danger in the street was minimally smaller than it was in the building.) The children immediately hurried down the small stairway, most of them without hats and coats, despite the damp, cold weather. I ran with them to the nearest crossroads, where the town hall was located. There I intended to put myself under police protection. About ten policemen were stationed there, a sufficient excuse for curious spectators to be waiting to see the sensational events in the offing. They didn't have long to wait: the chief constable, Freihahn, shouted back: 'Jews will get no protection from us. Get out of here, and take your children with you!'

At the same time, Freihahn herded us towards a side street, in the direction of the garden (rear) side of the orphanage. Since I could not give him the key to the garden gate, he drew his sidearm. I told him: 'Strike me and the children dead, and then the matter will be quickly settled.' The officer took in my remark with a cynical laugh and broke the gate open with his weapon. We were then ushered onto the wet grass of the orphanage's garden and told that for the time being we were not to leave this place under any circumstances.

From that vantage point, we could now see how the police officers stood aside while the men inside the building systematically destroyed the orphanage's inventory, shattering window panes, throwing books, chairs, beds, tables, linens, maps, valises, piano parts, etc. out of the windows and doors. Among the curious crowd that had gathered passively at the garden fence, we saw former suppliers of the orphanage.

Around 10.15, we heard a wail of sirens and saw an enormous cloud of smoke, whose location made it clear that the Nazis had set the synagogue on fire. Soon afterwards, we noticed other smoke clouds. As I later saw, Jewish buildings had been set on fire under the expert guidance of the fire brigade, or – if the buildings were not homes – completely reduced to ruins.

10.45: the police commissioner of D. came up to me, in order – as he put it – to discuss the situation. In a tone that was supposed to show his disapproval of what had happened, he told me that he wanted to go through the orphanage with me. He asked me about my plans. I answered him curtly: 'I want the authorities to give me, today, permission to emigrate with all the children to Belgium or Holland.'

While we were making our way over mountains of rubble (even the railings of the stairway had been ripped out), a young man in civilian clothes suddenly planted himself in front of us and shouted in a loud voice to the police commissioner who was standing there in an officer's uniform: 'What does that Jew want from you?' Whereupon this uniformed representative of the law shouted at me: 'Get back with your own kind right now!' All I could do was leave as quickly as possible and rejoin my wards.

In the meantime, a few police officers had gathered; they ordered us to line up in a column and march to the school for Jews in the centre of the city. On our way there, we once again found, of course, many curious onlookers lining the streets. At the head of the column strode two police officers, to whom their colleague Freihahn shouted from the kerb: 'Hey, boys! Why are you leading this bunch of Jews? They ought to know themselves where their stall is!' Thereupon the two police officers immediately left. We were now herded into the schoolyard, which was near the synagogue, so that we could all see clearly how D.'s fire brigade encouraged 'the work of burning the synagogues' by only keeping the fire from spreading to neighbouring buildings.

After a few minutes of waiting, a few more Jews from the city arrived. For the most part, they were poorly or lightly clad, since they had been ordered by the brown-shirted horde to leave their homes immediately. Once again, a curious crowd had assembled in order to watch us. Then a representative of the NSDAP in civilian garb shouted to them: 'Fellow Germans! Get away from the garden fence! Pay no attention to "them"! They're really not worth looking at!'

Our 'family' had by then grown to about ninety people. All were put into the little schoolroom. No one was allowed to leave the room. After a few minutes, men 'fit for military service' were called out again. Only the oldest – including 75-year-olds – could remain. As we soon learned, after they were arrested, all men under sixty were taken to the concentration camp in Dachau. So long as they were still in 'protective custody' in the court prison, they were allowed to procure lunch at their own cost. As Herr S. and Herr L. told me – and as I later also learned from police officers – most of the Jews held in the court prison were brutally slapped and kicked by National Socialists before being shipped off to Dachau. Those mistreated were highly decorated frontline veterans.

I myself had incredible luck. The 'ringmaster' told me that I must see to it that the Jews remained quiet and orderly and be the spokesman for all of them. They ordered me to draw up a list of all those interned in the schoolroom. Naturally, this took some time. There were constant disturbances. One woman grew faint, another asked for water and still another complained of a bad headache. The retired Jewish teacher of D., a very dignified-looking old man (he had once been a city council member and the director of the city of D.'s commercial college), sat groaning in a corner with a bandaged head, which was bleeding as a result of the blows he had received. I managed, using an old envelope, to provide water for those who felt ill or were wounded, literally 'stealing' it from the water pipe in the hall.

Sudden quiet. A Nazi in civilian clothes and wearing a peaked cap came in. He was accompanied by a very unprepossessing woman. The party representative had the floor:

'People, listen: unknown elements have committed the destruction that took place this morning. That's understandable. You have to imagine: in Düsseldorf, a German mother and a father are mourning the son for whom they had such high hopes, and who was murdered by a Jew. You have to understand that, you people! This woman is a German woman (pointing to his companion), and for that reason she will ensure that not a hair on the head of any Jew here will be harmed. You need not be afraid! We are, after all, not in Russia! The old people – if you want – can be taken to the hospital by ambulance. The doctor will be coming soon. If you are hungry, you must pool your money – you have enough of it – and someone can then go into town to get food.'

After a short pause, the Nazi representative demanded our attention again: 'I would also like to make it clear that we have ordered that the cow belonging to the orphanage, which is taken care of by a German farmer, will continue to be fed. Animals must not suffer on this day.'

In the meantime, a doctor had arrived and he treated the elderly people with obvious sympathy. The afternoon passed quickly. The mood among the adults was very bleak; people were wondering what was going to happen. On the other hand, the children did not take the events so seriously. Some of them thought it all exciting. Around 6.30 p.m., the National Socialist from the morning turned up again, this time in a brown uniform. He ordered that everyone detained in the schoolroom should immediately march to a room at an inn in the city. The children were to get into a large wagon and all the other Jewish people were to walk behind it. This programme was strictly adhered to. After about twenty minutes, the 'Jewish procession', which had to force its way through crowds lining the streets, arrived at its destination.

The dance floor in the room was covered with straw and a few pillows that had been brought from the orphanage. Over the stage hung a picture of Adolph [*sic*] Hitler, but it had been quickly covered with a cloth before we arrived. An SA leader told me that in accordance with my wishes, noodles and dried fruit had been prepared for that evening, 'and no National Socialist has put anything inappropriate into it!' At 8 o'clock, the police authorities informed us that all Jewish young men over the age of fifteen and all men (meaning disabled war veterans) would sleep elsewhere, namely in the stable owned by the Jew L.

At 10 p.m., everyone was supposed to go to sleep. But in the presence of forty uniformed and armed SA and SS men, this was simply not possible. The children had 'bedded down' in a long line on the floor. It was my opinion that the children, who had been brought up Orthodox, should not forgo their evening prayer, especially on this evening. I said the prayer to them in a loud, audible voice, and the children repeated each word in chorus. At this moment, all the National Socialists withdrew from the room, with a guard consisting of a police officer and an SA man remaining. Despite the guards' assurances, the adults did not want to go to sleep. Only when I stated that the officers had given their 'word of honour' that nothing more would happen did things grow quiet. But only for a short time! At three in the morning, three people had to be taken to the hospital by ambulance. Then there was the monotonous walking up and down of the Nazi sentry . . . It was the dead of night, but only a few people slept.

## The following days of protective custody

The next morning, a city official came to inform me that he had been appointed commissioner of food supplies for the Jews. In the orphanage, he had found a total of RM 132.50, and he had to keep very precise accounts with me. He would always present to me the receipts for the food bought. The official was no doubt serious about this precise accounting. But at this time it struck me as a bad or stupid joke. Just that morning, my pupil Arno G. had brought me a 20-mark note that he had seen sticking out of a pile of rubble of the former garden on a path leading to the orphanage (which was under SA supervision, of course) and that he had spirited it away in a moment when the SA man was not looking. To talk about correct accounting under such circumstances!

We were allowed to cook in the kitchen of the former boarding house. The oven and the water supply still worked, whereas everything else had been completely destroyed. The preserving jars full of fruits and vegetables had been used – as traces clearly showed – by the National Socialists as missiles to throw against the kitchen door. We soon got used to this situation and were no longer surprised by anything.

The police officers spoke at length – when alone with their Jewish prisoners – about what had happened. They repeated apologetically that they had had nothing to do with these monstrous and disgraceful acts, but after all that was how they earned their living. A police officer told me that on the night of 10 November he had been roused from his bed by the command to go immediately to D. town hall because a raid was being carried out there. The officer in question further told me:

> We were ordered only to make an official appearance as police officers at four in the afternoon (10 November) and until that time to keep the street clear for the National Socialists. Because of all this, the mood among my comrades was wretched. To be on duty for so many hours for such nonsense! Except for this Freihahn, we're all still good Social Democrats or Democrats. But what can we do in times like these?

One morning, a young man who was sleeping in the stable with other pupils and men told me that at night they had been visited by a drunken SA man. Even though there were police guards there, they had to obey the drunken man and at his command exercise for an hour and then in conclusion sing a verse of the Horst Wessel song.

A Jewish man, who was also sleeping in the stable and learned that the young man had told me about the nocturnal National Socialist intermezzo, implored me not to bring the matter to the attention of the authorities. 'It wasn't so bad, after all, and anyway it's over.'

Guards were assigned day and night to all rooms in the demolished orphanage in order to prevent looting. In many rooms, clothing, linens, etc. still lay under large piles of rubble and glass shards. When I had to go into the orphanage at seven in the morning on 13 November, a police officer came up and addressed me with the following words: 'You must excuse me; our guard here is really a waste of time. Last night, at the behest of the National Socialist district committee, lorries came in and hauled off everything that the district committee itself had ordered us to guard, after the school's stock of wine – about sixty bottles – had been drunk by the SA men. And on top of that, they also broke into the strongbox.'

At eleven in the morning on the same day, a car pulled up in front of our internment camp. An elegant lady with a distraught expression lurched into the hall and cried loudly: 'My husband is dead! He died in a prison cell on the border after being tortured by the Gestapo!' The police officer exclaimed: 'Died!' The woman went on: 'Yes, my husband has to be buried here. Is that possible?' The police officer could not say. After long negotiations, the burial in D.'s devastated Jewish cemetery was authorized, but the public had to be kept away.

And in the afternoon of this same day, the deputy police commissioner appeared in our prison camp and ordered me to go immediately to the orphanage, taking with me all the keys to the building that were still in my possession; the district leader wanted to see me. I immediately followed the official and was taken directly to the refectory in the former orphanage. Here about forty policemen and SA and SS leaders had gathered. The district leader, a former teacher's aide, a tall, gaunt man, immediately grabbed the keys out of my hand and ordered me to go into the courtyard. Then from the window of the refectory he shouted at me: 'Criminal, step forward! You criminal, you have complained that you were being treated badly!'

| | |
|---|---|
| I: | 'This has to be a mistake!' |
| District leader: | 'A police officer told me that, and an officer never lies.' |
| I: | 'The officer must have been mistaken!' |
| District leader: | 'Criminal, stand aside and wait until I call you again.' |

Young men in civilian clothes were busy carrying the building's library to the district leader's car. One of the youths shouted at me: 'What do you want, Jew?' I replied that I was supposed to wait for the district leader. The boy shouted to the latter, who was talking with the police commissioner: 'District leader, there's a Jew waiting here!' The district leader called me forward and dismissed me with the words: 'Take off, you criminal!'

In the evening, a very friendly SA man summoned me several times to the telephone, which was in the front room of the inn. Relatives or acquaintances of the children were calling – calls from Antwerp, Brussels, Amsterdam, The Hague, Berlin and Hamburg came in almost without interruption – in order to enquire about them. A National Socialist tried to disturb the conversations by making heckling remarks but was strongly rebuked by other guests. As I went out I heard: 'Jews are people just as we are. Foreign countries will eventually learn the whole truth!'

## We move again!

On 15 November, the police announced that all Jews could return to their homes. By 4 p.m., we had to leave the hall in the inn clean and in order because a boxing match organized by D.'s athletic club was to take place there. Naturally, the only solution was for several families to live together since most of the buildings were simply uninhabitable. With the remains of the food, the pots and pans and the beds, I moved with the orphans into the outlying 'Villa' C, and had two rooms there cleaned up – as far as that was possible – to provide a place for fifty people to sleep. Before we left the hall at the inn, the district leadership made it clear that nothing was to be delivered to us and that not the slightest favour was to be done for us. Thus, the orphans were forced to transport our last possessions to the new living quarters in a large handcart, and in fact, at the NSDAP's command, right down the city's main street. At night, with a few boys, I mounted guard in front of our 'home' because the police had withdrawn their permanent guard. I could not endure this terrible gypsy-like life for another night. Cold, wet, with no windows, no toilets.

I got in touch by telegraph with the Jewish authorities in Cologne. The very next day all the children were transported to Cologne, a large city about 120 kilometres away. I stayed behind alone in order to wait for the lorry from Cologne we had ordered, which was to transport what remained of the property belonging to our former orphanage. While waiting, I reported to the police authorities the transfer of all orphanage residents from D. to Cologne. In a corner of the office, I saw in a large crate the silver 'that the SA and the police sought to secure against looting' and had for that reason taken away from the orphanage. Between six and eight o'clock, I helped the driver load the beds and the last food supplies . . . and then began the five-hour trip to Cologne in an open lorry. The case of D. was now closed. The NSDAP used the money it had confiscated from the orphanage to build a new district administration building.

# 'ARALK'

## Manuscript 107 (8)

*Pseudonym indecipherable, probably an anagram for Klara; born 1895, wife of a businessman from Munich, three children; emigrated to the USA in 1939.*

The Munich agreement confirmed National Socialist foreign policy, while violence cemented their domestic power. The sporadic unrest among the people was repeatedly nipped in the bud by such successes, which the Nazis proudly presented to the masses in a highly embellished form as proof of their achievements. I have to admit that when things were seen, as they were by us Jews, through the lens of the sufferers, the anaesthesia that the Nazis spread among the people was remarkably effective. So many friends we had known for decades sooner or later turned their backs on us. We had the feeling that they were not at first entirely convinced that what they were doing was correct, but they gradually changed their minds. They learned that the party's recipes were the right ones for the German people and the fatherland. It was very painful for us to see and feel this.

A few exceptions remained steadfast and saw deeper and farther with us. It was these exceptions who saved our lives. First of all, they tried to protect my husband's life, since it was men who were most at risk. At the same time, when women were imprisoned, little gentleness was displayed either. Our maid was a protector who sacrificed herself for us in the truest sense of the word. The law regarding servants didn't apply to her, and I didn't have to dismiss her as I did my other staff. I repeatedly drew her attention to the possible danger of serving in a Jewish household, but she was an outspoken opponent of Hitler and moreover a practising Catholic bound by great love for our children. Thus she decided to remain. I was astonished by the constancy of a person who was in herself quite simple.

There were those who sought to shake her from her firm decision. Her dear friend from the neighbouring house who proudly told her that she was one of the old 'battlers for the Hitler party'; the associations that showed up a few times a week to inform her of the dangers she was subjecting herself to by serving Jews; and naturally, the party itself, which had her spied upon by the janitor, who held the honorary title of block warden in the house, in order to cause problems for her. Yet she bore all these tribulations with iron calm and without complaint. As a practising Catholic, she took the simple standpoint that no mortal had the right to judge his fellow man himself. She achieved great things! The emigration of our children, our young ones, was probably the hardest blow she had to endure in her long years in my house. During this time, the good woman had become a friend to me, true and sincere. Not only in her loyalty, which she showed right down to the final hour before our emigration, but also by keeping away from us people who were still trying to get us into trouble.

During the great 'cleansing operation' that took place on 10 November 1938, she was the one who saved my husband's life by keeping him out of the concentration camp and who helped us all to escape. We were assisted by good fortune. A brother-in-law in my husband's family had already been in prison for a few months because of a statement he had made to a group of friends. At their regular table where he had met with his friends for decades, he had said that some day, when Hitler was no longer in control, his friends would see how Germany had been ruined as a result of his policies. His dear friends' denunciation put him in prison. In this connection, my husband had to visit a man, at seven in the morning on that famous 10 November, to try to get his brother-in-law released. That turned out to be a stroke of luck for him.

In the street, he learned that during the night the synagogues had been set on fire. He heard that the Jews were all being arrested. And he saw how Nazis with their private cars, always in groups of four or more, were quietly taking away half-asleep men from the front of buildings. Ten minutes later, I was awakened by the telephone ringing, and my husband told me to go immediately to my friend's apartment. Sensing that something was amiss, dear Anna silently helped me get away.

As I left the building, who did I see coming towards me shrieking, with her hair down and only half-dressed? A neighbour, the mother of two small children, who screamed non-stop: 'They've taken my husband away, and I don't know where. What should I do?' and ran past me as if possessed. A few steps further on, I met our doctor's wife, very pale, trembling and quietly weeping. She said: 'The Nazis picked up my husband this morning at 5 o'clock, I don't know why. Where should I go to enquire about him?'

I was gripped by dread. I hurried to my husband as fast as I could. My friend's husband had already emigrated, and at first my husband felt safer at her place. Fortunately, the apartment had two exits, and necessity is the mother of invention. The two exits now played an important role for us. On that morning, the Gestapo knocked on my friend's front door three times, and we escaped their eagle eyes three times by going out of the back door. Our child was still in school, so about noon I decided to go and pick her up. She had been sitting there unsuspecting in her classroom while we battled to keep her father from being arrested.

I left my friend's building just as Hitler's car, with him sitting next to the driver, raced past me. It was completely surrounded by standing SS men, their weapons ready. It was like a thunderbolt emerging from a black sky. Loud and sinister. I picked up my daughter and after a while returned to my friend's apartment.

In the meantime, my husband had gone into the city without my knowing it. There he saw a scene of devastation and destruction. The madmen had wrought terrible damage in the shops. In one department store, sparkling wine was flowing down the stairs, and not a window in the five-storey building remained unbroken. During the night, they had taken the owner and his son from their beds and sent them to the camp at Dachau. They had detained the women in their houses. In the private home of some friends of ours, they had shoved the elegant lady into the maid's room, arrested her husband and maliciously destroyed the whole house, a particularly fine one. At these people's house, the Nazis used their rifle butts to destroy our friends' large and valuable collection of paintings by Spitzweg until not a single picture remained intact. Then they set everything on fire, and the lady was barely able to save herself by jumping out of the window and running to the neighbours' home. Only then was she finally able to get dressed.

On this memorable day of 10 November, we were hunted down like game. After the Gestapo had repeatedly come to my friend's apartment in order to inspect it, we fled for the fourth time out of the garden gate into the street. Since there was nothing specifically Jewish in our appearance, we gradually came to see our greatest safety lay in being in the midst of the crowd.

The organization of these Jewish arrests was kept secret from the population for an astonishingly long time. But as during the course of the day people saw the cars dashing around and the frightened faces of those affected, a vexed uneasiness became discernible. At the railway station, I tried somehow to reach my elderly mother, who lived with an aged uncle. I got her on the telephone, and she answered in a very upset voice. When I came out of the public telephone booth, what did I see? Two civilians arresting a Jew, who had happened to be standing alongside my husband in the open railway station hall. I assumed they would then arrest my husband, and with the presence of mind that necessity provides, I spoke to my husband in English, loudly and distinctly. We quickly vanished into the crowd. Our daughter, greatly astounded, hurried after us.

The three of us rushed to a taxi stand and in our excitement each of us told the driver to head in a different direction. The old fellow said, with a strong Munich accent and the greatest equanimity, 'You know, people, I can only drive to one place at a time.' In our great excitement, we couldn't help laughing, and that did us good. We felt ourselves again. We now went to my mother's home in order to check how things were. As our taxi turned into the street where my mother lived, I saw the Gestapo loading my elderly uncle into their car. I couldn't believe my eyes and hurried to my mother. As a precaution, I left my husband in the taxi. Here I found another sad scene.

At seven in the morning, my nearly 70-year-old uncle had been hauled out of bed and five men had announced to him that he had to pay 3,000 marks or be arrested. Since my uncle had only 100 marks at home, the gentlemen generously agreed that he should get the money from the bank before noon. They promised that, if he did, they wouldn't lock him up. The old man got the money from his bank, and then men, different ones, came back. They took the money and then told him that he had to go with them after all. And that was the moment when we turned up. My mother was upset and ill from all the agitation and commotion, and we stayed with her. The night was, as can easily be imagined, a torment.

In the meantime, we learned through our maid Anna that our house had already been searched twice. They were looking for my husband and our older son. Our Anna saved my husband from arrest – whether because she didn't understand or because she was embarrassed, I have never been able to determine. After they – the Gestapo that is – had searched the apartment again to see if my husband was there, she said, truthfully, that she expected us back for supper. Late in the evening, three other men appeared again, and now the good woman asked what was actually going on, what they wanted from her master. Then the SS men told her the following: We had to leave Munich and Bavaria within twenty-four hours since they could no longer guarantee our security in any form. Since Anna could not memorize all that, she asked the men to give it to her in writing. And she was handed the following note, which we still have: 'The National Socialist Party hereby demands that you leave the city of Munich and Bavaria within 24 hours, since your security cannot be guaranteed.'

I think I need not emphasize that this message caused us some consternation. Moreover, they had bitterly reproached Anna for working for Jews at all and said that she ought to be locked up along with us. The faithful Anna wept a great deal, of course, and was very upset. The next morning, in great uncertainty as to what was going to happen to us, I hurried home with my daughter to make the necessary preparations. We bundled up twenty-four small and large pieces of hand luggage in such a short time that today I am amazed that it was possible to do so. We slunk out of our building like two criminals and, with a taxi she had ordered, Anna brought the luggage to us at the next street corner. With the half-packed things, we drove to another part of the city in order to pick up my mother and my husband. In the meantime, my husband had organized another car with which we could continue our journey. I can still see in my mind how we transferred the luggage on the open street, to the astonishment of passers-by. Everyone helped and we threw the luggage into the car and we were on our way! But where?

My husband directed the driver, while we women sat in the back, our feet and sides encumbered by luggage. In just over an hour, we arrived in Augsburg, where we intended to look up a good friend of my husband's from the war. He informed us that the same thing had happened at his home the previous night, and that things were very tense. But he gave us a key to his private rooms, where we were to stay until he picked us up. The man was the owner of a hotel. He said we would be able to wait there undisturbed until he could see more clearly how to help us go further.

My mother was quite exhausted by the hasty journey, and we considered whether we should accept this generous proposal for her sake. For all his charitable offer and loyal friendship, we neither wanted to nor could put the good man in danger on our account. What would be the point when we had our papers in our pocket and a 24-hour deadline for leaving the homeland? So, we decided to flee further – but where, why, how? But time was pressing, and we couldn't consider our options for too long. The car, loaded with many pieces of luggage, bumped through the winding lanes. We could hardly move because of all the luggage. Finally, we emerged from the narrow streets of Augsburg and headed at high speed towards the city of Ulm. We wanted to cross the Bavarian border as soon as possible and preferably arrive in Stuttgart before dark.

As we sped down the autobahn, we again and again saw large transport lorries fully loaded with men and with armed SS men in the front. A cold shudder swept over us. We knew that this was a raid in progress that was affecting the whole country. We all nervously watched every car that approached us or came up to us from behind. Suddenly my husband and I saw a small and very familiar police car turn into one of the autobahn entrances and race up behind our heavy Mercedes. We both exchanged glances for just a second and immediately understood what it might mean. My husband told the driver to increase his speed to 120 kilometres an hour. It was a mad race. My mother fainted during this crazy ride. Our daughter constantly begged her grandmother to wake up and calm down. It would last only a little longer, and then we would be there. I myself sat as though held by iron bonds, just watching the car following us.

Our good driver, probably guessing that something was going on here that could not be called ordinary and customary, said not a word and drove. He drove the car so safely and so well that I, as a driver myself, had great respect for him. With the police car behind us, this diabolical trip, during which I thought I would rather be dead than imprisoned along with my whole family, was an unforgettable one. This trip full of fear and trembling – how would it end? That half an hour seems an eternity in my memory, but the much smaller police car finally seemed unable to keep up with us. And then we saw it turn off at one of the autobahn exits. At first we couldn't believe our eyes. Still far too agitated, we maintained our speed and only very gradually began to speak again. In constant fear that we were being followed by telephone from place to place, we raced on. Finally, we crossed the border. Exhausted and at the same time liberated, we began at last to slow down.

Off the main highway, we found a small road where we could rest for the first time.

# MARIE KAHLE

## Manuscript 185 (101)

*Born in 1893 in East Prussia as Marie Gisevius; wife of the Bonn
orientalist Paul Kahle; five sons; the family emigrated to England in
spring 1939; died in Sussex in 1948.*

The German Congress of Oriental Studies was held during the last
week of August 1938. My husband was the chairman of the meeting,
in close collaboration with the mayor and the local authorities.

In early September, the World Congress of Asian Studies took
place in Brussels. My husband was head of the German delegation,
appointed by the ministry. Even more fearful than I was in Germany,
in Brussels I avoided engaging in any kind of political discussion.
When foreigners asked me about my attitude towards National
Socialism, I certainly did not speak against the government, although
I avoided praising the Nazis as much as I could.

After the disappointment that Munich[1] brought us, we closed ourselves off from the outside world as much as possible.

On 10 November 1938, at 11.30 in the morning, the wife of a
Jewish colleague came to me and reported that both the synagogues
in Bonn had been set on fire and that SS men had destroyed the Jewish
shops, to which I replied: 'That can't be true!' She gave me a manuscript to keep, her husband's life work. Then one of my sons brought
the same news.

My third son immediately went, without my knowing it, to a
Jewish clockmaker's shop, helped the man's wife hide a few things
and brought home a chest with the most valuable jewellery and time-
pieces. Then he went to a chocolate shop, warned the owner and
helped her move tea, coffee, cocoa, etc., to a room in the very back
of the building. While three SS men in uniform were destroying

88

everything in the front of the shop, he slipped out the back door with a suitcase full of securities and rode home with it on his bicycle. Later on, he spent weeks selling these hidden things to our acquaintances and thus made money for the two shop owners that the Gestapo knew nothing about. A Jewish colleague of my husband's[2] stayed with us all day long on 10 November and thus avoided being arrested.

From 11 November on, my sons worked furiously to help the Jewish shopkeepers clear out their shops. I couldn't take part in this myself because I did not want to endanger my husband's position. I could only visit the poor people. During one of these visits, my eldest son and I were surprised by a policeman, who wrote down my name. The consequence was a newspaper article in Bonn's *Westdeutscher Beobachter* for 17 November 1938 headed 'This is a betrayal of the people: Frau Kahle and her son help the Jewess Goldstein clear out.'

On the basis of this newspaper article, my husband was immediately suspended and he was forbidden to enter the Department of Oriental Studies or the university buildings. My eldest son was also forbidden to enter the university. He was convicted by a disciplinary court; the judgement is enclosed [see below]. During the night, our house was attacked. Window panes were broken, etc. The youths probably came with the intention of taking me with them, but could not break down the door to the house. The police came a short time later but went away again immediately. One of the policemen advised me to look out into the street; there, we found written in large red letters on the pavement: 'Traitors to the People! Jew-lovers!' We washed the writing away with turpentine.

However, since the people were constantly coming back in their car, I openly rode away on my bicycle. I did not want to be beaten to death in front of my children and I was also only a danger to my family. I found shelter in a small Catholic convent, where the nuns were kind enough to look after me and my youngest child. During my interrogation by the Gestapo a few days later, I was asked whether I knew the licence number of the car whose occupants had made the attack. When I said 'no', I was released. As I came out of the Gestapo's building, this same car stood in front of the door. I even recognized the driver.

Particularly important in this whole period was a visit in 1939 by a well-known neurologist[3] who, as Reich Education Director (*Reichsschulungsleiter*), was well up on Jewish matters. He told me, on two afternoons when we were alone, what would happen to me and my family along the lines of 'Jews and friends of Jews must be exterminated. We are exterminating friends of Jews and all their offspring.' Then he said that I could not be saved, but my family could. When I asked what I should do, he gave his answer in the form of a couple of stories in which the wife committed suicide and thereby saved her family. Then he asked: 'How much Veronal do you have?' When I answered 'Only two grams', he wrote me a prescription for the quantity that was lacking. I carried the Veronal around with me for a few days, but then I decided not to die, but instead to try to escape abroad *with* my family.

In four months, only three of my husband's colleagues dared to visit us. I was not allowed to go out during the day. When one evening I met a colleague's wife and complained that no friends or acquaintances had dared to visit me, she said: 'That's not cowardice: we are just facing facts.'

When on 17 February 1939 the Gestapo forbade my husband to speak with his colleagues (my acquaintance's first point), I saw that it was time to leave Germany before the Nazis could put me and my boy in a concentration camp (his second point).

I assume that this acquaintance told the district leader that I would certainly take my own life and that my passport (which had been taken away from me after 17 November) should be returned to me. I can find no other explanation for the return of my passport. Three days later, I travelled with my eldest son to Holland and from there to England. Here, our English friends collected money for us, and an academic position was found for my husband. When all means of informing my husband that he should now also come to England failed, I travelled to Brussels and met my husband there. After almost insuperable difficulties, we succeeded in getting the other four children out of Germany. On 2 April, we all travelled back to England.

In conclusion, I would also like to say that I would not have been able to endure our last months in Germany, had I not had a friend. This friend was Professor Rademacher, a professor of Catholic theology at the University of Bonn. His last words to me were: 'Confide, filia, fides tua te salvam fecit!'[4]

Disciplinary Judgement

In the disciplinary proceedings against the student of musicology Wilhelm Kahle, born 12 June 1919, residing in Bonn, Kaiserstrasse 61

The three-man committee of the University, in the session of 5 December 1938, in which participated:
the University Rector, Professor Dr. Schmidt,
the head of the teaching staff, Prof. Dr. Chudoba,
The leader of the students, philosophy student Eitel,

90

as judges
University Councillor Dr. Wildt
as representative for the accused
University Head Inspector Stuesser
as recorder
has decided that:
The student of musicology Wilhelm Kahle will be punished, because of behaviour unworthy of a student in regard to the protest action against Jewish businesses, by
dismissal from the university and
denial of credit for the semester's work

On 10 November 1938, there occurred in Bonn, as a result of the murder of the legation councillor vom Rath, a demonstration against Jews, in which the corset shop owned by the Jewess E. Goldstein was affected. On the late afternoon of 12 November 1938, the accused went with his mother to this shop, in which the latter had earlier made purchases. When they arrived at the shop, around 6 or 6.30 p.m., three Jewish females were leaving it. In the shop, they met the owner and another Jewish person named Herz. The shop owner was busy putting boxes back on the shelves. After they had been there for about three minutes, Police Sergeant Peter Stammen entered the shop and wrote down the names of the Jewish persons and then also the name of the student Kahle's mother, and in doing so had some difficulties with the latter. He then turned to the student Kahle, who was putting the boxes that were on the counter back on the shelves, and asked him whether he was an interior decorator. The student said he was not, and then gave his name.

Contrary to the charge, the Disciplinary Court has not been able to determine that the accused intended from the outset, as he left home with his mother, to go to the Jewish shop. It is more of the opinion that no preconceived intention lay behind this visit, but rather that the visit took place only on the occasion of passing by the demolished shop. Further, the Disciplinary Court has not derived from the proceedings the impression that the student helped the Jewess put her merchandise back on the shelves but sees the student's actions simply as an effort, without any special intention, to help the Jewess in her work or to support her in some way.

Nonetheless, the student's behaviour is thoroughly reprehensible. By finding it justifiable to enter a Jewish shop after the given incidents, he seriously endangered the reputation and dignity of the university and thereby violated his academic duties. Articles II and III of the Disciplinary Code for Students, 1 April 1935. He was to be penalized.

The accused's behaviour requires a vigorous atonement. Since the accused seemed to be a little inept and awkward during the proceedings and was obviously under the influence of his mother, the

91

Disciplinary Court has decided in mitigation merely to dismiss him from the university and deny him credit for the current semester's work.

In imposing this punishment, which is mild in relation to the offence, the Disciplinary Court has acted on the basis of the expectation that the student will pursue his further education at a greater distance from his parents' home, so that in future he can mature into a more independent, more self-confident and more responsible person.

Bonn, 6 November 1938  
[stamp]  
Rector of the Rheinland Friedrich  
Wilhelm University in Bonn

The Rector of the University  
signed Schmidt  
Witnessed: Stuesser  
University Head Inspector

# — Part II —

## In The Camps

# KARL E. SCHWABE

## Manuscript 202 (207)

*Born in 1891 in Hanau; married, two children; shopkeeper, emigrated to London in April 1939, from there to the USA; died in Philadelphia in 1967.*

In early October, our son returned from school in Frankfurt in great distress. He had seen lorries full of Jewish people being taken to the railway station under SS and police guard. They were, he learned, Poles who were being expelled. They had been roused from their beds early in the morning and had not been allowed to take anything other than the most absolutely necessary hand luggage with them. The sight had been so terrible that even non-Jews had been scandalized by it. But what use was getting upset? This was not, after all, the first time the party had shown its brutality. The newspapers said that it was a defensive measure against Poland, and negotiations to settle the matter were under way. Then we heard that those expelled might soon return. Later events made the 'Poland action' seem less important; it had been a kind of dress rehearsal.

On the evening of 9 November, my [English] teacher, a Christian artist, came to visit. When he tried to leave at about 10.30 to go home, two SA men in uniform were standing in front of our garden gate. What did they want? We waited half an hour, a whole half hour, and they were still standing there. Finally Herr W. climbed over the garden fence behind the building and was fortunately able to get home without being noticed. I felt very uneasy and apprehensive. I told my wife how I felt, and we tried to calm each other.

The next morning I prepared to go to my shop as usual and stood there in hat and overcoat, waiting for my little daughter, whom I always took to school in the morning. The doorbell rang, and I myself

95

opened the door. Two men in civilian clothing stood there – Gestapo – 'Are you Herr Schwabe? Come with us!' We were all dreadfully frightened. They refused to explain the grounds for my arrest. I had a clear conscience and tried to console my wife. Marie quickly prepared a couple of sandwiches for me, and then I followed the officers. Outside stood the dark green police car. I sat alone in the semi-darkness on the journey, thought about my brother, and racked my brains to find the reason for my arrest. The car stopped again, and after a few minutes Herr O., who lived near me, got in. In the same way, the car picked up a number of other Jewish men, and then drove to the prison, the so-called Frohnhof.

At first, we were put into a dark cell where there were already a number of arrestees, and then one after another we were taken to register. We had to give our personal details and hand over the contents of our pockets; then we were allocated to various cells. Of course, the prison was not designed for such a massive number of arrests. More and more people came in from the city and surrounding areas; they had been arrested just as they were, wherever they were. Finally, there were nine people in our cell which was designed to hold two prisoners; only a few could sit down; the others stood. An earthenware jug of water stood on the table, and in the evening there was so-called coffee and bread. We were all much too upset to be able to eat anything. The slop-jar stank and destroyed what was left of our appetites.

For the night, a few straw mattresses were thrown on the floor, and then the lock clanked, the light went out, and I experienced my first night in prison. I lay with another man on one of the not-very-inviting beds; each of us had a rough woollen blanket. A few men immediately went to sleep, snored dreadfully, and some talked in their sleep, mumbled and sighed, while I lay awake most of the time. In the morning, we could wash ourselves a little, 'coffee' and bread appeared again, and then the nine of us were locked up once more in the cell. New prisoners were still being brought in; we heard voices and tramping feet in the stone corridor, the clanking of the locks.

The noon meal we left almost untouched. At 2 p.m. came the order: 'Everyone out of the cell!' We were given back the things that had been taken from us and made to go out into the prison courtyard. For a long time we stood there, and then Gestapo officials and the district administrator (*Landrat*) appeared. Sneering, the latter greeted every one of us as a special criminal and said that we would now be taken away, warning us against 'escape attempts', saying that we would be shot immediately. A column was formed, police on our left and right with loaded weapons, and we passed through the city to a gymnasium where a few hundred men had already been interned. We learned that the synagogue had been set afire and burned down, that shops had been demolished, window panes broken and homes devastated. How would it be at home?

Again, hours of waiting, and then came a brief medical examination. The elderly and ill were sent home, and the rest of us marched again in a long column to the railway station. The population had obviously been told what was happening. People were standing shoulder to shoulder and let us pass by them. Hardly any of them said anything; a few laughed, but sympathy and dismay could be seen on many faces.

We got on a train coming from Frankfurt in which several hundred people were already sitting. In each compartment a policeman served as a guard. In my compartment sat a few young men from Gehringshof, the Zionist educational institution.[1] They had been taken from there to Hanau in a lorry. They had full hampers of food and were unworried and almost cheerful, but I didn't feel that way. A short stop in Fulda; on the platform, travellers were waiting for their trains, girls looked in surprise into our compartment; how immensely far we were from that life as we wondered what fate had in store for us.

The policeman was not unfriendly, got water for us to drink, but didn't say a word. The train continued on and it grew dark; the landscape outside seemed to me unfamiliar in the moonlight, even though I had so often travelled along this stretch. The unlit stations swept past us: a short stop in Eisenach, then came Weimar. The train stopped, we got out, the policeman disappeared. Again, we were formed into a column and marched down the long platform. We turned right and proceeded towards the underpass. I heard noise, cries, curses. On the left and right of the stairway stood SS men and policemen who struck and kicked us as we hurried down. Today, I still don't know how I got downstairs.

In front of the station there was a long row of transport vehicles, and we all tried to get into one as soon as we could; those who failed to do so were beaten mercilessly. A harsh voice ordered us to put our heads on our knees and not to look up. The vehicles lurched forward and seemed to drive on endlessly. We went uphill, and it grew colder; finally we stopped. 'Out, you swine!' Everyone jumped quickly out of the lorry onto a great open place lit by searchlights. We were completely dazed and blinded. Cursing and beating us, the SS men herded us through a large gate; we had arrived in Buchenwald.

Overseers in strange, patchwork uniforms took charge of us. Each of them wore a coloured triangle on his coat. Later we learned that these were prisoners who had been given these positions because of their good behaviour. The colour of each triangle indicated why they were there: red for political criminals, black for professional criminals, green for Jehovah's Witnesses, etc. 'Don't worry,' they told us, 'now you've made it, you'll no longer be beaten.'

We were divided into groups and then made our way over piles of earth and tree roots to the barracks that had been prepared for us. In the dark they seemed enormous. Coming through the door, we entered a kind of anteroom from which narrow, dark passageways with tall racks on each side branched off to the left and right. A few electric lights were burning. The racks, made of rough, unplaned planks, held five bunks, each about three-quarters of a metre high. That was where we were to sleep. No blankets, no mattresses, no straw, only bare wood. The barracks had no wooden or paved floors, only the recently cleared and unlevelled forest floor.

I was too exhausted to look around much and, glad to be able to stretch out, I climbed into a bunk. The man next to me could not sleep and complained. He came from Breslau [now Wroclaw] and had been on a business trip. He had been taken out of the train in Wiesbaden and had been unable to inform his family.

At about 5 a.m., we were called out. There was a terrible crush in the narrow passageways; no one wanted to be the last. In front of the barracks there was indescribable confusion. It was dark and cold. No one knew what to do. The barracks were on a slope, separated from a wire fence by a strip of ground about 50–100 metres wide. The wire fence divided this strip of land from a levelled and tarred muster ground with the commandant's building on the second side and permanent barracks on the other two sides. On this muster ground, the long-term prisoners who had reported for the morning's work stood in endless lines. Silently, the columns moved out, and the ground was empty again.

The overseers from the previous evening reappeared. 'Here Frankfurt, here Hanau, here Fulda!' they called out, and people from the same area tried to find each other. We were led to the muster ground. Endless lining up and counting off. In the meantime, it had got light; the sun shone red through the forest trees behind the commandant's building, and it grew warmer. Now we could see how incredibly many people had been herded together.

We stood there all day for no apparent reason. Always lining up again, being inspected by SS men; old, ill people collapsing; beatings.

Finally, towards evening, we were taken back to the barracks. On that day, we were given nothing to eat or drink.

That was my first day in Buchenwald; many similar ones followed. I cannot and do not want to describe all the details. It was a series of endless physical and mental sufferings. The first days were the worst. We were made to go thirsty. Water was in short supply and none of it was given to us. Our mouths dried out completely, our throats burned, our tongues literally stuck to our palates. When on the third day bread was distributed, I couldn't get it down; I had no saliva. The nights were terrible. People had attacks of hysteria. One man shouted that they were trying to kill him, another delivered a kind of sermon. A third babbled about electrical waves. In between, cries, weeping, praying, cursing, coughing, dust, dirt, stink – it was as if all hell had broken out.

During the early days, we had to muster every day at the same time. We were registered, each one received a number. They began by stamping the numbers on the prisoners' wrists but after a few days they stopped doing that. Also, they stopped shearing off hair and beards. After a week, we were left to ourselves.

On Monday, 13 November,[2] after standing all morning, we sat from one o'clock to six on the cold, bare earth. No one was allowed to stand up or go to the toilet. SS men were constantly going up and down between the rows, checking the line-up and beating people and grossly insulting them. I saw people fall to the ground; an old man who could no longer endure sitting stood up, was dragged past us, kicked and beaten. On that day, people were literally beaten to death. Many soiled themselves. There was neither water for washing nor a change of linen. At night, the hysterics raged worse than ever. The sentries threatened to shoot into the barracks. Several people ran into the electrified barbed-wire fences; in the morning, I saw their naked bodies lying in the mud.

Slowly things got a little better. The mistreatment lessened. The worst thing was the lack of anything to drink. At first, there was no water at all. When it rained, the water that dripped from the trees and roofs of the barracks was collected. Coffee – on average, a quarter of a litre per day. Sometimes a little more, sometimes none at all.

One morning, from seven o'clock on, I stood on the muster ground in front of our barracks. Far ahead, coffee was being handed out. Slowly, our group moved forward. About 10.30, we could see the coffee being distributed. It was cold, the ground was damp and muddy, and our thirst grew. Suddenly, the overseers attacked the people with clubs and drove them off – the coffee was all gone, and the poor thirsty devils had refused to go away. In later weeks, water was occasionally provided; that is, a bowl was held in front of us and we were allowed to drink a few sips. Food was in short supply and sometimes almost inedible; it was handed out at very irregular intervals. Under these circumstances, mortality was high. Every day we saw shrouded biers and coffins being carried away.

The sanitary conditions defy description. Jewish doctors who had been taken prisoner with us did what they could, but there was hardly any way to help. People ill with pneumonia, suppurating middle ears and other diseases lay feverish in the barracks. Almost everyone had diarrhoea. Money for medicine was collected, and now and then we got a few drops of opium or charcoal tablets, but as soon as this was known patients crowded in and most people got nothing. Later on, a sickroom was set up in a cold, dark wash house, and here the dying lay on dirty straw mattresses; anyone who had to go to the wash house was given up for dead.

The barracks were overfilled. I lay with an acquaintance from Hanau very high up, on the 'fifth floor'. Reaching it was a gymnastic feat, but there was more light and air there; I could even stand up, if hunched over, and more importantly, no dirt fell down from above, as it did on the lower levels. Above me, an air hole had been cut in the roof, which was a great blessing. Naturally, under these circumstances all of us were extremely irritable and tried somehow to calm our nerves. Rumours emerged and were eagerly taken up and debated. We were to be released – special trains were standing ready in Weimar; England and Holland had made camps available for us; Jews in other countries were to pay a ransom for us – nothing was too fantastic.

How much we all had to endure. A 38-year-old man had been hauled off in his dressing gown and slippers, a regional court judge from Frankfurt arrived in his bathrobe. I saw a crooked, dwarf-like man who had a shirt and a kind of overcoat, and literally nothing else, not even shoes. A confectioner from Frankfurt had been beaten until he destroyed his own shop, while others had looked on while their apartments were demolished and ruined and their property burned up. The director of the Gross Breesen educational institution[3] described how non-uniformed SS men had driven up and destroyed everything. The local police knew nothing about it, and tried to resist the unknown intruders; only when they enquired by telephone did they learn about the 'spontaneous' wrath of the people. After ten days, we were allowed to write a postcard bearing a prescribed message.

The first releases followed, very old and very young people; there were 90-year-olds and 13-year-olds. One day, there was enormous excitement. People who had been decorated with the Front Soldiers' Cross of Honour and who had the certificate with them were to report for release. Astonishingly, more than twelve hundred of them had brought along the precious piece of paper. We others were allowed to write postcards asking that the certificate be sent to us. The hope of being released rose. Now the first packages also arrived. From then on, our whole lives were one great waiting. Loudspeakers hung inside and in front of the barracks. When they started to crackle, noise and conversation stopped – no one wanted to miss hearing his name. When the loudspeaker fell silent, the din in the barracks began again.

After a fortnight, I ran into my cousin from Mainz. Each of us knew that the other was also there [i.e., on the Ettersberg, where the Buchenwald camp was located], and we had looked for each other, but in the indescribable throng of people we had only now found each other. Richard's head had been completely shaved, while my hair stuck out wildly, and both of us had stubbly beards. He tried to give me a kiss, and it was like two hedgehogs embracing. We were happy to be together. He told me that his shop – one of the most elegant in Mainz – had been completely demolished, and that afterwards he had been arrested among the ruins. From that time on, we were together every day. As a veteran, the man who slept next to me was released. He left me his travel rug. I had the usual camp diarrhoea, with acute pain, especially during the night. Now that I could stay a little warmer, I felt better.

A great event: I received a package. My wife had written the address, the first sign of life. She had found everything: underwear, shirts, socks, handkerchiefs and my ski boots. The latter gave me the greatest joy. The rain had loosened the clay soil so much that my light, low shoes literally got stuck in the mud. A big, warm blanket was also in the package, and Richard got my other one. A canteen was opened up. The prices were outrageous, but sales were brisk.

Wild excitement gripped the whole camp when cases full of mineral water were unloaded; we were parched with thirst. Normally quite reasonable people became enraged when at 10 o'clock one evening coffee was handed out and the distribution wasn't fast enough. Each person got only four sips, no more. People tore the bowl away from each other's mouth. Finally, the mineral water was distributed, two men to each bottle, and we could have drunk ten of them. You can get really drunk on water.

More and more people were now being released. Every day, sometimes once, sometimes twice, the loudspeaker crackled and everyone waited to find out when his turn would come. The camp became noticeably emptier, and Richard and I stayed outside as much as we could and 'went for walks'. Through the barbed-wire fence, we watched the long-term prisoners when they came back in the evening from the quarries, each with a heavy stone on his shoulder. Emaciated, listless and infinitely sad, they slunk back, and kicks and blows with rifle butts rained down on them when they did not find their places fast enough. They were half-starved. Once, we saw one of the large pots in which the food was brought fall over. In a second the prisoners were on their knees, licking the food off the ground.

The SS men were, with few exceptions, fiendish brutes. The commandant, a big fellow with a ruddy bullish face, always had his riding whip with him, and not for nothing.[4] They were all crude and mean. We were called 'the Jewish swine'. A boy whose father had died up there was told about the death with the words: 'The bird's dead. Dismissed!' An SS man said, as a coffin was carried past him: 'Let me see the dead Jew.' I saw and experienced something similar every day. About ten days after our arrival, they stopped giving us spoons with our meals. Anyone who didn't have one or couldn't get one ate out of the bowl like a dog. I was happy when the previously mentioned bedfellow left me his spoon as a farewell gift.

The canteen constantly suffered from a 'lack of change', and thus sold only in lots at five marks. For example, anyone who wanted to buy cigarettes had to buy chocolates, canned fish, packages of dried figs, etc., along with them. Thus all day long 'dealers' stood there and tried to sell the things they didn't need. The prices were three to ten times the usual ones. Items such as socks, scarves, shirts and blankets that came from Jewish shops in Halle were sold, and the labels with the original prices hadn't even been removed.

Along with all the misery, there were also tragicomic moments. For example, every morning one could hear someone cursing and complaining: 'The syrup!' Syrup, that sticky stuff, was given to us in paper cartons to spread on our bread. These cartons had a nasty tendency to fall over if you weren't careful. The syrup ran out, spread and dripped, and when people woke in the morning they had to struggle with strings of the stuff, like Laocoön with the serpents.

Another scene: because of the colossal overcrowding, some of the most recently arrived Jews were put in the permanent barracks. They were made to wear the greyish-blue striped camp uniforms and caps without peaks, and they were all given shoes in the largest available sizes. In them they were made to march up and down and do callisthenics all day.

We were allowed to go to the toilet at night only with permission, and the guards used this to show their sense of 'humour'. For example, a rather portly older gentleman who had failed to join his group when it reported back was punished by being forced to do twenty squats and then sing the song 'Die Vöglein im Walde'.

The days went by, and it was always the same thing. Dirt, diarrhoea, boredom and the constant waiting strained our nerves. I did not feel well and spent much time lying on my fifth-level bunk, reading. A comrade had brought along a big book he had taken out of a lending library. I read *Jakob Gontard und die Genien der Liebe*[5] at least ten times. In my situation, the marvellous banquets described in this book were more interesting than the sad fates of Hölderlin and Susette Gontard.

I had once again fasted, because fasting was the only way to avoid diarrhoea, and felt somewhat better. I went out of the barracks and waited for Richard. Suddenly, unusually early, at 8.30, the loudspeaker up in the tree crackled. Everyone paid attention because Hanau names were being read: 'Julius Reis, Alexander Schwab, Karl Schwabe'. An indescribable feeling shot through me like a lightning bolt. I was benumbed; I could no longer see or hear. I pushed through the people waiting there, raced into the barracks, packed up my things, gave my underwear to comrades and hurried off at a run through the 'little gate' on the muster ground to the commandant's office.

Our names were read out, about two hundred of us; some were so excited that they hardly knew their own names. First, we were sent to see a doctor who did not examine us but instead looked each of us over to see if there were any signs of mistreatment; if there were, he would not be released. Then we marched to the orderly room where various forms had to be signed; we had to promise not to say anything about what we had experienced, acknowledge that we had been properly treated, and so on.

Next came the barber. Our hair and beards were shorn off. I was shocked when I looked at myself in a little mirror; I hardly recognized myself. We got through that, too, and we were then taken to the 'post office' to pick up any money that had come in for us. My wife had sent me RM 60; I was given RM 17, and they kept the rest – supposedly for prisoners who had nothing.

It was now 2.30 in the afternoon. I happened to have a little bread tucked away; otherwise I would have had to go on fasting. We were taken back to the commandant's office. Each of us was given a brush and we tried to clean off the worst of the filth, with little success. Finally, finally we passed through the big gate; it was Saturday, 10 December, precisely one month after my arrest. But we had still not been released.

We had to stand for hours in a long hallway in one of the buildings adjacent to the gate. On the left and right, doors marked 'Sturmbann-führer X', 'Kriminalkommissar Y', and so on.

An obnoxious young coxcomb lectured us. We had had a little taste of the concentration camp, and that would probably be enough for us this time, etc., etc. We made it past that, too. In conclusion, he demanded that we make, as a special concession, a contribution to the SS Winter Aid programme, and then we were allowed to get out of the hallway and into the open air! This time, buses were waiting in front of the door, and we climbed in. The buses started up, and with each turn of the wheels we moved farther away from the hell of Buchenwald. On the way downhill, we saw numerous roadblocks and guard posts. We finally turned onto a main road, and after a few minutes the first buildings of Weimar came into view. We drove through side streets to the railway station; it was almost dark.

A man in civilian clothing walked up to us: 'Please follow me.' He led us to the same passageway through which we had so hurriedly bolted to the trucks a month earlier.

Police officers were there again: 'Please go to the back, gentlemen, you will be given something to eat.' We could hardly believe our ears. Was such courtesy possible? At the back stood Jewish women with coffee and white rolls. For two days I had eaten nothing but a few bites of dry bread, and all at once I realized how starved I was. The coffee and rolls tasted unbelievably good. The friendliness with which they were given us also did us good, and it was amazing how well the ladies worked together with the police. One man got us train tickets; we men from Hanau had to report to Gestapo headquarters in Kassel.

At last the train came and we could get in. We were, of course, very noticeable with our shaven heads and ragged clothing, but no one said anything. One after another, we went to the washroom to clean ourselves up. For a month, I had not been able to wash myself even once. We arrived in Kassel at 8.30 p.m. The big square in front of the station was brightly illuminated, and we looked with wonder at the traffic, which had become unfamiliar to us. Could we take a taxi to the Gestapo? We didn't know. In Buchenwald one day, owners of cars had been ordered to assemble, and the commandant had read them a decree saying that in future Jews would no longer be allowed to own cars. Then they had to sell their vehicles at scandalously low prices.

A taxi driver was glad to take us on, and a few minutes later we were at the local Gestapo headquarters, where we were released without further formalities. Now at last we were really free. The taxi took us back to the railway station. We went into the waiting room and soon had coffee, bread and sausage on our table. I ordered three times, but the hole in my stomach still was not plugged. There was no direct train to Hanau. We travelled via Fulda, and there we had to wait from 12.30 a.m. to 5 a.m. Here, too, we went into the waiting room to get something to eat. It was full of customers who were dining there because the restaurants in the city had already closed. We attracted attention, and loud remarks were made; we sat there as if on hot coals. We quickly choked down our food and were glad to get outside again.

With a comrade, I walked through the dark, empty streets. The city was decorated for Christmas. Green garlands had been strung from lamppost to lamppost; despite the late hour, the shop windows were still brightly lit. Had I also once had a shop? Had I, too, once displayed things there, planned, worked?

We walked all around Fulda and finally passed by the old castle and into its grounds. I sat down on a bench, took off my ski boots, put on the lighter low shoes and brushed from my trousers as much of the Buchenwald mud, which was now dry, as I could.

The hours dragged on endlessly; twice, the train was reported delayed. Finally, it came. It was growing light, and I saw the landscape gradually become more familiar as it passed by me. How would we find our homes, our lives again? The man at the ticket barrier, whom I knew well, looked at me meaningfully and gave me a friendly greeting. As we hurried towards the centre of the city, one after another turned off. Herr H., one of my neighbours, and I had the farthest to go.

The house stood peacefully there, its shutters closed. With trembling fingers, I put the key into the lock, quietly opened the door, tiptoed the few steps to the door of my apartment and unlocked it. The carpet in the vestibule had disappeared, and on the coat rack hung an unfamiliar overcoat. I was startled. Did someone else now live in this apartment? Then a door opened and our maid Marie appeared in her nightgown and screamed when she saw me. My wife came laughing and crying at once, our boy appeared, and our sleepy little girl blinked at me: 'Papa, how funny you look. People would think you were 53 years old.' I didn't look like the same man.

The bath of which all the men returning home dreamed was soon drawn. A delight to be able to get clean again. I was feverishly excited, told stories and listened to others' stories, my mother came, and I went on soaping and scrubbing as if I could wash off everything, everything. Then, all clean and wearing fresh linen and a fresh suit, I sat down to the breakfast table. The tablecloth was white, the cups, plates and cutlery sparkled, and there was food and drink, good bread, sausage, butter, cheese, eggs and coffee, as much as I wanted of them. It was incredible, and I kept on telling my family how incredible it was.

My wife had kept going splendidly. Immediately after my arrest, she had tried to get me released. Although he had been warned not to do anything for Jews, our family doctor had given her an attestation that I had recently had an operation, and she took this to the Gestapo. When this attempt was thwarted, she tried to get permission to bring me warm food to eat, but this was also refused. In the meantime, our faithful Frau K. had gone to the shop in order to put the money and the most important account book with the accounts receivable in a safe place.

Our little shop, which was in a side street, was the last one in the city to be destroyed. Furniture, mirrors, window panes, the cash register, typewriter and sewing machine were all smashed.

The goods had been thrown on the floor, the business papers and account books torn up. The next day, the two women and our boy cleaned up the worst of it. My wife called a dealer, who until recently had still been purchasing from us every Saturday, and sold her what goods were still there, naturally at a price far below our own costs, but a little was saved.

The first days must have been terrible. After I was arrested, the landlord had demanded that the apartment be immediately vacated, which was, of course, impossible. My family heard that in other parts of the city Jewish homes had been plundered and wrecked, and they moved carpets and valuables to hiding places (that was why I hadn't seen the carpet when I came home) and waited, trembling, for the gangs to come to them. While they were putting things away, my mother slipped coming down the stairs and broke her collar bone. She had to be taken to the hospital late in the evening. She was splinted and bandaged under anaesthetic.

Thanks to the vigorous protests of our district's local group leader, the apartments in our neighbourhood were spared. In other parts of the city, there were terrible beatings. All the remaining men were mistreated, and a few had to go to the hospital with serious injuries. Most of them were arrested and held in prison for weeks. Three days later a number of people appeared at the home of our friend Dr K., who is crippled, and beat and threatened both him and his 84-year-old mother with a pistol. They forced him to hand over all the money he had in his safe, smashed everything, slit open the eiderdowns and then took off. The police, who had been called by a neighbour, did nothing.

My family thought it was too dangerous to remain in Hanau. They fled to relatives in Frankfurt for a few days, and my wife drove back and forth between Frankfurt and Hanau every day. Then things calmed down. The landlord presented his excuses, and the eviction notice was withdrawn. My wife worked and did what she could for me, dealt with business matters and wrote to everyone in an attempt to find a way to emigrate. On top of that, she had the household to run and my sick mother to care for; my wife's achievements were truly amazing. All this I discovered only gradually, of course.

At first, after I had once eaten my fill, I was very, very tired. Then I lay in the darkened bedroom. The unfamiliar quiet made me nervous. Where was the relentless noise of the barracks? Where was the constant cougher who always put on a special performance for hours before we went to sleep? Where was the rumble of conversations, the whistling, cursing, singing, praying – all the noises that a thousand people make? Despite my fatigue, I could not go to sleep. I turned on the reading light, and good old Wallace [presumably Edgar Wallace] helped me. The lines swam before my eyes; my wife came to look in on me, put out the light, and I slept.

A few hours later, I woke up, hungry. Again, I ate as if I had had nothing to eat all day, and we were all glad to be together again. I called various acquaintances, women to whom I gave news of their husbands, my cousin in Mainz, whom I told about Richard, and then I became very tired again. Once again I was amazed by the quiet. I woke up in the middle of the night. The street lights in front of the building, shining through the Venetian blind, made yellow stripes on the wall. The cracks in the barrack walls had also made stripes when the light of the rotating searchlights fell on them. It would go dark again soon! Wasn't that Ludwig's snoring? Where was H.'s foot, which I always hit when I stretched out? I could no longer get my bearings. Bathed in sweat, even though I was cold, I tried to form a clear idea of where I was, and breathing a sigh of relief I realized that I was at home and safe, and lay down again to really sleep. This went on for weeks. Night after night I saw the images, heard the sounds and thought I was back in Buchenwald.

The next morning we were sitting at the breakfast table when we received an unexpected visit. Two city officials handed me a writ of attachment for no less than RM 7,000. Immediately after the 'people's wrath' had taken its revenge on my window panes, the city had demanded that they be immediately repaired. Now there was also a law that these repairs had to be paid for, not by the owner of the building (in many cases a non-Jew), but rather by the Jewish shopkeepers. Through Dr K., my wife had protested this requirement, but that didn't bother the city. The Jew had to pay. Naturally, the women were very upset, but I remained calm. I had experienced too many infamies in Buchenwald to be surprised or upset by one more. There I had gained another view of the value of life, and had become harder.

The officials exercised their office, and soon every item in our home bore an attachment mark – a 'cuckoo', to use the popular expression. One of these officials obviously found this disagreeable and tried to help us as far as he could, intentionally overlooking money in the desk drawer. Later, he returned alone and made his excuses; he had to do his duty.

Naturally, we immediately filed an appeal and submitted one petition after another. Finally, the landlord, Herr B., had the facade of the building renovated and thus put an end to the matter. The law alone would not have prevented the city from ruining us. The homes of almost all the Jews in Hanau were subjected to similar writs of attachment. Nothing was too bad to serve as a pretext for robbing Jews in one way or another.

After a few days, I had an outbreak of a skin disease that I had caught in Buchenwald; the itching was unbearable, I could have torn my skin off. I went to see Dr P. He looked at my emaciated body (I had lost 15 pounds), shook his head and congratulated me on my strong constitution which had made it possible for me to survive. He attributed the skin problem to nutrition and prescribed baths and unguents. It took weeks before it gradually went away.

After a few days, I was ready to get to grips with our affairs. We were hoping to get a visa for England, and we now had to get the necessary papers and permissions. For all the pressure being put on Jews to emigrate, everything was done to make it as hard as possible for them to do so. It was not only that heavy fees had to be paid, making the property that remained practically worthless, and that surcharges of 100 to 300 per cent were added to all purchases made in preparation for emigration, but also that endless errands and red tape were required in order to acquire all the necessary certificates. You had to go to the passport office, the police, the customs investigation office, the currency exchange bureau, the city treasury, the advice centre for emigrants, the registry office and other offices to which you had to make multiple visits to get even the simplest certificate. You would wait for hours and when it was your turn, an 'Aryan' client would often show up and be served first.

In my particular case, the chief difficulties were with the tax office. In the declaration of assets required of Jews by the regulation issued in April, I had assessed my real estate in accordance with the generally valid rules. Now in November an (unpublished) instruction was issued that for Jewish property no more than the so-called unit value – the taxable value, on the basis of which property taxes were calculated – could be paid. As a result, the sales value of my property was a great deal lower because the unit value was in most cases barely half as much as the market value. The tax office had not taken this into account in assessing the payment of 20 per cent (later 25 per cent) of assets that Jews had to make as an 'atonement levy', and had refused to make any adjustment. For me, of course, this was particularly important, and I was fortunate enough to succeed in getting an adjustment made, but it took three months of constant battling to do so.

Besides all these problems with the authorities, we also had a thousand other matters to take care of. The household had to be dissolved. Under the rules imposed by Sprenger, the governor of Hesse, you had to have special permission for the sale of each individual item. Advertisements could not be put in the newspaper; no newspaper would take them. Luckily, a few customers had proven to be true friends, and they helped us all they could, purchasing food for us that we ourselves could not buy in Hanau, buying the furniture that we could not take with us, or found buyers. Without these friends, we would scarcely have been able to cope with all this.

# GERTRUD WICKERHAUSER LEDERER

## Manuscript 74a (130)

*Born in 1895 in Vienna, Catholic, writer and translator; married since 1922 to her second husband, the Viennese medical specialist in internal diseases Kurt Lederer, who was arrested on 7 July 1938 and deported to Buchenwald in early October; the text gives Lederer's account after his release on 15 February 1939 in the form of a dialogue with his wife. In early March, Lederer emigrated via France to the USA; his wife and their young son followed in early July.*

On 5 November, if I remember correctly, the young Grynszpan shot Herr vom Rath in Paris. That was bad news. The *Völkischer Beobachter* fumed and the SS reacted as if their own children had been stabbed. It's good that we're already in a concentration camp, we thought. Because we knew that bad times would come for Jews and their minions. But we had no idea that the terrible era of Buchenwald, the worst for us and the most lucrative for the SS, was about to begin.

Around 10 November, the Gestapo tried to arrest every male Jew in Germany but did not succeed in snatching all of them. Moreover, they realized that in any event they would run out of space. They took 10,000 harmless and completely innocent Jews to Buchenwald from all districts of the old Reich. These must have been impeccable citizens because otherwise they would not have been left alone up until that point.

Ten thousand distraught, helpless people were being pumped into a camp that was already overcrowded. No preparations for such an influx had been made, and the sloppiness and mismanagement typical of such places did more damage. People were sleeping – no, my God, they couldn't sleep . . . they lay next to one another, on top of one another, in unfinished shacks. They couldn't wash themselves; they couldn't wash their linen. What was particularly bad during this time is that we were given canned whale meat goulash. Either whale meat is not edible, or the cans had gone bad. I can't decide. We all suffered the consequences; everyone in the camp got dysentery. I cannot and will not describe how people looked and stank. It was hell.

We, the people who had been arrested by the Viennese police, had by now organized our lives a bit. We could get ourselves a little water and use empty jam containers – in return for payment, of course – to wash our clothes, more or less. When a block elder began to require payment from his comrades for the little water that they were allotted, they beat him to death one night. And they were right to do so.

*What did the camp management say about that?*

Nothing. They didn't get involved in domestic matters between prisoners. The SS thought that if the prisoners found it necessary to kill a flagrant exploiter, a spy or a traitor in their midst, that was clearly their own affair. There was not a high price put on human life in Buchenwald. A single complaint about a fellow prisoner filed with the camp management – and the complainant was a dead man. That was all to the good. Here we were, the prisoners, and there was the administration, the SS, the enemy. Anyone who collaborated with them in any way was our enemy, an enemy in our midst, who had to be eliminated.

These 10,000 new, unfortunate prisoners upset the little order we had created. They included madmen – people who were really, certifiably, insane – whom the Nazis, full of racial pride, had thrown out of the insane asylums and offloaded on Buchenwald. You can hardly ask a poor madman to observe the rules, or rather, you can ask him, but it does no good. Many men entered the camp with serious neuroses and when they had to live in those conditions alongside the insane, they didn't get better. On the contrary. A couple of dozen lunatics among 10,000 reasonably normal men create more turmoil than you can imagine.

After a few days, the SS had had enough, and they let us know unofficially that if we didn't establish order in the special camp by ourselves, they would come in with machine guns and shoot us.

Dr Kriss, a Berlin gynaecologist, and I dealt with this together by establishing an asylum for the insane in the wash house.

111

*What was the wash house?*

The wash house was a sloppily constructed building full of holes that stood on the boundary between the secondary camp and the main camp, and was intended to serve as a laundry. Water pipes and wash basins had been installed, but since the water supply didn't work, the room had never been used and was in a lamentable condition. But it had a concrete floor and a roof.

We identified the mentally ill and neurotics who endangered our activities and our lives, and brought them to the wash house. Twenty volunteers agreed to help us and were at our disposal – a Berlin gynaecologist, a Viennese internist, lawyers, industrialists and journalists who were willing to help but had no idea what to do.

During these first weeks, the wash house . . . was hell. No medicines other than a little Luminal. No room. No blankets, no straw mattresses. Those we got later. We took a collection from the prisoners so that an SS man could buy us medicine in Weimar. The first SS man pocketed the money. The second collection brought us the medicine, but it took two weeks. At first, we were kept busy restraining the raving madmen and isolating them in a partitioned-off area of the wash house. The camp administration had willingly made large quantities of electrical wire available to us. We wrestled day and night with the mentally ill and restrained them and tied them up by force.

I have already said that we all suffered from severe diarrhoea. The floor was a morass of refuse and blood and excrement. No one could imagine the appalling filth in the camp! A few helpers went mad on us, and it was a while before we noticed it. And more ill people from all over the barracks were constantly being brought into the wash house. At the peak, we must have had about 150–60 patients. However, many of them died.

From the first day, I tried to write up a history for each patient; and naturally this included his personal data. With mentally ill people and under the circumstances, this was not easy . . . When we had laid out the fifth dead man, whom we could not identify, the second camp leader, the famous Jonny, a sadistic thug of the first order, threatened to give me fifty lashes because it was clearly my fault. The whole camp was made to file past the dead man, but no one recognized him, not even his own brother. It was only later, in the course of a more detailed examination, that we discovered who had actually been burned in the Weimar crematorium. On the same day that the second camp leader threatened to beat me because of the sloppy way I ran the wash house, Herr Rödl,[1] the camp commandant, gave me a packet of cigarettes in recognition of my achievements. I don't smoke, as you know, but naturally I took them in order to give them away, and because I understood that they were a reward.

*What did the SS do in the wash house?*

For the most part, nothing. They liked to stand at the window that looked out onto the main camp, and there were also a couple of holes in the tarpaper wall there, and they looked in there with their revolvers in their hands and waited to see if they could help us in our struggles with the madmen by firing a well-aimed shot.

It was hard to tell the sick men and the helpers apart. We, the doctors and the aides, tied handkerchiefs around our left arms as an insignia. The mental patients were crafty. A few of them imitated us. Helpers lost their armbands and were beaten down and tied up by their colleagues. We were all more or less mad. Finally, we used ink to write admission numbers on the patients' foreheads. But this was not a sure means of help, either. The men rubbed the numbers off. Kriss and I once worked 36 hours without a break.

One day, an SS man came and examined this hell from within. 'Look here, Herr Doctor,' he said benevolently, 'we see how hard you're working here. We recognize that. But as long as you have to deal with these raving lunatics, you can't establish any real order. Select the twenty most difficult cases for me, and we'll take them off your hands. Then it will be easier.' Finally, someone with a glimmer of understanding. Now they'll give the poor devils proper care, I thought, and chose twenty incurables who could not be pacified.

Then Kriss came back from his meal and I went to eat mine. When I came back, 35 patients had disappeared. These included very easy cases, harmless neurotics. I recall one old man who had done no one any harm, but who incessantly talked, talked, talked. His son, a nice boy, had volunteered as a helper in order to remain with his father. He hoped that in time he could have a calming influence on him. They took the old man away, too. They killed the 35 men in the bunker.

*I gulped. What is the bunker?*

The detention room. Thank God I never saw the inside of it. Few came out of the bunker alive and those who did were never unharmed. There were also standing cells [*Stehbunker*] . . .

*(Kurt remained silent for a long time, staring into the fire. He had lived in this hell and he had survived it without breaking down.)*

113

Once, an SS man came and looked at us. An old, bearded Jew was praying and sobbing. The SS man bellowed at him. The old man hardly heard him. He prayed loudly to his God and sobbed. This is getting dangerous, I thought, and quickly intervened. A harmless neurosis, I explained. Give me time; I can calm the man down. He shrugged and said: Give it a try.

'I want to help you,' I told the old man. 'If you take these pills, it will be easier. You have bad headaches, don't you; isn't that why you are crying? This is a good medicine for headaches. I'm a doctor, and I know. I take it myself when I have a headache.' I tried to reach him by means of quiet, simple words. That takes a while when you're dealing with a very disturbed man. The SS man looked on, watch in his hand. After two minutes he said: 'You can see that you're not getting anywhere.' And he knocked the old man down with his baton. Then he followed this with a couple of kicks in the head with his heavy boots . . . The old man died three hours later. A basal skull fracture. Yes, that was the wash house . . .

It was the terrible era of Buchenwald in another respect as well. In the rush, the money belonging to the 'November action Jews', as they were called, had not been taken off them. There were rich men down there: businessmen, industrialists, men from the liberal professions. Some of them had a couple of thousand marks on them, and almost all had a couple of hundred. We calculated that at least a million marks flowed into the camp at that time, not to mention the money that was sent in later on.

# KARL ROSENTHAL

## Manuscript 235 (192)

*Born in 1885; married, two sons; from 1924, rabbi of the Berlin reform community; arrested on 11 November, released from Sachsenhausen on 16 December 1938; died in Oxford in 1952.*

So there I was a prisoner, exactly twenty years to the day after the armistice of 1918. When the Nazis had come to power, they declared that the rights of Jewish veterans of the World War would not be restricted. Hitler broke this promise like all his others. From 1914 to 1918, I fought for Germany on the front, was twice wounded, and was decorated with the Iron Cross and other honours. We were five brothers in the field at the same time; two of us died for the fatherland, and the three of us who survived were all wounded. One of my brothers, who had suffered a serious gunshot wound to his head during the battle against Russia, was arrested on the same day as I and taken to the Buchenwald concentration camp near Weimar.

When the two Gestapo men arrived with me at the police headquarters, Alexanderplatz was filled with an enormous crowd gawking curiously at the stream of people who had been arrested. I was taken into the inner courtyard of the large building, where about twenty people were standing. We were arranged in lines of five. In front of me stood a man whose face I could not see, and facing him was a young Gestapo man who repeatedly tried to intimidate him: 'Now we've got you, Herr Attorney N. We'll make a note of your name, and you'll get a warm reception!' he said, making threatening gestures.

It was about 6.15 when I was detained there. We stood for hours on the same spot in the courtyard in the freezing cold. Our feet began to hurt. In the gloom, I recognized the man on my right as another

Berlin rabbi. We secretly shook hands. Every few minutes a new victim of the Nazis was brought in. One hour after another went by in agonizing uncertainty. Not a word was said about what was supposed to happen to us.

At last, after standing and freezing in the cold November night for about four hours, we were led into a second courtyard, where large police vehicles stood ready, three of which were already full. We were ordered harshly to get into the last vehicle. There were about sixty of us. Two police guards in uniform with rifles hanging over their shoulders got in last and we were driven away towards an unknown destination.

For a long time, I was silently worrying that we would be taken to a concentration camp. I tried to determine the direction we were taking. At last, by looking backwards through the half-open canvas top of the truck, I succeeded in recognizing the sign over the entrance to an underground station: Gesundbrunnen, in north Berlin. Now it became clear to me where we were going: we were travelling north, towards Oranienburg, that is, towards the notorious Sachsenhausen concentration camp! The very idea of it was terrifying. I had already heard so many dreadful things about it. But exhaustion resulting from the anxiety and the long period of standing outside in the cold had made me sleepy.

Berlin's sea of buildings and the bright lights of the great city were now behind us. We drove down the dark country roads. The trees on both sides swept eerily by us in the light of the headlamps of the vehicles behind us. But finally it grew brighter. Large electric arc lights lit up the terrain. One of the two policemen suddenly gave us an order: 'Take off your hats!' I didn't know why, but five minutes later I realized that this was a friendly gesture on his part that was intended to spare us worse things.

It was about 10.45 when our four police vehicles drove into Sachsenhausen concentration camp. I saw that the camp was surrounded by high walls and barbed wire. A large iron gate opened, the truck turned sharply into the road leading to the gate and suddenly stopped with such a hard jolt that we literally banged into each other. What happened then cannot be told as quickly as it happened. The two policemen leapt out of the truck, and we heard a medley of raucous voices shouting: 'Out, you Jewish swine, get down out of the truck! Are you not down yet?'

We hurried to get out of the truck, but as we were jumping down, SS men armed with batons and whips attacked us. Amid wild shouts and curses, they beat us mercilessly; on the back, on the legs, on the

116

head and face. Two SS men climbed onto the truck and kicked the prisoners getting out. 'You swine still have your hats on your heads!' cried an SS man and savagely struck the long-since bared heads. I received a terrible kick in the back, so that I flew off the truck. My leather bag, in which I had my few possessions, fell on the ground and broke open. When I bent down and tried to collect the scattered things, I got another kick: 'Will you get a move on, you old Jewish pig!' At the same time he hit me with his riding whip.

At this moment, one of my unfortunate fellow sufferers was thrown off the truck by such a terrible blow that he remained lying on the ground with large, gaping wounds on his head and forehead. Blood was streaming over his face and his overcoat. 'Get going, you damned Jews,' the SS men were shouting. In the meantime, I had found my bag and my hat and stumbled after the other fellows who were running away like a herd being hunted by wolves. The SS men drove us along with blows from their batons and whips and repeated kicks.

It was not easy to determine exactly where we were. Powerful sweeping searchlights fell on us from the roofs of the buildings surrounding the area. They dazzled us so that we couldn't see clearly what was going on. At first, only two things were obvious: first, that the long columns of prisoners were constantly being driven at a fast pace across a large open area; and second, that the SS men were striking us, incessantly shouting and cursing.

SS men were standing all over the open area, and we had to pass by them. As soon as we got near them, we had to expect to get kicks and blows on the head. At every moment, in the constant alternation between the bright light cast by the searchlights and the sudden half-darkness, one of us stumbled and fell. Then an SS man shouted, 'Will you move on, you dirty Jewish swine!' giving the fallen man a kick. One man would lose his hat, another would drop his bag or package – if he tried to pick the things up, the SS men fell on him and drove him on with savage blows.

An old man near me began to groan: 'My heart! I can't go on!' He stumbled and fell, and remained lying on the ground. I tried to help him up, but the SS men had already come over and started beating him, shouting: 'Get going, you stinking old Jew!' I myself soon started to feel heart pains. I had had angina a few years earlier and, since then, I had to avoid walking too fast or any strenuous movements. But despite my troubles, I had to continue running along in the ranks of my fellows. Finally – the pursuit must have lasted about thirty minutes – I collided with the man in front of me. The column had stopped, and we stood still. Out of breath, gasping, coughing, trembling, hearts pounding, hundreds of hounded men stood there. The big searchlights lit the area from all sides. Sometimes their light swept over low barracks, sometimes it showed a tower, from which other searchlights shone down. Cautiously, I looked around at my comrades. Most of them had dishevelled clothing as a result of the frenzied hounding, the SS men's blows, and stumbling and falling. 'How are you, comrade?' I quietly asked my neighbour. 'Not too bad,' came his answer with a weary smile.

Bringing us to the point of extreme exhaustion by chasing us across the large area was the first premeditated way of mistreating us. Now the second method began: contrived, systematic bullying. We had to stand still on the same spot. At first, standing still felt good after the terrible, half-hour-long run. Gradually, however, we began to feel cold; it was, after all, November! We still had our hats in our hands but were not allowed to put them on.

Men with blue-and-white striped trousers, on which white strips with big numbers had been sewn, put us into rows of five men, one behind the other. They also cursed us – but only when SS men approached. They were prisoners, some of whom had already been in the concentration camp for years, and were now ordered to oversee us.

In the searchlights, I now saw that at least six large columns of about 300 men were in formation. The SS men went down the long rows, every few moments stopping and giving one or another of the prisoners a shove: 'How are you standing there, you old Jewish shit-swine? Hold your head up!' One of them struck an old man under the chin with his fist so hard that his teeth cracked. Another SS man holding a riding whip walked slowly past us. After four or five steps, he stopped, peered at one of us and shouted: 'Why are you looking at me so stupidly, you dirty old Jew?' Then he struck the man in the face three times with his riding whip. Next, he stopped in front of another prisoner and began to hit him on the nose with his fist, at first softly, then harder and harder.

'What's your name?'

'So and so.'

'Your profession?'

'Lawyer.'

'What? A lawyer? You're a damned nasty crook!' And then he gave him an especially hard punch in the nose.

One of the older prisoners who had to supervise us had to bring along a sign that was attached to a stake. An SS man ordered each of us to hold up the sign for a while and then hand it on to the next

118

man. On the sign was painted, in large letters, WE ARE RESPON-
SIBLE FOR THE MURDER OF HERR VOM RATH. The SS man
saw to it that each of us held the sign high enough. Suddenly, he
quietly slipped up to one of us who was just about to hold up the
sign and gave him such a dreadful blow that blood flowed out of his
mouth. Why he hit him, I don't know.

After a time, a second sign was brought. It read: WE ARE THE
DESTROYERS OF GERMAN CULTURE! It also had to be held by
each man in our column, and then handed on to the next. About fifty
yards away, I heard an SS man raging and shouting. He ordered us
all to say in unison: 'We are responsible for the murder of Herr vom
Rath!' We didn't say it loud enough for him, so we had to shout the
same sentence over and over for at least a quarter of an hour. Then
it was the other sentence's turn. While we were forced to shout the
first and then the second one, SS men went up and down the rows.
'Why didn't you join in, you damned Jew?' and punched people in
the face again. We had to bellow the two stupid sentences louder and
louder, and the alternating chorus of several hundred men rang eerily
through the cold winter night: 'We are responsible for the murder of
Herr vom Rath! – We are the destroyers of German culture!'

Meanwhile, the SS men were continuing their senseless and arbi-
trary beatings. Not for a moment could we be sure that we would
not be kicked or struck on the head from behind, or receive from the
SS man in front of us a blow in the face. The fear of these repeated
abuses wore us down. We had not yet come to terms with our dreadful and unexpected situation. Then I heard a deep voice saying
quietly: 'Take it easy, boys, keep your chin up, friends – things will
soon improve, it's only at the beginning that it's so bad!'

It was one of the old prisoners whom the SS men had ordered to
help us who was trying to reassure us. In this inferno of barbarous
Nazi brutality, his calming words sounded as if they came from
another world. He went slowly down the rows with his encouraging
'Take it easy, boys!' I dare not give his name – he may still be lan-
guishing in Sachsenhausen, and Gestapo criminals might still punish
him for the fact that in a state-organized hell full of evil and brutality
he managed for four years to retain his humanity. But full of deep
gratitude, I will always think of this splendid man who over the following weeks showed himself generous to us and who, because of
his dissident political views, was cruelly detained in the concentration
camp for years.

In the meantime, the hundreds of newly arrived prisoners began to
be registered. A low, wooden barracks served as the concentration

camp secretariat or orderly room. Each time, a few of our men were forced to go in there and exit through another door. Two SS men stood at the entrance and kicked and beat those who had to go in. An elderly man who hobbled in somewhat slowly was given such a kick in the behind that he fell and hit his face on the doorpost. Blood ran out of his nose. 'Can't you be more careful, you old Jewish swine?' snarled the same SS man who had caused him to fall.

When it was my turn to go into the orderly room, the SS man kicked at me, but I am quite agile and sprang with one long stride over the low threshold into the secretariat. Here sat numerous older prisoners who had to enter us into a card file. As I came out, I saw the comrade who had been thrown out of the truck by the SS men when we arrived at the camp. His head was bound with white bandages, but blood had seeped through, and the large red bloodstains contrasted dreadfully with his white, deadly pale face. Two other prisoners were supporting him; he could hardly stand up. Later I heard that he died the same night; when he fell from the truck his skull had been fractured.

It was now about 1.30 a.m. The last men in our column were registered in the card file. The night was getting colder and colder. Freezing and shivering, we still stood on the same spot. Then orders rang out: we had to run across the area, but now running felt like a relief after two hours of standing still. Near the two-storey gate building, we were ordered to halt. We had to about-face and now stood in front of a wall about five yards high that surrounded the whole of the camp square. Electrified barbed wire had been strung along the wall at about twenty-inch intervals, with white insulators. In front of this wall, protected by electrified wire, there was a wire entanglement about two yards high and three yards deep, which was separated from a narrow gravel path by a three-yard-wide strip of grass.

Every fifty paces, a sign had been put up on the grass, showing a white skull and crossbones against a black background.[1] Every time the searchlight fell on the sign, the grinning skull was eerily lit up; then it disappeared again into the gloom. Other signs that had been put up at short intervals read: YOU WILL BE SHOT WITHOUT WARNING! We were forced to keep looking at the high, grey wall, the electrified barbed wire and the skulls. This was part of the criminally and sadistically planned tactics for wearing us down, to which we were exposed over endlessly long hours.

Here I must say something about the cunning, the insidiousness, with which not only the physical abuse but also, just as much, the moral and mental abuse of the prisoners was conceived. We were all already in a state of high mental agitation as a result of our arrest and transfer to the concentration camp. Then came the inhumanely savage abuse on our arrival at the camp, after several hours of which more than one of us had already broken down. Now, completely exhausted, we were made to stand in front of this threatening wall and the electrified barbed wire in order to show us that escape from the camp was impossible. And these skulls that we had before our eyes for hours portended the horrible fate that awaited anyone who, despite everything, attempted in desperation to escape.

The searchlights swept incessantly over the area. We stood still and wondered, full of uncertainty, what was in store for us next. The SS men now remained at a distance from us and approached us less often. Suddenly we heard shouts: we had to hand over our cigarettes, which the SS men pocketed. The hours went by. We were still standing on the same spot with the skulls grinning at us. Only a few SS men were patrolling the camp square. It grew quieter. The lights in the nearby barracks were put out. But the searchlights kept moving. And we stood and stood and stood . . .

I felt hungry and took the sausage out of my leather bag, ate a piece and gave my neighbour some. Another man shared some bread, and a third shared his chocolate bar. I tried to sleep a little standing up. But I couldn't do it. The cold became increasingly intense. The clock over the gate showed 4 a.m. . . . I wondered whether the SS men or the camp commandant had forgotten to give us the order to go into the barracks. My knees were trembling. I grew dizzy. But soon I got hold of myself again.

A few metres away, a man fainted. His comrades put a package under his head. An SS man who was standing nearby came over. He pushed the fallen man with his foot and asked: 'What's wrong with him?' When we tried to make the unfortunate man stand up, we found that he was dead. 'Doesn't matter,' the SS man said, 'far too few of you croak anyway.' Two of us had to drag the dead man away to the medical barracks.

Suddenly we heard a siren. It was 4.30 a.m. Lights came on in the barracks. Voices became audible. The camp, which had for several hours lain as if dead, was coming back to life. In the searchlights, I saw people with large urns coming out of the barracks and walking across the open area. After a short time, they came back, each pair of them carrying a heavy urn that was filled with the morning tea. I quietly rejoiced in the idea that after this terrible night we would now soon get hot tea. That should refresh us! I calculated that we had had to stand for about eleven hours straight. Who would have thought

121

that one could endure something like that? The tea-bearers disappeared with their urns into the barracks. The old prisoners had to
have their breakfast first; then it would be our turn, I thought. But
another hour went by – and we were still standing on the same spot!

However, there was movement in front of the barracks. Loud
orders echoed through the camp. Large groups of prisoners marched
up. They lined up behind our backs in the middle of the muster
ground. Suddenly, there was a curt order and all the prisoners whipped
off their caps; it rang out like an iron bell. They all stood still, as if
nailed to the spot. The clock struck six. It was the daily morning
roll-call. More orders. And then the columns separated and some
marched back to the barracks, while others moved through the
entrance gate to work. Now – I thought – we will finally get our tea
and a little bread, after they probably forgot to take us into the barracks to sleep. In the meantime, it had grown somewhat lighter. On
the horizon, a bright strip heralded the dawn.

When the columns of long-term prisoners had marched away, the
SS men who had been on duty for the roll-call came over to us. I
thought they would probably order us to go into the barracks; we
had been on our feet since six o'clock the previous evening, that is,
for over twelve hours straight! How good it would be to rest. Then
not far away I heard an SS man shout: 'Hold your snout up, you old
Jewish piece of shit!' That was his morning greeting to us. He stopped
in front of the man in front of me, who was, I later learned, 63 years
old. 'What's your name?' the SS man said, using the familiar *Du* form
(in German, a very impolite way of addressing an adult). 'Glücksmann [lucky man].'

'Your profession?'
'Former mayor.'
'Where were you mayor?'
'In G.'[2]

The SS man, with a triumphant grin on his face: 'Ah, now I've got
you. You once threw me out when I was in your office. Just wait,
we're going to play a little trick on you! Look here,' he said to another
SS man, 'this dirty Jew used to be the mayor of G. . . . and once threw
me out. We'll show him!'

The SS men then went up and down all the rows of the new
prisoners. Here and there, they asked them their names and professions. And this was usually followed by insults and often blows
in the face or kicks. An older man with a grey beard was asked
about his profession. When he said 'businessman', the SS man shouted
in rage:

122

'You're a dirty old Jew! Say again what you are!'
The old man: 'I'm a Jew!'
'Say "I'm a dirty Jew." '
'I'm a Jew.'

A box on the ear was the SS man's reply. A few minutes later another man was asked: 'Your profession?'
'Former lawyer.'
'Bullshit, you're a pimp! Repeat it!' The man kept silent. The SS man said once again: 'You're a pimp!' and with a scornful laugh hit him in the nose. We saw how much the SS men enjoyed throwing the most vulgar insults at those men who had had high social standing.

It was now broad daylight. SS men came and went. I saw the columns of new prisoners standing all along the edges of the muster ground. We all held our caps in our hands. In the neighbouring columns, two men held up signs with the previously mentioned words. One of them must have held the sign for several hours; his comrades supported his arm when the SS men moved away a bit.

I now felt a raging thirst. I hadn't had a drop to drink since 4 p.m. the day before and on top of that there was the pursuit in the night and the mental turmoil. It was now 10 a.m. In a low voice, I exchanged a few words with my comrades. They were also thirsty. But what could we do? The SS men were nearby. We were constantly under observation. I saw that between the gate and the gatehouse there was a large crossbeam. On it was mounted a machine gun that was aimed threateningly down at us. SS men with steel helmets on their heads were watching us through binoculars. Whenever a group of prisoners came near the main building, the machine gun was immediately aimed at them. About every 150–200 yards, massive stone towers rose from the perimeter wall of the camp. In each of them, several SS men were posted, who also aimed their machine guns at us. At night, strong searchlights beamed down on us from each of the towers.

The whole camp was laid out in rows radiating from the gatehouse, whose searchlights and machine guns could cover all the barracks and all the paths between the barracks. In front of the gatehouse was the muster ground, about 500 yards across. Approximately in the middle was a stake. It was here that all orders were given, three times a day during the roll-call. Near the muster ground were the medical buildings, the orderly room, the kitchen, the shower-block and a wash house. The barracks extended almost to the high perimeter walls, from which they were separated by broad strips of sand and the previously mentioned barbed-wire barricade. Naturally, we worked out the details of this whole layout only in the course of the following days.

For the time being, we were still standing, as if we had grown roots there, on the same spot where we had been for many, many hours. We were hungry and thirsty. Among the prisoners who were crossing the muster ground I suddenly saw the man who had so kindly spoken words of encouragement to us during the terrible night. He came up to us and once again he found a few friendly words. We asked him why we had to remain standing still where we were and whether we would not soon be allowed to go into the barracks. He shrugged his shoulders and said with his deep, calm voice: 'Just keep your chins up, comrades, you've survived the worst of it.' We told him how thirsty we were and asked whether we couldn't have something to drink. 'Well, I'll see,' he replied.

A quarter of an hour later he secretly brought us a pail of water and a cup. He put the pail in the middle, between the columns, so that the SS men couldn't see it. The pail and the cup were handed on and everyone got a drink. That was the only nourishment we'd had in more than twenty-four hours! When the pail was empty, the man brought more water. SS superior officers came across the ground. They passed by us with contemptuous looks. People with large cauldrons came by again. Soon they came back, the cauldrons steaming. The smell of hot soup invaded our nostrils.

Now large groups of prisoners were again coming out of all the barracks and going through the entrance gate. Again they arranged themselves in dense, rectangular blocks in the middle of the muster ground. When the clock struck 11.30, orders rang out, caps flew off the prisoners' heads, and everyone stood still. Then there was another loud command, the prisoners returned to the barracks for their noonday meal. Now – I thought – we too will get something to eat. Our stomachs had been rumbling for a long time, but when we saw the steaming cauldrons our hunger grew even greater. But nothing changed for us. We stood and stood and stood. In front of us, the wall with the electrified barbed wire and the skulls; above us, on the towers and the gate building, the threatening machine guns. SS officers came and went. Either they acted as if we were invisible and did not exist for them or they looked at us with inexpressible contempt.

The hours slipped by. Every quarter of an hour was an eternity. The men carrying urns came back again. They were bringing tea for the evening meal. It was shortly before 4 p.m., and through the entrance gate the groups of prisoners were returning from work.

124

Others came out of the barracks. At 4 p.m., there was another roll-call. It lasted until about 5 p.m.

It had grown dark. Electric arc lamps came on. The searchlights on the towers on the wall and on the main building began turning again; their beams swept over the muster ground. SS men came towards us again. This was never a good sign, as we had already learned. One of the SS men stopped in front of a pale, wretched and sickly man. 'Scared, aren't you, Jew?' Then he asked: 'What's your name?' – 'So and so.' – 'Open your overcoat!' When the man had unbuttoned his coat, the SS man ordered: 'Shirt up!' Then he held his pistol to the poor man's naked chest and said: 'Now you'll be shot!' Finally, he struck the man on the chest with his pistol and moved on. He asked another prisoner what his profession was.

'I'm a teacher.'

'Where?'

'Berlin.' The SS man said: 'Well, you won't need to teach any more – tonight 3,000 Jewish kids will be shot in Berlin.' We saw how much pleasure he took in frightening and tormenting us with such remarks.

Another painful hour went by – what could still be to come! At about 6 p.m., our friend who had brought us drinking water that morning returned. 'Well, boys, now things will soon change.' We had to march across the muster ground to the wash barracks. It was such a relief to be able to walk these couple of hundred yards. We were completely stiff from standing there in the cold. We'd been on our feet for a full twenty-four hours! In front of the wash barracks we had to take off our collars and ties, untie our shoes and get ready for the bath. Under the supervision of SS men, all the food, cigars and cigarettes that were still in our possession were taken away from us. Except for a handkerchief, we were not allowed to keep anything in our pockets. I nonetheless stuck my toothbrush in one of my shoes.

Groups of about 100 men each were led into the wash barracks. When they came out, I saw that their heads had been completely shorn – like convicts in a penitentiary. After we had waited half an hour outside, it was finally our turn. We had to get undressed in an anteroom with benches and clothes hooks. We had to tie our clothes in a bundle and were given a number to attach to them. Later, we had to wear this number on our clothing. Money and other valuables had to be handed over for safe keeping under the same number.

When we had all undressed, we went into the actual wash room. Several SS men stood ready to 'receive' us. They were holding long canes. As we passed by them, they hit our naked bodies with the canes. In a corner of the large room several people with hair clippers

125

were at work. With a shudder, I saw how my comrades' heads were shaved completely bare. Then it was my turn. As my hair fell, my thoughts turned towards home: what would my family say, what would my community say, when they saw me looking like this? But it was already done . . . my head was shaven! I looked like a convict.

Then we went under the showers. Nearby, an SS man sat on the edge of a table, holding his cane. A prisoner who was ahead of me – a weak, dried-up-looking man – hesitated a moment to go under the shower. The SS man immediately began beating him. To be sure, the cold shower on our half-frozen bodies was not pleasant. But when I saw that the SS man was especially inclined to beat those who looked frightened, I acted as though I found the cold water refreshing – and the SS man left me alone.

I had to dry myself with a small towel and then I received the clothing I was to wear as a concentration camp prisoner: a completely torn, thin shirt, ragged, ancient stockings, a pair of trousers and a coat. I had recently had an attack of lumbago and feared that I would suffer another if I wore these wretched, tattered clothes. But even though I was now quite cold, I felt refreshed by the cold shower after more than twenty-four hours of standing in the cold winter wind. Many a comrade later said that the shower had been the best thing in the concentration camp.

We all had to line up again in front of the barracks. We were a ghoulish sight. Our heads were shaved. We felt so undignified! And then there was the convicts' clothing. But since we all looked the same, we very quickly became accustomed to our new, unattractive image. We waited for the rest of our comrades, who were still in the shower. Our helpful friend – let's call him 'P.' – had us line up in rows of five, one behind the other. A couple of SS men walked down the rows. 'Your profession?' one of them asked a gigantic young man. 'Butcher,' was the answer. 'Ah, so you're the kind of skunk who practises his kosher butchery on Christian children, right?'

Then he came up to me: 'What's your profession?'

'Rabbi.'

'Aha, a damned Talmudic Jew! Fine things are written in your Talmud!' he said, ironically.

'Indeed,' I said, 'fine things are written in it.'

The SS man, snorting with rage: 'What's that you say? Fine things are written in it? What, for example?'

I replied: 'Love thy neighbour as thyself!' The SS man hesitated a moment and then, after a moment of embarrassment, said: 'But that holds only for Jews and other Jews!'

I answered, 'No, it holds for all people, because the Talmud also repeats that other Bible saying: "Thou shalt not oppress the stranger and thou shalt love him as thyself!"'

The SS man: 'That's in the Talmud?'

I replied: 'Indeed it is.' Then the SS man fell silent and walked away. But one of the long-term prisoners who was standing nearby came over to me and said, 'Man, you did that right. Just don't be scared! Give it to these brothers to their face – and right away they shut up and take off!'

In the meantime, the last members of our group had come out of the showers, and P. asked an SS man whether he could leave with us. The SS man said he could, and we immediately ran at the double across the muster ground to one of the barracks that was to be our home for the coming weeks. It was almost 7.30 p.m. when we finally stood in front of the barracks. Hitler's elite corps had kept us standing out in the wintry cold without anything to eat for more than twenty-five hours! As we stood hour after hour freezing, facing the electrified barbed-wire fence, hoping in vain again and again to be led into one of the barracks so that we could finally lie down and sleep, I had still believed – not guessing the evil depths the Nazi regime can sink to – that through an organizational error of some kind someone had forgotten to grant us rest. Only later, when I saw that all the prisoners who had the misfortune to be sent to the Sachsenhausen concentration camp were subjected to such brutal exhaustion, did I recognize with horror that it was all part of a satanic and inhuman plan. It was part of the previously mentioned 'wearing-down tactic' that was supposed to drive us in desperation to attack the SS men (who would then have immediately shot us) or to commit suicide.

This terrible first night in the concentration camp was the pinnacle of this godless, diabolical barbarism and cruelty that is the hallmark of Hitler's new 'religion', National Socialism! It was this criminal barbarism that led Hitler to have his own friends murdered when they stood in his way (30 June 1934!), and it was the same barbarism that led to the bloody terror in Czechoslovakia and in unfortunate Poland.

When we entered the barracks, two large cauldrons with steaming soup were waiting for us. A few of the long-term prisoners who knew from their own experience what we had gone through over the preceding twenty-four hours distributed the food. The soup was pretty thin, but that didn't matter so much. It was hot, and the warmth did us good! Our friend P. was now our block elder; that is, he was responsible for order in his barracks. In addition to him, about ten other prisoners had been assigned as room orderlies.

The wooden barracks consisted of two identical wings built to accommodate 120 people altogether, not the 150 who were now crowded into each of them. They both had a day room with several long tables and benches and a couple of camp beds for the orderlies. Next door was our 'dormitory' – it was completely empty. Between the two wings of the barracks were a common washroom and a latrine with eight toilets (for 300 men).

After we had eaten our soup, which we slurped down as if it had been the most splendid meal, we could go into the dormitory. Each of us received two cotton blankets in which we could wrap ourselves. Dead tired, we lay down. It was almost impossible for 150 men to find room to lie down in an area about 10 yards by 15 yards. And yet we managed somehow. Friend P., now our block elder and leader, explained that it had been ordered that we must all lie only on our sides; it was forbidden to lie on our backs! We lay literally packed like sardines in a can. And yet we were happy to be able to lie down at all. Our legs were trembling from the strain of the previous twenty-four hours. But not the slightest complaint was heard. Of course, there were a few words of rage and disgust at the subhuman cruelty of the Nazi system; but almost everyone bore the trials and psychological humiliations with strength and dignified forbearance.

Next to me lay an elderly man; when we exchanged names, it turned out that he was the former mayor who had been so threatened by an SS man that morning. 'So,' I said, 'you're the unfortunate fellow with the auspicious name of Glücksmann [lucky man]! What did you actually do to that SS man?' He assured me that he had never seen the man before in his life, and that the SS man's claim that he had once been thrown out by him was a blatant lie. In other words, it was one of those typical cases in which the SS men tormented and tried to scare one of us for no reason at all.

Suddenly we heard loud voices in the day room. Someone shouted *Achtung!* and an SS man, accompanied by P., came into the dormitory. With his heavy military boots, he stamped through the rows of sleeping men, carelessly stepping on the feet of some of us. 'You Jews keep quiet in here or I'll come and drive you all across the muster ground again, and then you'll be finished sleeping!' That was the goodnight we received from this warm-hearted German man!

When he had left, P. came back in again. 'Comrades,' he said in his informal way, 'you've had a hard day. But it was certainly also the worst, and now things will get better. You mustn't lose heart. The SS men love it when you break down. So stand tall. Be comradely and help each other. Life here in the camp is difficult and hard and can be endured only if we draw on our inner strength. I will do what I can to help you. I wish you all a good night!'

This splendid person had already been in the Nazi hell of Sachsenhausen for more than four years, but despite that fact – or perhaps precisely because of it – he was able to find such humane words for us.

I soon fell into a deep and dreamless sleep. The bright electric arc-lamps and the searchlights that constantly shone through the large, unshuttered window didn't bother me. We were all far too exhausted. It was about 8.30 p.m. when we fell asleep. About three in the morning, I woke up. I was freezing. The thin blankets were not warm enough. But I went back to sleep. Suddenly I heard the siren. In the other room, where P. slept, an alarm clock went off. The electric light in the dormitory was turned on.

We jumped up from our hard beds, on which we had slept more soundly than many other people do on the softest beds. It was four in the morning. An orderly handed each of us a hand towel. Then we hurried to the washroom. Within a few minutes at least fifty people were in there, even though the room was only 4.5 by 6 yards. It was almost impossible to move. While we were washing our upper bodies, two SS men appeared in the doorway and without any reason immediately began to shout and bluster in the early morning.

I hurried back to the dormitory. Since there were neither wardrobes nor hooks, we stuck the hand towels in our pockets. In the meantime, the food distributors had brought two big urns full of tea. Each of us received, as his daily ration, a small loaf of army bread and a bit of margarine. At 5.15 a.m., we had to line up in front of the barracks. We were supposed to form a long column of thirty sections consisting of ten men each. But since many of us had never had any military training, it took a long time to put the dense mass of men into a proper military formation.

Shortly before six o'clock, we marched to the muster ground for the morning roll-call. Groups of about 300 men marched out from all the barracks, as we had seen from afar the night before. When we got near the stake, I saw large groups of new prisoners standing on the left and right of the entrance gate; they had arrived the preceding night. They were standing – as we had stood on our first night – bare-headed, facing the electrified barbed wire and the skulls. With a shudder, I thought what these poor men would probably have to endure and how they must now be longing for rest!

In the meantime, the whole muster ground had been filled with columns of prisoners. Only with great effort could the block elders and the orderlies put the large groups of men into military order. The ranks and files had to be just right. Loud orders resounded everywhere, with the shouts of the SS men in between. The searchlights swept over us from all sides and the machine guns were aimed at us. An SS man, our squad leader, came up to us. Friend P. took off his cap, stood to attention in front of him, and reported: 'Block no. . . . with 300 men, in formation!' The SS man checked the formation, and then commanded us: 'Eyes left!' and reported us to the Sturmführer who stood near the stake.

When the clock struck six, we received the orders: 'Attention!' and 'Caps off!' When the thousands of long-term prisoners whipped off their caps all at once, it sounded like rifle butts hitting the ground. Meanwhile the SS men were walking up and down the blocks of men, here and there dealing out pokes in the ribs, kicks or blows to the head. Finally came the order: 'Dismissed!' and immediately thereafter: 'Jew blocks stay where you are!' We had to stand still again for about half an hour in the morning cold. The SS men were apparently receiving instructions as to what to do with us. Then we too marched back to the barracks. SS men came at us again from all sides: 'On the double, you Jewish swine!' In doing so, they repeatedly kicked us. In front of the barracks, we had to stand to attention for another half an hour.

Around 7.30 a.m., we marched back to the muster ground. Under the command of the SS men, we had to do drill the whole length of the muster ground. There were many people among us who were ill and crippled, people with hernias or pain in their legs and feet. No allowance was made for them! Even trained soldiers find it difficult to march in perfect step in columns of 300 men or more. But here were an untrained motley group of men of all ages, and it was completely impossible to carry out military movements correctly. Sometimes two or three blocks were mustered together, and then of course the exercises were even more poorly executed. But as soon as an exercise was not carried out properly, the SS men made the whole enormous column run across the ground. Ill and elderly people could not run as fast as others. We held them under the arms and carried them along with us. It was an appalling sight, these old, fragile or ill people, driven by brutish SS men, doing exercises or running across the muster ground!

Often the SS men forced us to go down into a deep knee-bend and then stay in that position for five to ten minutes. Then they went up and down the rows, doing their usual checks. Older people whose legs were now too stiff for such knee-bends were pulled backwards by their shoulders to the ground or kicked in the kneecaps with the heavy military boots, so that they fell over backwards. On this occasion, an SS man of about 25 years old screamed at an old, white-haired man: 'There we have it, you Jews can eat and whore, but you can't do exercises properly.'

After an hour, many of us were already completely exhausted. But without any consideration we were marched and exercised further. One hour after another went by. I remember my time as a soldier in the old Germany. It was hard, to be sure, but when we had drilled about half an hour on the parade ground, we were always granted a brief rest period. And we were then 20–25 years old. But now these criminals Hitler had unleashed on us made us drill for hours, relentlessly, without rest, until we were completely exhausted. Every day people would faint. Then medical personnel came with stretchers and carried them away.

At last, after these pointless torments had gone on for four hours (!), we were given a little time to rest. The clock over the gate building struck 11.30. It was lunchtime. First, however, there was another roll-call, which lasted until 12. Only then did we march back to our barracks, where the orderlies had two cauldrons of soup ready for us. We ate a piece of our bread with it. Some of the men were so exhausted, however, that they couldn't eat anything at all. After the meal, some of them wanted to lie down on the floor of the dormitory for a while in order to rest – but the block elder came and said that that had been forbidden by the Scharführer!

One 83-year-old man from near Bromberg was allowed by P., the block elder, on his own responsibility, to rest a bit in a corner. From then on, this man no longer needed to exercise with the rest of us, but he had to be at the roll-call three times a day and sometimes endure the hours-long stand in the cold. We held him under his arms and supported his trembling knees. After about two days, he collapsed and ended up in the infirmary where, as I heard several days later, he died.

Shortly before 1 p.m., we had to line up again in front of the barracks. Once again, we went to the muster ground where the drilling began all over again. This time it went on for three hours without a rest – with the usual insults from the SS men and with the same torments as in the morning. At 4 p.m., the third and longest roll-call of the day took place, which this time lasted almost two hours. The cold wind swept over our shaved heads because the Nazi thugs had taken away our own hats but had not given us caps like the ones worn by the other prisoners. As we later heard, this was a calculated plan on the part of the commandant: it was hoped that in this way many of us would get bad colds and die from them!

After the roll-call had been carried out in the usual way, we were again ordered to stand to attention. The 12,000 men stood silently. And now the camp commander, SS-Oberführer Baranowski,[3] delivered his 'welcome speech' to the 6,000 or so Jewish prisoners who had been interned over the previous three days. In a shrill voice – like that of a true Prussian nobleman – he bellowed out over the muster ground: 'You have been incarcerated here in order to be educated. Among the means of education at our disposal are physical punishments. No resistance on the part of Jews will be tolerated. Should any of you dare to resist or attempt to escape, my SS men will immediately use their weapons. And my SS men are good shots! Dismissed!'

After this friendly welcome, we returned to the barracks, but on the way we had once again to run the gauntlet of SS men who hit and kicked us. In the barracks, there was tea but it was no longer hot, and we ate the rest of our bread with it. After this 'supper' we were allowed to move freely between the barracks, but only in front of the so-called Jewish barracks. We were not permitted to go into other parts of the camp in which about 6,000 'Aryan' prisoners were held.

When I came out in front of the barracks, I saw hundreds of new prisoners similarly standing in front of the doors or walking about. Each felt glad to have a few minutes when he was not being hounded or abused, but even this free time did not pass undisturbed. SS men patrolled between the barracks, and their proximity was generally signalled by loud shouts and insults. If they saw someone who had put his hands in his trouser pockets to keep them warm, they fell on him and kicked him.

As I was walking between the barracks, I met a large number of people who were known to me from my work in Berlin. We were all sad and surprised, of course, to encounter one another here, shaved bald and in convict's clothing. [. . .] now I want to briefly describe the conclusion to my second day in the concentration camp.

As on the preceding evening, we were packed together into the dormitory. Once again, we all lay on our sides, and it was carefully ensured that no one was lying on his back. There were a few small disputes among the prisoners themselves, for example if someone thought his neighbour was taking up too much room. Hardly had we all lain down on the floor – the light had not yet been put out – when a few of us were already snoring so loudly that the room shook. The snoring was almost unbearable for us all. Because of the lack of space, it was so difficult to breathe freely that more and more people began to snore. This caused many of us to be repeatedly disturbed in our sleep, which we all needed so badly. If you gave your snoring neighbour a little poke in the ribs, the snoring would stop for a few minutes, but would begin again soon afterwards, louder than ever.

Another hardship was the severe cold in the thin, wooden barracks. On the second evening, we received some straw to lie on, but we had to leave a few of the windows open in order to provide sufficient ventilation for the relatively small room in which about 150 men were trying to sleep. As a result of eating the indefinable soups that constituted our main meal, many of us suffered from severe flatulence. A third problem, caused by the cold on the muster ground, was the bladder infections from which many prisoners suffered, so that all night long people were constantly getting up to go to the toilet. But since we were lying very close together, no one could walk through the room without walking on others or bumping into them and thus disturbing their sleep. Some of these bladder problems contracted in the concentration camp became chronic.

Shortly before the light was turned off on our second night, P., the block elder, came in to give us a few necessary instructions. On this occasion, he appealed to our community spirit and the comradeship among prisoners as a way of improving our situation. Once again, he urged us not to lose heart or fall into despair. Afterwards, the light was turned off, and then I experienced, for the first time in two days in the camp, a pleasant surprise. I was just going over the ghastly and terrible events of the past two days in my mind when I heard music coming from the other room. It was an accordion. The door to the dormitory opened, and one of the orderlies from B wing of our barracks came in. He played one or two folk songs and then a hit from some film or other. With the next piece, he began to sing as well. It was dark in the dormitory, and we all listened as if we were present at the most beautiful concert.

What this little night music, so insignificant in itself, meant to us prisoners can be understood only if one recalls how deeply we had suffered over the past two days – not only physically: we were all also very profoundly traumatized. The brutality to which we had been exposed in the camp during these two harrowing days had caused some of us to despair of humanity. We no longer believed that anyone could exist here who would want to provide us with a little joy. Had an SS man come in and forced us to get up and do exercises at night, we would not have been surprised. But now a simple man appeared who wanted to cheer us up with his accordion after all the horrors of the preceding days! More than one of us had tears in his eyes. It was mediocre music, and the singer's voice was not good, but what did that matter? For a few minutes we had heard, in the hell of the concentration camp, the VOICE OF HUMANITY!

Feeling a little better, we went to sleep. But not all of us were strong enough to face the coming day with inner strength: the next morning we saw several of the new prisoners hanging on the electrified barbed wire! They had preferred a quick death to slow Nazi torture.

# GEORG ABRAHAM

## Manuscript 90 (1)

*Born in 1905 in Bromberg; married; sales representative in the tobacco and cigar trade, lost all permits in 1938; arrested on 10 November, released from Sachsenhausen on 14 December; emigrated to England in early 1939.*

Since I was now unemployed and my wife and I wanted to emigrate as soon as possible, I decided to retrain in agriculture. In the meantime, my wife could wrap up the business. I arranged with a Jewish farmer who lived in a village of 500 people to work until my emigration alongside his two sons on his 40-acre farm. The latter had been owned by the family for over a hundred years. He also ran a general store nearby. This was shut down, however, because in this little locality the [Nazi] party's spies watched the customers so closely that they could no longer patronize the store. The farm itself was highly productive, so that the party had no influence insofar as it could not alter the laws of nature. Although the party made it difficult for this man to acquire seeds and sell his products, the long-serving local police, and especially the mayor, were well-disposed towards him and tried to mitigate the hardships of the time. They knew the Jewish farmer to be helpful and just as hard-working as anyone else.

Despite all the respect he enjoyed, the farmer had long been considering the idea of selling his property and emigrating. But many obstacles were put in his way and, by the time it came to transferring ownership, it was no longer possible to transfer Reichsmarks, nor was there even any chance of his taking the machinery that he would need to establish a new farm.

I had been employed there for two months doing all kinds of work when that terrible November in the year 1938 fell upon the Jews of

Germany and left all their plans for emigration and every kind of orderliness in ruins.

For that reason, I can never forget the deeds of my brave wife and her brave mother. The drama played out at that time in every Jewish family, but what we heard about in other cases, was nonetheless quite different to our fate. The leaders of the National Socialist German Worker's Party are solely responsible for all our misfortune. For that reason, we were convinced, when on 8 [read: 9] November German radio reported the death of the official vom Rath, that the party would also exploit this opportunity to the hilt at the expense of the Jews. On that evening, we said to ourselves that the criminal had been arrested. We ourselves were not to blame and had no reason to fear for our lives. With this in mind and enraged by this crime, we left on the morning of 9 [read: 10] November in order to work in the fields. At 10 a.m., a messenger came to tell us to return home, because a rural constable wanted to speak with us.

After taking down our personal data, he then told us we were under arrest. Until he received further instructions, we were to follow him as inconspicuously as possible to the local fire station.

The young men took their leave of their parents and their sister without saying a word. But the pain on the faces of their family was indescribable.

We were now treated as dangerous criminals in a room with bars on the windows. The prison warden, a former friend of the family, looked after us and assured us that he would do everything he could to make our situation as bearable as possible. But unfortunately he had to do his duty. His wife sent her best wishes; she had been a maid in my cellmates' parents' house and had known my comrades when they went to school together in the village. The constable who had arrested us was a good friend of my two friends' parents. He arranged for the parents and also my wife, who had arrived in the meantime, to visit us as it was getting dark. Since six o'clock that morning, my wife told me, all the Jews in my home town had been arrested, with the exception of one old, sick man. My wife had taken our car and tried to save me and the [farmer's] two sons before we were arrested. Unfortunately, she got there half an hour too late and was inconsolable.

Our nerves were strained to breaking point. None of us had ever been arrested, and we did not know what surprises the next day might bring, especially in view of our inadequate housing and our being at the mercy, or lack of mercy, of the Gestapo and the party. We will always remember the people who tried to console us and give us new hope during those fateful days. The constable visited us in our cell a few times. He told us that he sympathized with us and could very well imagine how we felt. The Gestapo had wanted to send us to a concentration camp, but he had argued for keeping us here. A special guard for our relatives had been set up around the only Jewish house in the village. The arrested men's parents and my wife were thus protected. From the villagers themselves there was nothing to fear, but in these unpredictable times the mayor had recommended that this step be taken. Nonetheless, the guards had not been able to prevent a car from driving up and a few large stones being thrown through the gable window into the parents' bedroom. No one was hit, however, since they were all visiting us in the cell.

Then the constable told us about his own life, that he came from East Prussia, had been an active soldier in the old Prussian army and for the past nine years a country constable. He had joined the party because otherwise he would have lost his job. Unfortunately, the efforts he and the mayor made to keep us in the village for more than a week were not successful. At his own risk, he had tried to make it clear to the Gestapo that we were needed there for the very important task of cultivating the fields that the people urgently needed for their food supply. But the Gestapo remained deaf to all objections. Our transfer to the concentration camp was ordered.

At six o'clock the next morning, the night watchman came and informed us that we had to leave at noon. In the meantime, our family members came and there were heart-rending scenes between the young men and their old parents that I will never forget as long as I live.

I was myself deeply shaken, but my belief in our innocence and my trust in my young wife gave me the strength to endure this farewell.

I gave my wife full power of attorney and full use of my assets so that she could do everything that was necessary to win our release, and in case we never saw each other again.

The constable, who undertook to transfer us to the concentration camp, found it difficult to tear us away from our loved ones. He wanted to do us a last favour and, against orders, drove us in his own car to the main railway station. He didn't want us to use the tramway and allow us to be gawked at by people.

At the main railway station, a great number of trains came in with other Jews in them. In addition, there were buses from various smaller places. We could see the infinite sadness and evident distress in their faces. Many of them had already been in prison for days, while others had had first to see their shops ruined and their livelihoods destroyed. Among them were old, fragile people, including one who was crippled and couldn't walk. His wife had to bring this unfortunate man to the station in a handcart.

The police officers accompanying us allowed us as much freedom as they could. As the train left the Berlin railway station, the officers told us that we should prepare ourselves because we would arrive at our destination in fifteen minutes. Then suddenly the doors were ripped open, there was loud shouting and cursing, we were half pulled out of the carriages and found ourselves standing on a dark platform. The first blows were already falling on us, and a wild mob signalled that we were in the hands of the SS.

About 300 men were ordered, with kicks and punches, to line up. A number of SS men walked alongside us, in front of us and behind us, with their weapons ready. In order to make the large group of people move faster, the lorries following them drove into the crowd. This made people run forward in panic. The old were held fast by the young to keep them from falling and being trampled. One of my cellmates took the cripple on his strong shoulders.

After about ten minutes of breathless running, we came to a vast muster ground that was illuminated by a large searchlight mounted on a tower. Behind it were guards with a machine gun. There were four such towers in the camp. We were made to line up in rows in front of a long barracks, all along which there were signs with the inscription: 'We are guilty and we are the murderers of the diplomat vom Rath.' We had to read out these signs in a loud voice and were then kicked and punched. After three hours, we were driven in groups of five to the reception barracks where we were medically examined, although only to find out if anyone was homosexual. After that, we went into the shower-block, and then exchanged our clothing for thin prison clothes.

Our future block elder, a political prisoner who was to supervise us, led us into the dormitory. This barracks was now so densely packed that people had to step on each other's heads when they needed to go out. Our clothes and shoes served as pillows. After we had squeezed ourselves in, our block elder explained the situation to us. He warned us against losing our nerve and resisting, even if we got beaten. The concentration camp had 13,000 prisoners, of whom 6,000 were of the Jewish faith. Many had been there since 1933, and he himself had been there for two years because he had belonged to the Social Democratic Party for the past two years [sic].

Here in this camp he had acquired a fundamental knowledge of the [Nazi] party, and he was sure that he would never want to belong to it. Our situation was not hopeless, he said, because no provisions had been made to hold us here for a long time. These barracks had been built for us during the summer.

Up to this point, the party had simply lacked a reason to bring us here. Had the opportunity not presented itself in Paris, then another reason would have been found sooner or later. We should just trust his guidance, he said, because he was an old trooper and knew how things worked here in the concentration camp.

In these late hours of the night, this man seemed to us like a father who was taking us under his wing – us poor children who had been abandoned and repudiated by everyone. The next morning we were given cloth insignias and numbers which we all had to sew onto our threadbare clothing. Our insignias were in yellow fabric, while political prisoners had red insignias, the work-shy [*Arbeitscheue*] green insignias, homosexuals pink insignias, and so on.

In the morning, we got up at 5.30, washed, dressed and ate breakfast. At 6.30, each block elder had to appear with his inmates lined up in rows on the previously mentioned muster ground. Two thousand men then marched to a large construction site, where I myself worked until I was released. The other inmates were assigned to all kinds of work.

It was very hard to endure this long march because we were driven like dogs by the SS guards who accompanied us. For those who could no longer endure it, there was little choice but to be transported from this world to the next. They could choose to be either trampled to death or beaten to death.

My work consisted of loading a truck with sand, along with 25 comrades. This truck was pulled by us for about 500 metres and then unloaded. So long as the foremen, themselves prisoners, were directing this work, everything went quietly and smoothly. But if a block leader [*Blockführer*] came, then we had to do everything at the double. On several occasions, people tried to escape from this large construction site through the cordons that had been set up. Such an attempt was a matter of life and death because as soon as an unfortunate man came near [the cordon] he was picked off by the guard. But people no longer had much to lose, so escape attempts were often made. Once we heard shots and I later saw a dead man and a seriously injured one being carried back on a stretcher. The injured man recovered, and the SS guard must have been demoted because he had aimed so poorly.

139

Another time we were not allowed to march back [to the barracks] because one man was missing. After hours of searching, he was found hanged in a ditch. He had stolen a piece of bread from one of his fellow workers. He expected to be given 25 lashes for the offence and had preferred to commit suicide. Prisoners who had been in the camp for two years or longer were starving so that they were thankful for every bit of bread.

People who were 60 or 70 years old could not endure these many hardships, however, and soon died. According to the comrades whose job it was to carry away the dead men, there were 80 of them a day.

Inmates who became sick were very badly treated. There was only one SS camp doctor, and he had his own special way of treating inmates with frozen hands and feet. After standing for hours in front of the sick bay, they were sent away with kicks and got another supplementary punishment: they had to stand for six hours or more at the entrance gate. This gate was located under the watchtower, and the man standing there could not move from the spot. The electrified wires, the empty stomachs and the bitter cold did the rest. In addition, they got no supper or midday meal. However, this prohibition was usually circumvented since the block elder would save the half-frozen fellows' food.

Once, as we were returning from work, we were not dismissed because we were supposed to see what happened to those who tried to escape. As we heard, the person involved was a house painter who had been here for two years, and one day was assigned to decorate the camp doctor's apartment. Since he was not under guard, he decided to escape. Wearing the doctor's uniform, he was able to get past the guards. Hours later, he was missed. For weeks, they looked for him, broadcasting his description over the radio and using the camp police. As punishment, all the prisoners had to stand every day for three hours and more on the muster ground. The prisoner had gone to Berlin and had there disappeared underground in some dive. Months later he was caught, and he got the kind of welcome back that he deserved, as they put it.

An enormous wreath made of fir boughs, with an inscription in the middle that read 'A Hearty Welcome', was carried in front, and behind came a man with a huge drum that he had to beat constantly. In the enormous rectangle that we had to form, a scaffold had been erected. Here the man was tied up, and twelve SS men gave him 25 lashes. Then another prisoner had to yell: 'This is what happens to anyone who tries to escape.' The man was then put in a special cell

and then in a punishment unit. And that's another story. It was isolated, and the prisoners in it, about 400 of them, had to work especially hard. A particularly brutal SS man dealt out more blows than
food.

Among these prisoners, there were some who belonged to one of
the sects most persecuted by the party, the Jehovah's Witnesses. The
majority of the men who belonged to this religious community were
Aryans. Every year at Christmas they were offered release if they
would promise to disavow their convictions. But none of them agreed
to do so, and so year after year they remained there. It was a sad-
looking group, and the men seemed to be on the verge of collapse
from hunger and deprivation. I had an opportunity to speak with one
of these victims.

He told me that he believed that a higher being ruled the world.
Their sufferings were merely temporary. Some day the heavenly
Father would take pity on them and destroy their tormentors. This
regime had to perish because it had burdened itself with too much
guilt and its crimes cried out to Heaven.

The SS guards trained for duty in the concentration camp consisted
of 1,200 men. They were so filled with hatred and had become so
sadistic that they regarded the prisoners as so many cattle. But here,
too, there were exceptions. I got to know one of these. He sat down
with us after he had made sure that the coast was clear, as he put it.
He asked where we came from and encouraged us to believe that we
would not remain here long if we got our relatives to make preparations for our emigration as soon as possible. We should be glad, he
said, to have come here at this time because six months earlier it had
been hell. People had died of thirst in the heat of this sandy wasteland
because they had no water. The death rate was so high that the
authorities had to intervene.

Earlier, he had been a guard in Buchenwald concentration camp,
he told us, and this camp [Sachsenhausen] was incomparably better.
In Buchenwald, there had been no sanitation facilities but a far
greater number of men. Near the camp, there was a beech forest
[Buchenwald]. There, the unwanted and already earmarked inmates
were simply hanged on trees. He could still hear them screaming and
reciting prayers. Far more people were housed in each barracks at
Buchenwald, and still more were beaten to death. He himself was the
son of a police officer. He had not wanted to join the party. But since
he'd had no job, he had had to work with farmers. He couldn't do
that work and so he had to choose either to join the party or to be
put in this concentration camp as a work dodger. He suffered a great

141

deal when he saw all this wretchedness; he had imagined that the party had higher ideals.

Among my workmates was a very nice, bright young man. He told me that he had been arrested three months earlier, when the SA was making a raid on so-called work-dodging elements. He was immediately interned along with thousands of other innocent people. At that time, he had been unable to find work as a confectioner and earned his living by producing and selling sweets at fairs. Our shared suffering made for great comradeship. We all stuck together through thick and thin. Never did I hear a word of anti-Semitism, nor were there any racial distinctions. Because of what these men had had to take from members of their own race, they were anything but anti-Jewish.

We worked on Sundays and holidays as well. How well we worked, we heard from the most brutal *Blockführer*. If a job had to be done quickly, and the foreman had doubts as to whether it would be, the *Blockführer* said: 'Take the Jews to do it; they'll manage.'

In the evening we had an hour of free time. This I used to visit my father-in-law and my many friends who were housed in other huts. Each of them had experienced terrible things on 9 November. Of the many individual accounts I heard, I have here chosen a few cases that I was able to confirm after I was released.

One story concerns a 65-year-old man who ran a thriving business and had a small farm in a village of 500 inhabitants. The house where he had been born was on his land.

On 9 November, all the Jewish men in this village, along with their wives and children, had been taken from their beds. The synagogue was already burning, and the SA, accompanied by a hooting and jeering mob, hastened to set fire to this man's business, which was stocked with goods. The real value of what went up in flames was about 70,000 marks. All the men were loaded into a lorry to be transported with many others from the nearby town to Sachsen-hausen. The man died a few days after this conversation and was thus spared hearing how his son was later tricked out of his land. In addition, he still had to pay his telephone bill to the post office. The party leadership presented a bill for RM 45.60 for the petrol they had used to set fire to the synagogue and the house. The son still has this bill; it is the proof of his former property, which he took with him to Palestine.

All of the furnishings belonging to my best friend in my home town were destroyed. The goods that were not stolen were ruined by the SA with paint. His wife, who protested against this crazy destruction, had to flee with her 10-year-old child to her aged parents, because the SA men threatened to beat her to death. The friends who took her in were secret members of the Jehovah's Witnesses. They prayed with them that the night might pass without loss of life. These people consoled the victimized Jews with their strong belief in a better future. God, they said, meant well for the Jews by making them the subject of persecution. Because here there was great distress and war. This was all written in the Bible.

My friend, whose fate I have just recounted, got out of the concentration camp much later than I. He had volunteered for military service in the [First] World War and, after it ended, fought against Bolshevism for two more years in Finland under General Mannerheim. But what did everything we had done matter on 9 November? We were all responsible for the [death of] the diplomat Rath.

Thanks to the tireless efforts of my wife and the establishment of this camp[1] with generous help from England, my wife was able to obtain my release. The Gestapo needed proof of my intended emigration. It wasn't easy. An official asked her about her race and what her concern was. Then an iron grille came down. My wife thought she herself had now become a prisoner. After checking the papers, the official told her that I would be released in a week. When my wife still didn't leave, he telephoned the order to Sachsenhausen.

I will never forget the day and the hour that I left this concentration camp – even if my joy was mitigated by my concern about my father-in-law and all the other people who remained behind. I left them with the firm intention of doing everything I could to help them. A series of formalities still had to be gone through before our release. In particular, we had to sign a promise not to speak to anyone about what we had seen and experienced. The long arm of the Gestapo reached beyond the German border, the camp commandant told us. Our first steps to freedom, if it could be called that, were accompanied by fear about the way our fellow citizens would treat us outcasts. We were all pleasantly surprised. Even at the railway station we encountered friendly people. Everyone could tell where we had been and gave us sympathetic glances. People offered us money and refreshments. No one asked how it had been; they all knew.

In our home towns, our friends were the same. In general, they considered what had happened to us unjust. In their opinion, the party and Minister Goebbels were mainly to blame. A party member who was present when the synagogue was burned down told me how it happened.

On the evening of 8 [read: 9] November, the town's SS men were summoned to the town hall by the mayor, who was himself an SS man. Here they were instructed to break the windows of all Jewish shops at 5.00 in the morning of 9 November. Beforehand, the temple was to be set on fire and Jewish men arrested and sent to Sachsenhausen. The police were not to intervene and the fire brigade was merely to protect adjacent buildings. The fire was to be put out only after the building had burned to the ground. Beforehand, all the ritual objects in the temple were to be removed. During the demolition of old temples, workers were to search for gold coins. The action was to begin at 3 a.m. and be carried out within 24 hours throughout the whole Reich. These were the orders, he said, that he had been given by his superiors. Every SS man had to carry out the command.

Another friend who lived in an adjacent apartment building near the temple told me that his attention had been attracted by the constant noise of people coming and going. He saw about twenty SS men, led by the mayor, break down the doors of the temple. Then some men carried a few objects out of the building while others remained inside with firewood and paper. When they came out, he watched as it slowly grew brighter inside the large building. But since the fire didn't really catch hold, they broke the panes of the arched windows. Then torches were brought in, and he saw how the SS men's hands trembled and one match after another went out without igniting the torches, until the mayor himself stepped in.

When in spite of their efforts, the huge building failed to catch fire, he sent a few men away who came back with petrol cans and took them inside. Then bright flames flared up inside the building. The residents, except for the Jews, were woken and told that they should get up because the temple was on fire. So that is what the seething popular ferment that the Nazis propagated actually looked like. Nothing was actually done by the German people themselves. They were just as helpless as we were in the face of this violation. To be sure, there were elements that rejoiced in this destruction because they themselves had nothing. But the majority thought that it would have been better to preserve these enormously valuable objects.

The Jewish shop owners had to replace their broken windows at their own expense. Since all the shop windows were insured, the insurance companies had to cover the damages. But the government arranged for these payments to go solely to the Reich rather than to those who had suffered damage.

For businesses and shops whose owners had been taken to concentration camps, so-called trustees were nominated; their task was to

transfer these enterprises to Aryan ownership. The signatures necessary for this were very often demanded of Jewish shop owners in the
concentration camps, and when particular problems arose, they were
released from custody after an agreement to sell had been extorted
from them. I hardly need point out that the interests of the Jewish
proprietors were not respected in these matters.

The Reich carried out further plunder through the sale of real estate
and commercial plant. These had to be sold at a price below the unit
value (see p. 109). The difference between the latter and the amount
actually paid was assigned to the new owner in the form of a mortgage held by the Reich. The proceeds had to be put in a special
account from which the seller was allowed to withdraw only a small
amount to cover his living costs. Special permission had to be obtained
to use these funds for any other purpose.

In addition, the authorities undertook an inventory of gold, silver
and jewellery owned by Jews. These possessions had to be handed
over in March 1939, with the exception of wedding rings and one
set of table silverware. These objects were paid for by weight. This
legally authorized fraud was worthy of the other crimes committed
by Germany's ruling clique. The old people in particular had tears in
their eyes when surrendering objects that had been in their families
for generations and for which they received a few worthless marks.
It was not so much the monetary value as the memories that they
clung to that made it so hard for them to part with these objects.

After all these events, the rate of emigration increased enormously.
The action on 9 November had shown even the greatest of optimists
that the regime was bent on destroying German Jewry and that there
was now no alternative.

One might have thought that the Nazi regime would have done all
it could to get rid of the Jews as quickly as possible. But the following
description will give an idea of the obstacles that had to be overcome
in order to be able to leave Germany.

Everyone who wanted to emigrate had to provide the local currency exchange office with a list of the objects he wanted to take with
him. Up to that point, it had been possible to take anything, so long
as the requisite fee was paid. Now, however, only a small number of
things were approved, and no new possessions could be taken out of
the country. And the high charges levied on old things bore no relationship to their value.

In practice, as I myself experienced it, this is how the situation
looked: the value of all the assets I planned to take with me amounted
to 1,340 marks. This inventory went to the currency exchange office,

and one morning the head of this office appeared at my door with several officials. He bellowed at me: 'Do you have the goods you want to move ready? Can't you stand up straight the way you learned in the concentration camp?' Then he asked who was there. My parents-in-law and my wife were in the house. A search of the house immediately began, during which they came across a letter that my father-in-law was writing to his relatives in Brazil. The letter referred to their current situation and the fact that their financial resources were almost exhausted. They could no longer live in this witches' cauldron, my father-in-law's letter said. His son was seventeen and still an apprentice lathe-operator in a machine shop. He couldn't finish his training there because the anti-Semitic abuse was making his life miserable.

When the SS man had read the letter, he shouted at my father-in-law, saying that this was lies and propaganda and asked him whether he wanted to go back to the concentration camp. However, after my father-in-law's military documents had been found – he had served as a medical officer from 1914 to 1918 – and another official had put in a good word for him, nothing further was said.

Turning to me, the official demanded that I tell him how much I was owed and what other assets I had. He immediately blocked the payments, and I had to sign a document allowing me access to the sum of 4,000 marks only with his permission. I apparently had so little that only one official was left in the apartment to inspect the possessions I was planning to take with me.

He had great trust in us, said the official, and was glad to see the order and cleanliness that prevailed in our house. But unfortunately he could not exempt us from the payment to the Reich, because his superior had set the amount of 3,000 marks. He said he would take it upon himself to reduce the payment to 1,560 marks and would see to it that everything was in order. There was no standard fee. It was determined in each case by the emigrant's assets. The goal was to prevent Jews from using any funds for purchases. I would be wise to write a cheque immediately because he knew for certain that further, severe restrictions would follow. We were young, he said, and could earn back abroad what we had lost here. Our things had practical value for us, and we would certainly not be in a position to make any new purchases. I objected that I still had duties to my parents, whom I had to support for a long time, and that freight and travel costs were also considerable. He was sorry, he said, but he had done what he could for us and he was being straight with us.

Then he gave a few examples from his office.

A property owner whom I knew well had assets of one million marks after the forced sale of his real estate holdings. He had had to pay 850,000 marks in taxes, property levies and other costs. He could not account for the remaining 150,000 marks and his [the official's] superior had had the man arrested.

They had also dealt with my former boss. He had had to pay 15,000 marks and, since they liked the young man, they had permitted him to take silverware with him in exchange for a special payment. But they left him enough to allow him to flee with his wife to Australia.

He had also gone with his boss to the home of another Jew to look for gold stocks. The owner did not stand up straight and smoked his cigar. His boss had yelled at the old man, asking him if he couldn't stand up straight. 'In my own house I can do and stand as I wish,' the man replied. Thereupon his boss had punched him and imposed a fine of 1,500 marks. Later, he also arranged for the man to be arrested.

After hearing all this I realized that I was still better off paying. The man left, wishing us the best for the future.

It was still months before I could emigrate. I had to leave my wife behind, reassuring her that I would do everything I could to get her out as well. I succeeded in doing so shortly, thanks to the help provided by this country [England]. But during these months of anxious waiting, fate continued to deal us hard blows. I had to bury my dearly beloved father who could not understand what was happening. The constant harassment and his concern for his children hastened his end. In the many quiet moments that I was fortunate enough to spend with him, he spoke of soon emigrating but he never received permission to do so.

# HERTHA NATHORFF

## Manuscript 114 (162)

*Born Hertha Einstein in 1895 in Laupheim/Württemberg; married Dr Erich Nathorff. Until September 1938, she was head physician in the Charlottenburg Hospital in Berlin. One son; emigrated to the USA in 1939; died in New York in 1993.*

### 10 November 1938

It is late at night – I want to try to write down, with a trembling hand, today's events, events that have engraved themselves in flaming letters on my heart. I want to write them down for my child, so that some day he can read how they destroyed his life.

I want to relate my experience – at this midnight hour, sitting alone and trembling at my desk, groaning painfully like a wounded animal – I want to write, in order not to scream out loud in the still of the night.

Yesterday a murder was committed in Paris – a Polish Jew shot a secretary at the German embassy.

Now all Jews must atone for it!

Yesterday there were already questions being asked: 'How could the man have got so far inside the building? You can't just walk into any embassy in the world.' And they said: 'This is a second Reichstag fire; the man was hired by the Nazis themselves. Herr vom Rath – who was in any case a seriously ill man – was on the blacklist . . .'

This morning my maid said to me: 'It looks like they were at it again last night. In the fur shop next door, the windows were smashed and everything was stolen.' I only half-listened to her. By that time we were used to such things. Shortly afterwards, I was on my way

148

to the clinic. It was odd that there was so much broken glass in the street! In the beautiful, elegant dress shop all the windows were broken, and the displays were empty. And it was the same in the shop next door and at Etam, the fine stocking shop across the street. What have they done now, I wondered. Then I heard a well-dressed woman say to her husband as she walked past me: 'Serves the damned Jews right – revenge is sweet!' Only then did I begin to understand what had happened and really looked around me. Broken glass everywhere, demolished shops, insofar as there are still any Jewish shops in the Kaiserallee. Nauseated, I turned away and returned home. I heard a few passers-by remarking sadly about these events; but most of them just walked timidly and quietly through the streets.

When I got home, my maid said: 'Herr Doctor has already left. He was called out urgently for a heart attack.' Right, here were the numbers in the order that my husband made his visits. There were so many of them today. I was very anxious for him to come home, as I had things to do all morning. The telephone rang constantly. One urgent call after another for Herr Doctor. I managed to contact him – I made six or seven calls before I finally reached him – and told him: 'You have to go to so-and-so immediately, it's a heart attack.'

'But I can't leave here yet,' my husband said. 'If it's really so urgent, please call a colleague.' I tried to reach one. Impossible! He too was very busy.

The whole morning was like that. I ate lunch with our son. He told me: 'Can you believe it, Mummy? The synagogue on Prinzregentenstrasse is burning. I saw it on the way home, and there is broken glass all over the streets. People say the Nazis did all that.' But I wasn't really listening to what my son was saying. I was still preoccupied with my husband's return. It was now 3 p.m. The first patients were arriving for afternoon surgery. I had to put them off, telling them that they would have to wait a bit. These were new patients, who didn't know me. One of them said: 'Do you know that our temple is burning? What else is going to happen today?' I didn't have time to gossip.

The doorbell rang again. My sister had arrived. How pale she looked today, I thought: she was probably still upset at having to say goodbye to her brothers and sisters, or they had given her husband trouble with his science tours. I didn't have time to talk to her. The telephone and the doorbell kept ringing. My sister said: 'Even today you're not going to stop working like mad?' But I couldn't stop to explain myself at that moment.

Then my husband arrived – weary, exhausted. 'I can't eat anything; I'll just grab a quick cup of coffee.' He hastily greeted my sister. 'Can I speak with you alone for a moment?' she asked. Thinking that she wanted medical advice, I left the room. After a few minutes, my husband came back and said: 'I don't want you to be alarmed, but they've picked up her husband.'

'Picked up? How? Why?' I asked.

'It looks like another raid is underway,' he said. 'Some of my patients have also been arrested. That's why there are so many heart attacks. They even took away all the men at a wedding party.' I asked my husband to call my brother-in-law's brother immediately. His wife answered the telephone and said: 'He has no surgery today. He's on an excursion with his friends in the Grunewald. Please come over right away!'

Then my husband held his surgery! Afterwards, he accompanied my sister to her sister-in-law's home. Their son opened the door and said: 'They picked up Papa as well.' Then they phoned me at home with this news. I asked my husband not to come home. I brought everything he needed for his evening calls out to the street, met him there and accompanied him on his rounds with a desperately sad heart. What should we do, what should we do? Again, I begged my husband not to come home. 'Sleep at a friend's house – someone recently said to me that there was always room for you.' But my husband? He thought only of his patients. Of the men and women who were having heart attacks today because their loved ones had been summarily taken away, no one knew where to.

It was now late evening. The newspaper said the attacks were over. And my husband said that in any case he wanted to come home. 'Don't you realize yet how their newspapers lie?' I asked him. But I couldn't stop him from continuing to do his duty. It was 9 p.m. I went back anyway; I had to take care of my son. My old cook had already gone home for the night. I was all alone in the apartment in the eerie silence.

As usual, I locked the front rooms of our apartment. I sat down next to the radio to find out what was happening and to wait for my husband.

9.30 p.m. The doorbell rang twice, briefly and urgently. I went to the door. 'Who's there?'

'Open up! Police!' Trembling, I opened the door. I knew what they wanted.

'Where's the doctor?' 'He's not in,' I said.

'What? The concierge saw him come home.'

'He was at home, but then he was called out again.' They went up to the first door. Locked. The second door. Locked. 'These are our examination rooms,' I explained. 'Ever since we were robbed, I always lock up in the evening when I'm home alone.' They went to the next door. 'Please don't rattle the handle,' I said. 'My child is asleep in there.' – 'We know your Jewish tricks.' He held his revolver under my nose and said: 'One more word and the bullet's in your brain. Where have you hidden your husband?' My knees were shaking. Just stay calm, stay calm, I said to myself. 'I'm not lying. My husband is not at home – but please, shoot my child first, and then me. And aim well.' And I opened the door that led to the room where my son was sleeping.

But the two men were already getting ready to leave. At last, they appeared to believe me. Then I heard the door to our apartment opening. My husband had arrived. He arrived, poor man, at the very moment when I thought I'd saved him. And they took him away, just like that. 'Just thank your God that your wife doesn't have a bullet in her head.' The man dared to say that again, and he dared to utter the name of God. And they went away with my husband. I ran after them into the street. 'Where are you taking my husband? What has he done?' They shoved me away roughly. 'You can ask about him tomorrow on Alexanderplatz.' And I saw them get into a car and drive him away into the dark night.

Our doorman was standing at the door to the building. He took my arm and said: 'If I'd realized what was going to happen, I'd have hidden our good doctor under the coal in the cellar. Yes, yes, they've come a long way since Herr v. B.[1] (whom they had shot in 1934!) to our doctor! From one floor to the next! But what they're doing will not turn out well.'

My legs would barely carry me up the stairs. What should I do? I tried to reach friends and colleagues by telephone. Always the same answer: 'Not at home.' With feverish haste, I searched my husband's desk. I found nothing, nothing that could incriminate him. I jumped at every sound. I had to be prepared at any moment for them to search the house.

Then I remembered: the small firearm from my husband's time in the military was in the kitchen. Yesterday I'd taken it down from the attic where it had been kept as a memento, along with other curios. Jews were no longer allowed to have weapons. The punishment was death. I'd intended to hand it over to the police the next day. What should I do with it until tomorrow? I ran across the street with the weapon. I dared not throw it away. It might be found and incriminate us twice over. I had to go home again. Something might happen to my son. At midnight a woman came to me. Secretly and quietly. She had seen the flickering light in my lonely room. Silently, she made tea for me and asked me what else she could do for me. Speechless, I held her hand. 'No one can do anything for me.' Then I thought of the sidearm. 'Just look after this until tomorrow morning.'

Now it will soon be 3 a.m. I am sitting fully clothed in my apartment, which seems so empty. They have not come back. From the adjoining room I hear my son's regular breathing. And where might his father be? I want to lie down, put out the light, as today in me a sacred, glowing light has been put out: my belief that people are fundamentally good.

## 11 November 1938

I sent my son to school. 'Be careful, son,' I told him. 'Daddy has already gone out; he has to visit his patients very early.' Then I made coffee and sandwiches for my husband, whose whereabouts I didn't know. My old housekeeper, Frau H., came in the early morning. She was going to stay with me. 'If anyone phones, say that the doctor is not here.' I didn't want to tell the whole truth, but I didn't want to lie, either. My sister and her little niece (who both lived through and saw the closing of the Jewish rest home in Lehnitz and how the Nazis stole all the supplies and confiscated everything for the NSV) picked me up and we drove to police headquarters. On the way, I bought some bananas, hoping that we would be allowed to give them to the men.

At the police headquarters, they wouldn't let us in. 'Go home. You'll be given written notification: your husband is no longer being held here,' said the officer at the door. Written notification! Frau v. B. also got written notification four years ago when she was summoned to pick up her husband's ashes, I recalled. But I didn't dare say what I was thinking . . . At that moment a lady saw me, a member of the board of the Jewish Women's Association. She had probably been trying to get information about the fate of the thousands of arrested men. 'You, too?' she said to me. 'But there is really no point. Go home; there is nothing to be learned here. We're trying to get information through the organization. The fact is that the men are no longer here.' And she simply put me in the car.

At home, the telephone rang incessantly. 'Where is Herr Doctor? Who is replacing him?' I didn't know what I should say. Earlier, when my husband was ill, I was at least allowed to substitute for him. But I couldn't do that any more. I called the medical association. They gave me the name of a replacement, who told me: 'If the medical association has decreed it, I have to do it, but please spare me too many of your patients.' My home had become a madhouse. People were coming and going, eating here, asking whether they or their acquaintances could sleep here. My home was not endangered at that point. They would probably not search it again, now that my husband had been taken away. Nonetheless, the wife of an Aryan colleague examined our books in case. There might be one that offended them if they did search the house. My son came home from school. 'Is Daddy still not home? Where is he, anyway?' I didn't answer. I couldn't lie to my son.

In the evening, I called a friend in my home town. She sobbed despairingly into the telephone. Her husband had been taken away. 'In the early morning, they even roused my 74-year-old father from his bed and put him in prison, despite his heart problems.' Neither of us could say anything else because the connection was broken. At least the small firearm was out of the building. My doorman had given it to the police first thing that morning.

## 12 November 1938

How many people spent last night at our apartment? I don't know. I know only that a large breakfast table was set when I left early in the morning for the American consulate in order to request confirmation that we had submitted our affidavit in August. Countless people stood with me on the cold, dark November morning in the damp grounds in front of the American consulate. Pale, aggrieved women from Berlin, Leipzig, Breslau [Wroclaw] all bore the same pain, and they stood quietly, acting on behalf of their husbands and weeping in their hearts – a women's crusade! For hours I stood like them in the damp and cold, in the rain and snow, and suddenly it occurred to me – my husband had played in this garden when he was a boy, in the rooms in which the American consulate were now located.[2] He had spent many happy hours of a golden childhood there. Grandpa Nathorff had lived there for many, many years, until he died. And now I was standing there begging, freezing outside the door, hour after hour!

When at last it was my turn to present my request, the blond man said to me and the lady behind me, the last to be let into the building: 'Closed. It's one o'clock. Come back Monday.' I had stood there for more than six hours, and he didn't have two minutes to answer my brief question. Sad and weary, I went home. Again, there were guests at the table. On Monday I would have to go to the bank to get money, I thought. I didn't have access to my husband's account. It was possible that mine would also have been frozen.

Again my son asked: 'Where is Daddy?' After we'd eaten, I took him into the surgery and told him: 'You know, my son, that your mother doesn't lie and that you are my best friend, to whom I want always to tell everything, just as you should always tell me.' And then I slowly explained to him that Daddy had, as it were, been called up, that like so many other fathers he had to do military exercises that might last a few weeks. 'Now you have to be my best comrade.' I looked deeply into his big child's eyes, in which tears were secretly welling up. I gave him a kiss and pressed his hand. 'Mummy, I'm with you, but I already thought as much. They've been talking about it at school.'

## 13 November 1938

Sunday, and there was still no news of my husband. Where was he, where? I feared for his life. The venerable old gentleman came early in the morning, accompanied by his wife. He said I should go to their home, stay with them. Several friends had already made similar offers. No, I said, I would stay where I was to protect our home until my husband came back. More than one friend advised me to send the boy away. He too was in danger. What should I do? All the time, patients were coming in whose husband had also been arrested. 'What should I do? What should I do?' they all asked. These people were desperate. There were not enough doctors. I didn't know how my husband treated some of the new patients. I knew that he had developed a special approach and a new drug for one seriously ill patient. I couldn't find the dosage for the injection in the card file. I wrote to him, asked for him; maybe the letter might reach him via police headquarters.

An Aryan patient called; her little girl had suffered a nervous breakdown. The horrors of the last few days had been too much for the sensitive child's nerves. The girl wanted to get out of Germany, out of the Hitler Youth. I couldn't help. I could only tremble and act as if I were calm. Other people had never seen me cry.

## 14 November 1938

A letter from the medical association. 'For the next four weeks, we have approved Dr N. as the replacement for your husband. After this time, please get in touch with us again.' For the next four weeks! That said it all! I had to get on with my life. I had to take care of my child and my house until my husband returned.

Today I couldn't go to the consulate. I felt so weak; I hadn't eaten anything the entire day. How could I, with the thought that my husband must be starving? At the bank I was able to withdraw another large sum from my account. How relieved I was. Now at least I had no money worries for the time being. If only so many visitors were not coming all the time! I couldn't bear these sympathy visits, no matter how well-meant they were. And the noon post still brought no news of my husband. I finally knew what it meant to suffer to the point of madness!

## 16 November 1938

Now I want to try to write down what happened, so that my child can read what was done to his mother, why she will say to him: 'Don't ever come back to this country if we manage to leave it alive.'

But let me begin:

## Monday, 14 November 1938

I was so tired. At about 1.00 p.m., someone called me to say: 'Your husband sends his greetings; he is alive. I spoke to him this morning before I was released.' That put me in such turmoil. I lay down for a few minutes on the sofa. My son was still at school. My old cook was back in the kitchen; my housekeeper had gone out for a short time to do errands. Shortly before 2.00 p.m., the doorbell rang. I opened the door myself. A slender, blond man stood in the doorway and asked if I was Frau Doctor. 'I come as your friend. Can anyone see me? I am an officer, a detective, you know. I've come because I want to help your husband.'

He had already put his foot in my door. I let him come in.

'Give me your word of honour never to say anything about what I am going to tell you. Only then can I help you. I'm an officer, and

155

you can be sure that my neck would be on the line if I were seen in your house, if people learned that I have gone out of my way to help you.'

'You want to help us?' I asked, incredulous. 'Then tell me where my husband is.'

'Your husband? In Tegel, in prison, incarcerated. Indicted because of 218.[3] But I know the man who informed on him and I know that this is only a jealous man's act of revenge on the girl involved. This girl is a friend of my girlfriend, who was once your husband's patient and who has asked me to help your husband. It was easy to find the complaint. Here it is.'

And then he took a letter from his pocket that he refused to show me or let me read. As an officer, he couldn't do that. 'My husband? 218? Out of the question,' I said. 'I'd swear to that.'

'But Frau Doctor, don't be silly. A Jew is always guilty. Just think of Dr G., of how long he's already been in prison. Your husband would not survive even investigative custody. We have to act quickly to pay the guy off and force him to retract his complaint.'

I went ice cold. 'My husband is innocent,' I said, 'and I have no money.'

'But you must have illegal money here.'

'Not a penny,' I said truthfully.

'Or outside Germany?'

'We have nothing abroad either.'

'Well, where do you keep all your money?' His tone was steadily hardening and he was becoming increasingly pushy. 'Hurry up. At 3.00 p.m. I have to go on duty. I have the complaint against your husband here, which I will have to hand on.'

I got scared. If only my housekeeper would come home. I got up. I tried to reach for the telephone. The telephone with my handbag next to it. The handbag with all the money that I had taken out of the bank a few hours before. Like a lightning bolt, the idea struck me. What if he –? If only I could call for help! The window was a few steps away. He guessed what I was thinking. 'And you think that I'd put myself at your mercy?' I heard him say. 'You seem to be unaware that we have a secret order to immediately shoot dead any Jew.' And again I saw a sparkling revolver pointed at me! I opened my handbag. 'Here, take what I withdrew from the bank this morning, as you undoubtedly already know. It should be enough. If not, I'm in the telephone book. Go. You needn't be afraid of me. I'll keep quiet, as I promised you. I keep my word, even to an extortionist.'

He took the money, all the money, and left. I heard the door close. Then I fainted. My housekeeper found me lying on the floor against the door to the surgery. 'Who was that creepy guy who was rushing down the stairs so quickly when I came home? Was he here with you?' she asked me. I only shook my head. She helped me to my bed, and I asked her to call a doctor who was a friend of mine. But now I was afraid at every turn. Would he come back? Would he secretly watch me, for fear that I would denounce him? That same evening I went to a lawyer and reported everything to him. He advised me against filing a complaint with the police. The priority was getting my husband home again. Then we would see what could be done.

I then sent my son to stay with an Aryan colleague, where he would sleep more safely than at home. Valuables, silver, jewellery, carpets I put into storage. I wanted my husband to find them again when he came home. I myself henceforth only slept fully clothed, if this brief dozing off could be called sleep. I was on edge all the time, wondering what would happen next. I knew that Aryan friends often passed by my house late at night in order to check if my lights were still on, if the lamps had been smashed, if our house had been ransacked, as had happened to so many others in recent days. My husband's physician sign had been torn down. I didn't have another put up; I felt endangered by it.

Because it was Atonement Day, all offices were closed today. I could do nothing but wait, wait like so many other people who are waiting with heavy hearts for their husbands, their fathers.

## 17 November 1938

A telegram inviting us to California. Now, when it is too late. But I went to the consulate with the telegram. For hours, I stood again in the cold and damp. I'd never even made a streetwalker wait as long at the door of my clinic as I now had to stand, along with other women tortured with worry. I stood for five hours, without eating a morsel. The Wertheim tea room was on the ground floor of the consulate, but the usual sign, 'Jews unwelcome', told us clearly enough that we wouldn't even get a cup of tea there. Finally, it was my turn. 'Visitor's visa for America – out of the question, you can't obtain certification that we have filed the affidavit.' No one took pity on me; no one would help me – me, who had spent my whole life trying to help others. So much for good friends and generous people.

157

On the way home, I met an Aryan who was a former patient. At first, she hardly recognized me. She too had heard about the Jewish pogroms and asked after my husband. I could only tell her: 'Him, too!' She took me along to her apartment. I let her take me there, in spite of the peril she would have been in had anyone seen me in her home. Her husband even came and had some kind words with me. Here in someone else's house for the first time I spent a peaceful hour where I could pull myself together without the fear of something happening to me. It's good that even high officials in the Nazi party still occasionally recalled that Jews had done things for them in the past. Here, too, I was advised to get my boy away to a safe place since new raids were constantly feared. At any rate, Herr Göring and Herr Goebbels seemed not to be of the same opinion concerning the events of 10 November. Herr Göring feared that the raids could have seriously damaged Germany abroad and that they were also not entirely in keeping with his four-year plan. Herr Goebbels seemed rather more eager for further raids.

My boy is sleeping somewhere else again. Some stranger who is also fleeing will sleep in his bed tonight. But where is my husband?

## 20 November 1938

I had been warned not to sleep at home, if possible. I wandered through the streets and no longer knew where I was going. I was constantly hearing of new abominations, but at least I'd heard that my husband was still alive. Another man who'd been released had brought me greetings from him. He told me that many old schoolmates from the Wilhelm secondary school had had an involuntary class reunion and were helping each other. But I should do all I could, he told me, to get my husband released as soon as possible. I could learn nothing more from the man.

## 24 November 1938

Yet new fear and distress. I ran from one government office to another. I waited for hours at the Emigration Advice Office for a certificate that would allow me to get a passport. I didn't succeed, though I sensed that the friendly official would like to have helped me: 'A passport can only be issued if you can designate an exact departure date.' I couldn't do that. I asked friends what I should do.

Book a passage somewhere, anywhere, I was advised. I sent telegrams all over the world. I received outlandish offers. A visa to Chile for 3,000 marks – courtesy of an Austrian Nazi. They get rich on our misfortune. I was completely desperate. I couldn't get access to that kind of money.

A patient of my husband's who had come from England for a conference sent his secretary to see if he could do anything for me. 'Save my child.' I couldn't think of anything else to say. In the meantime, after hours of negotiation, a travel agency offered me a booking to Cuba in February. It was the only legal booking that I could still make. I cabled America and implored that the required advance payment be made.

## 30 November 1938

The money for Cuba was supposed to have been deposited from America. At last I could go back to the Emigration Office and apply for a valid passport.

## 2 December 1938

I stood for hours at the Emigration Office, waiting on a narrow, twisting, precarious stairway, a special entrance for Jews. But I got the certificate necessary for the issue of a passport for emigration to Cuba. 'Come back tomorrow morning about ten o'clock and I'll give you a number,' the friendly official said. 'Come to me and you won't need to wait so long again.' If only he knew who I was! I knew precisely who he was and how he suffered when witnessing the fate of others, which was clear to him in all its tragedy every moment he was on duty.

## 3 December 1938

I got the certificate from the Emigration Office. The friendly man gave it to me. 'I'm very grateful to you, Herr X.' I addressed him by name. Astounded, he stared at me. 'Thank you again,' I said. 'Now I want to tell you whom you have been helping. The doctor of your friends, the X family.' He looked at me: 'Dear lady, that's you?' But I was already out of the door.

## 4 December 1938

Advent Sunday, and I'm all alone. I've even sent my boy away. The fear and insecurity in my own home is too great. I am sitting writing letters to patients to ask them to pay their bills. For the first time in my life, I have to ask for money. In point of fact, I have money, a great deal of money, in the bank, but I can't get at it. Then I have to calculate my taxes. Our old tax consultant, who knows more about this than I do because I've never paid much attention to these things, made two appointments to help me. The first time he had something to do for the party and was not in his office. The second time he was dead drunk. The party had had something else to celebrate.

Yesterday, my cousin Fritz flew in haste to England. He preferred to wait there until he could emigrate to Australia. And an hour later they had indeed come to arrest him. They got there too late, I was told by his brother, who has been a loyal friend to me and who has always been there for me without my having to ask. He is one of the few who has stood quietly by me and who doesn't torment me with tales of new atrocities and advice I can't act on.

I cabled my husband to tell him that I needed full power of attorney to arrange our departure for Cuba. That way, I hoped, he would at least know that I was doing everything I could for him, that is, if police headquarters would only forward the telegram to him!

## 5 December 1938

I applied to the police for the passport and took our so-called tax clearance certificates to the various tax offices. A loyal old official told me: 'Frau Doctor, you want to go away? I have to sit down!' On to police headquarters. I'd brought all the papers with me. The certificate for the Cuba booking. I received no information at all regarding the date of my husband's release.

Back to the American consulate. And again in vain! I was almost collapsing from hunger and cold. Two in the afternoon. I'd been on my feet since seven in the morning, and at three I had to be at the lawyer's. I didn't have time, even with a car, to get home and back again. But where, where could I get something to drink? Just a cup of tea or a drink of water! Where was there no sign, so that I dared go in? A Zuntz coffee shop on Potsdamer Platz. I hurried across the street. A car almost hit me. I had not been watching the traffic. The policeman at the corner warned me. 'Look out, little lady, the next time that will cost you a couple of marks!' I started. If he'd known who he had said that to – had he realized that I was a Jew – I would have been immediately locked up at the very time when it was essential that I was free to be able to act on behalf of my husband and child.

I dashed into the coffee shop. 'Fräulein,' I said at the counter, 'a quick cup of coffee. I'm in a hurry; I have to catch a train.' That was an outright lie, and I was ashamed of myself. But how else could I explain why I was gulping down a cup of coffee at the counter and didn't dare sit at a table? Someone might see me and know who I was. Even in a city the size of Berlin, I was well known. I had patients everywhere. How easily might one of them have had me, a Jewess, thrown out of the coffee shop.

At home a patient was waiting for me. Weeping, she told me that she had lost a valuable diamond brooch and reported the loss to the police. 'You've probably smuggled it abroad,' they replied. She was a Jew, after all. What could she do? Her husband wasn't there.

## 8 December 1938

At last I received the long-sought priority number from the consulate. Now I would try to get a stopover in England with the help of English friends. The Cuba thing seemed not to be proceeding as straightforwardly as I had been promised it would.

## 12 December 1938

I was receiving greetings from my husband almost every day. So many acquaintances had now been released from the camp. No one knew what determined these releases. People who were over fifty years old, business people who had or wanted to Aryanize their shops . . .

I heard that, at Herr Göring's instigation, 'veterans' were to be released at Christmas.

I waited and waited.

I had gone on several occasions to the children's transportation office. There I had recounted, in a confidential discussion, my experience with the extortionist and urgently asked the head of the office to include my son in the next group transport to England because his life was in danger. Thus I was completely cutting all ties. No longer any career, my husband in the concentration camp, my child soon in a foreign land! What would I have left?

161

## 15 December 1938

Today I went to the tax office to make the payment required of German Jews to atone for the murder committed by a young Pole in Paris. They had Jewish people murdered in order to get their money!

When I tried to make this payment, I learned to my horror that I was about RM 1,000 short because I had brought the amount that an official had told me – mistakenly, as it turned out – would be enough. What now? I had no more money.

'Frau Doctor, we know you,' the official told me. 'You can pay the rest when your husband is back. However, you'll have to pay interest then. I'll give you a certificate. We have to take the money from you. We officials can't do anything about it. We have to do what we are ordered to do.' But I drove to the bank quickly and managed to withdraw the missing thousand marks from my account so I could put them in the state's purse in accordance with the rules. I drove back to the tax office with the rest of the prescribed payment. It was still very busy. How many thousands, indeed hundreds of thousands, of marks of Jewish assets were handed over today?

## 16 December 1938

My husband returned. Suddenly, surprisingly. They had shaved his head and his beard, and his hair was growing back sparse and grey. It didn't matter. The first silver threads were also visible in my hair. And it was not age that had whitened them.

My husband was back; the main thing was that he was alive, he was there. 'I'm fine, and I managed. Don't ask any more questions,' he said.

I knew that, before they were released, they had all had to promise not to talk about it, and I didn't ask. I just looked at his blue, frozen, scratched, wounded hands. These hands that had once been so fine, so well groomed, and that patients had loved so much. Hands that could never cause pain, as people had often said. And now – I could have wept, just to see his hands. But – I saw more. His face had also changed. I knew how many people had been tortured to death, physically and mentally, behind those walls.

Our child was radiant. Courageous little soul! I had seen and felt what the boy had silently suffered during the weeks of fruitless waiting for his daddy to come home. And now we were together again, and I could even laugh about the overcoat that had been com-

162

pletely ruined during the disinfection in the concentration camp, the utterly unusable suit, the leather gloves that had shrunk to the size of children's gloves.

Tonight we will all sleep at home again, and hope that we have nothing more to fear.

## 17 December 1938

My husband had to return to the police headquarters in order to report that he was back. I went once more with him to this terrible building. Amazingly enough, he was somehow exempt from the dreadful decree that everyone had to report every few days to the local police. He only had to declare that he was travelling to Cuba in early February.

We hope that now nothing more will happen to us before our departure, but the fear, the incessant fear, day and night, refuses to abate.

## 20 December 1938

Constant running around and turmoil.

Our English friend said he would do everything he could to get us a permit, if we could only find out from the American consulate approximately when we would be able to emigrate to America.

But that was hopeless. We had no information.

We didn't yet know anything about our son's departure, either. And I was inwardly happy to have him still at home over Christmas. They said that nothing would happen over this period. They wanted to give their own staff a short break.

My husband had been visited by comrades from the camp. What firm friendships had been formed during those weeks of suffering. They had had to endure such dreadful things there!

I only heard fragments of the conversation. 'The most terrible thing was the bricks,' one of them said. If only I knew what that meant. My husband said nothing about it. He, too, must have had to carry heavy loads. I could see it in the way he walked, in his still stooped posture.

## 24 December 1938

Christmas Eve. The last one in our home. No tree, no twinkling lights. My old cook also refused to have a little tree in her room.

Even her Christmas gifts seemed this year to give her less pleasure than they had in earlier years. She too knows that, after thirteen years of working in our household, this is the last Christmas.

And tomorrow I will have guests again, dinner guests; lonely people who have no one else and whom I have invited. I have hardly yet thought about what they are going to eat.

## New Year's Eve 1938

The year is coming to an end. It has taken away from me everything that made my life happy and fortunate. The last few months have completely changed me. I no longer recognize myself. No wonder others no longer recognize me. I'm just counting the days until we can get out of this hell.

Many people come and go in our home every day. Jews and well-meaning Aryans. All of them have only one wish: to get out of this country, and they do not hesitate to say so openly.

# CARL HECHT

## Manuscript 83 (91)

*Born in 1891 in Metz; single; commercial clerk who worked for a wine and beer distributor in Frankfurt am Main; emigrated to the USA in 1939.*

During the night of 9–10 November 1938, all the synagogues in Germany were set on fire and burned to the ground. Allegedly, they were the target of popular wrath. But this cannot be true because it happened in all regions of Germany abruptly and followed an organized plan. Had it been a spontaneous expression of the people, it might have occurred in a few places, but not at the same time all over the country.

On the night of 9–10 November itself, Jews in Frankfurt and other places were arrested, beaten and transferred to concentration camps. In many cities and especially in smaller places, Jewish homes and shops were systematically demolished, but on the whole they were not looted and robbed.

Now I come to my own experiences, which I have had to write from memory, as I didn't dare make any notes in Germany because it was too dangerous. Although more than a year has passed since that time, I can still see it all as if it happened yesterday.

On the morning of 10 November, I left my apartment in Rankenstrasse[1] at eight o'clock to go to work in Windmühlstrasse.

A car stopped in front of the door to the building, and I saw two Jewish residents (H. and his brother, who was hard of hearing and had speech problems) standing in the street; they seemed to me rather upset, but I only knew them superficially, so I did nothing and didn't give the matter another thought. I mention this here because I later

165

saw both of them again in Buchenwald, where they told me that was when they had been arrested and deported.

I arrived in Kronprinzenstrasse[2] around 8.30; there, I saw a police car stop in front of the Europäischer Hof hotel (owned by a Jew). The proprietor was forced to lower and lock the shutters. When I saw this, I had a strong premonition of what was to happen. I continued on my way and, as I passed the Moselstrasse post office, I picked up the post from our box and took it with me to the office. I began my work as I would any day. Soon afterwards, my boss came in and told me that a man he knew well had called to say that the synagogue in Freiherr-vom-Stein-Strasse had been set on fire and was burning. My boss left quickly; he wanted to go to the cellar and take care of other business matters.

At about eleven o'clock, our cellarman called me from the cellar in Kronprinzenstrasse. The mob was smashing Jewish shops there and demolishing everything. The cellarman recommended that we lock the cellar and take down the business sign. I instructed him to do so and then immediately come to me, which he did. In the meantime, the boss had also returned to the office. We – the boss, the cellarman and myself – then conferred and waited to see what would happen.

At 12.30 p.m., I left work. Contrary to my usual practice, I left the office on time, and then set off to have my midday meal in my pension at Peterstor. Since I knew what was going on in the city, I avoided the main streets and took side streets, Hirschgraben, Töngasse, etc. Everywhere I saw small shops that I didn't even realize belonged to Jews which had been completely destroyed. When I arrived at my pension, I saw that there, too, the window panes had been broken. I said to myself: 'You'd better go to your sister's house; you can eat there', although of course I'd lost my appetite.

As I continued on from the pension, I saw in the distance a crowd of people approaching from the old part of the city. I thought it wiser to keep out of the way of the mob, and I turned into the park. The crowd followed me; it consisted in part of well-dressed, mainly young, people, many of them with bicycles. At their head marched a fellow who inspired me with little confidence, a real gypsy type with a cloth bound around his head and brandishing a club. He urged the crowd to go after me, using the well-known Stürmer slogans (I've had it up to here, beat the Jew to death, etc.). Fortunately, it went no further than words; had they attacked me, I'd have been done for, and I did for a moment think my hour had come.

Then I fled to Unterweg, where I met a lady I knew (Dr W.), who was also going to the pension for her midday meal. I told her what had happened and advised her to go home as quickly as she could. She said that the windows in a cigar shop in Oederweg had already been broken, so we should make a detour and I should accompany her home. I did so.

From there, I sought safety in my sister's apartment. I was no sooner through the door than my sister said to me: 'The cellarman just called. Your boss has been arrested and taken away.' I then spoke to the cellarman on the telephone, and he told me that my boss had been arrested by three men (they said they were Gestapo) shortly after I left. Thus I'd had the good luck to have left work punctually, otherwise I would also have been arrested. In the afternoon, the cellarman came over, and I gave him the key to the shop and the apartment because he wanted to wait all afternoon to see if our boss came back, as we hoped.

The cellarman had already called L. B., a friend of my boss's. I considered it my duty to go to see L. B. immediately after dinner, even though I knew that he couldn't do anything at this time either. L. B. lived right near me, but I took a detour in order to avoid the main streets. On the way, I met my cousin G. S. and another acquaintance and said to them: 'For God's sake, boys, go home and don't run around like headless chickens. In the current climate with your typical Jewish appearance, you're only going to have problems' – problems that I personally wanted to avoid.

I met my boss's friend at the apartment. He told me that the cellarman had just reached him at his mother's apartment. He had been called there because his brother had been arrested. He had already got in touch with the lawyer who acted for his brother and my boss. For the moment, however, there was nothing more he could do since he was travelling to Mainz to stay with an 80-year-old uncle in order to escape the same fate (that is, arrest). I gave him a piece of friendly advice: to avoid the main streets going to the railway station and take side streets instead, even though he looks very Nordic.

On 11 November 1938 (Friday), I went as always to the shop, but feared any moment that I might be arrested, all the more because an amiable lady who lived in the building and who always had the latest news told me that people were being arrested on the street. The day before, I had wanted to move to my sister's; it is only a few steps from my previous apartment. In view of what was happening, I decided it was safer not to move until Friday, and our cellarman helped me. Strangely, the move went very smoothly. In the shop, my boss's girlfriend, Frau D., called to ask about him. Since I knew that telephone conversations were being tapped – one had to be very

167

careful about spies, even in personal conversations – I said that Herr
S. was not there; the rest I could only tell her in person.

Then she came to the office. When she understood what had happened, she lamented: 'Poor Max hasn't even got a blanket; he won't
come back alive' (this turned out to be true, too, because the poor
man died in Buchenwald). 'We have to take blankets for him to the
Festhalle.'³ But in the same breath, she added: 'You can't get in. Lots
of women are being turned away.' I then said: 'My dear lady, the
cellarman and I are prepared to do all we can for S. You just have
to ask.' Then I called the lawyer. He told me that for the time being
he could do nothing. I should try to get a medical certificate, he said,
and then he would try to get my boss released. I called various
doctors, but I got the same answer everywhere: that they were not
in. I knew where they were.

On Saturday, I went to the shop until 1 p.m., and then went home.
After all that had happened, I was expecting to be arrested at any
moment. Therefore, I made certain preparations. One of my tenants
came and brought me money; I accepted it with outward calm, as he
acknowledged with admiration after my return. I gave my sister a
large amount of money to keep for me because I feared that, if I were
arrested, everything would be taken off me. I stayed at home; we had
various acquaintances in for coffee (Herr and Frau S., Fräulein L. S.,
etc.). Between 4 p.m. and 5 p.m., I went to the building's mailboxes
and brought up the post. As I was going to the mailbox, a civilian (a
Gestapo officer) came up to me and asked, 'Do any Jews live in this
building?' I replied: 'On the ground floor and the second floor, as far
as I know.' Then he said: 'Later I'll come for you, too.' Naturally, I
knew what was going on because he asked: 'Where do you live?'
(After they had arrested all the people whose names they knew, the
Gestapo started hunting down those they had missed by combing the
streets and apartment buildings.)

As I was enjoying my afternoon cup of coffee – I had acquired the
habit of doing this on Saturdays and other free afternoons since, as
a Jew, it had become almost impossible to enter a café – the same
man came back and told me that I should get ready and to take a
warm blanket with me; it was quite cold in the Festhalle. I took a
leather bag with a little soap and underwear, things in the main that
I was not able to use later on, while I neglected to take useful things.
The officer then told me that when I had finished I should join the
SS man waiting downstairs, but not be too long about it. Whereupon
I answered that he shouldn't worry, I wasn't thinking of trying to
escape or to commit suicide. I then said goodbye to the acquaintances

present and went to join the SS man on the street, where two people were already waiting with him.

Then we walked to Sachsenlager where we had to wait on the street while more people were picked up in apartment buildings; the Gestapo then went into two buildings on Gärtnerweg. I should also mention that for the most part the crowds looked at us with sympathy and not with hatred. From Gärtnerweg, we were taken to Unterlindau police station, where our personal details were logged; from there, we were taken to a relatively undamaged side room in the Unterlindau synagogue, where 15–20 people were already waiting. It was now 7 p.m. Then a bus came that was packed full of fellow Jews; to judge by their appearance, they came from the Ostend district. We were pushed into the bus and transported to the Festhalle.

We were met by the obligatory shouts from the mob assembled there. In the Festhalle, my watch, money and so on were taken away from me. I had RM 50 on me; I was told that half would be kept to cover my room and board, and that 'RM 25 is enough for you.'

In the Festhalle, we were then divided into groups, and had to do exercises and calisthenics under the supervision of SS men. This was good because it was very cold in there. The hall was crawling with a fine set of criminals (SS, civilians, police) who tormented some people in downright sadistic and perverse ways, making them crawl on the floor, do somersaults, and so on; some people were also kicked and abused in other ways. One man had a heart attack, probably because of the stress, and was dragged out dead; later, I saw dead men carried away every day in the camp, which no longer bothered me because I had become immune to it. A few groups were lucky and got a little tea and bread, while the rest of us had to just look on. I estimated that there were about a thousand people in the hall that Saturday evening.

Then – it must have been about midnight – we were loaded into buses and taken to the Südbahnhof. Here, at 1.00 a.m., holding our hands up, we had to pass in front of an assembled crowd that greeted us with jeers and insults. Then we were loaded into third-class carriages. We were extremely fortunate not to be further harassed during the journey; others were mistreated in the most vicious way and were not given a moment's peace. One of my fellow sufferers, a lawyer from Wiesbaden, gave me a little cognac which did me good in the cold. I had chocolate with me which I divided among the people in our compartment.

We arrived in Weimar at 6.30 a.m. the next day (Sunday, 13 November) and were there taken into custody by policemen (I

CARL HECHT

assume that they were SS men wearing police uniforms) and herded into a tunnel, where we were kicked, hit with truncheons and harassed – that is, when we went slowly, we had to run, and vice versa; many men had bloody heads and noses. From Weimar, we were transported like criminals in open lorries – we had to keep our heads bowed – to Buchenwald. There, we had to stand out in the cold all day; there was nothing to eat or drink; we were divided into groups. There were about 11,000 men.

In the evening, we were taken into rough wooden barracks with wooden cages (three bunks one above the other). We had to sleep on the bare wood without blankets, etc. There were about 2,000 men in each of the five barracks. During the night, I got water and coffee from a comrade; where he had got them from, I don't know and I didn't ask either. The first few nights were terrible. We heard hysterical screams and cries for help where people were being beaten. I was also suffering from shock but told myself to stay calm and not panic, whatever happened. I had heard descriptions of Siberia but, compared to Buchenwald, that must have been paradise. At first, I assumed that some night our tormentors would set fire to the camp, to our barracks, and then no one would escape alive.

The camp itself was a large place with barracks surrounded by barbed wire that was electrified at night. Every two hundred metres, there was a watchtower with SS guards, a machine gun and a searchlight. By Monday, most of the prisoners had diarrhoea. We had to appear for roll-call and sit for hours on muddy stones, which resulted in our clothes being totally soiled. I mention in passing that I did not change my clothes for a full fourteen weeks and hardly had a chance to wash myself.

Some people went to pieces. At roll-call, an old man began to pray loudly and call upon God, asking if he was going to permit such a disgrace; he was ruthlessly beaten up, which was hardly surprising, given that the camp commandant was said to have been a butcher.[4]

In my early days in the camp, I saw dead men being carried away every day; in the course of two months about a thousand people died. This was no wonder since neither doctors nor medicines were on hand. The ill were put in a wash house (barracks), got pneumonia and died. Others, if they did not die from mistreatment, committed suicide by running into the barbed wire on a daily basis.

The doctors who were interned with us did what was humanly possible with the most primitive means and cannot be praised highly enough, especially the Austrian doctors. That anyone at all survived in such terrible hygienic conditions still amazes me; but we found

170

that human beings can endure a great deal. The intention of Hitler and his comrades was to destroy these poor people, and many of them came away with permanent injuries, and more than one wasted away even after he returned. The distribution of food and so on was left to us, and for this purpose we had our own orderlies, some of whom, such as Moritz Meier from Worms (an officer in the Great War who had been highly decorated for bravery), carried out this task very fairly and skilfully.

On the other hand, there were the others. After Herr Meier was lucky enough to be released, the three Weil brothers from the Mainz area seized control of my barracks. They were scoundrels who held onto the rations and gave them only to people who bribed them. Not everyone is noble.

The days passed in endless monotony. After I had recovered from dysentery (early December), I was able to eat but unfortunately I got almost nothing because the fewer we were, the more closely the rations were supervised. In fourteen weeks, I saw no eggs, fat or meat. The food was of the lowest quality and consisted mainly of broth, e.g., cabbage soup, whale meat soup, peas or lentils. The bread was edible only when we toasted it. Now and then, a few of us got military bread. In time, I became completely infested with lice. Washing, teeth-brushing, changing clothes, and so on was out of the question. During the entire time, I received two cards and was allowed to write twice. Most of our post was sent back. Many of my acquaintances received letters which had been torn in half.

Luckily, I still had good friends who encouraged me; otherwise I would not have made it through. Because I had no blanket, my foot was frostbitten. We whiled away the time talking and smoking. Initially, I was happy to get a cigarette for 20 pfennig. Of course, we were only allowed to smoke outside. In the canteen, we had to pay a mark for a bar of chocolate that normally cost 30 pfennig, and the same went for cakes. A bottle of mineral water also cost one mark. At first, we almost died of thirst because there was a shortage of water in Buchenwald, and in addition we were denied anything to drink as a form of harassment. Later on, our fellow prisoners sometimes gave lectures in the evenings that served to stimulate us intellectually since we had nothing to read or otherwise distract us.

The building I owned in Frankfurt was taken away from me. That is to say, I was forced to sign it away after I had stood for at least five hours in severe cold and was no longer capable of thinking or reflecting. Early on, I even saw a blind man in the camp; epileptics and other ill and handicapped people were also among the interned.

171

As glad as we were that, starting in early December, inmates began to be released, it was hard to be among the last 250 men and to come home months later than others did.

On 13 February 1939, we – the remaining 350 men – were put in our own camp and dressed as prisoners. This scared me because, as I said to myself, 'You are going to have to stand for hours at roll-call in the cold and you already have a frostbitten foot.' Fortunately, on 15 February, the time came for my release. On that morning, our names were read out at roll-call, those of about seventy men, and at 6.30 a.m. we joyfully climbed into the bus that was to take us from Buchenwald to Frankfurt, where we arrived at 1.00 a.m. We had to pay the cost of our return trip ourselves. The next day we had to report to the Gestapo, where I was given until 30 April 1939 to leave Germany, otherwise I would be imprisoned again.

I should mention that on 21 December the whole camp had to turn out to watch the hanging of a prisoner who had escaped during the summer and killed an SA man when doing so.

On leaving the camp, I was forced to sign documents – for what, I still don't know. In addition, we were told that anyone who said anything or talked of atrocities would be imprisoned again; even abroad, the party had organizations, we were told, and Jews who had remained behind in Germany would have to atone for such offences. Furthermore, even abroad a blabbermouth could be 'liquidated'.

When I got my visa for America and was about to depart – my steamer, the *Deutschland*, was to leave on 11 May from Hamburg, and I had to travel to Hamburg on the evening of 9 May – I received on Saturday, 6 May, yet another summons from the Gestapo to present myself on Tuesday morning at 8.30. My acquaintances, whom I told about this, all advised me either not to go or to leave earlier. However, I did not take this advice because, as I said to myself: 'I have nothing to fear, since I am not aware that I am guilty of anything, and if I was accused of something, they would not ask me to come in but simply arrest me.'

I appeared there punctually on Tuesday morning. From the officials' courteous tone, of which I was particularly conscious after the way I had been addressed during the preceding three months, I sensed that I was not going to be accused of a political crime. The issue was this: when I was arrested, RM 25 had been taken from me in the Festhalle in Frankfurt, or, as the official put it, 'safeguarded'. I corrected him: 'taken away'. I was to get this money back. The official told me that it had been twenty marks, whereupon I said I didn't want to argue about it. Then he asked me when I wanted to emigrate, and I answered: 'In about two weeks' time.' The official said it might be a few weeks before I received the money, and asked whether I had a bank account. I said the money should be sent to my sister. Of the RM 25 (allegedly only RM 20), she finally received RM 15, less postage, leaving RM 14.90.

I mention this only to show how the people currently in power in Germany operate, since the money was given back to me only so that I couldn't say that there is no order and decency in Germany; according to them, everything is properly accounted for, the rule of law exists and political opponents and even Jews are treated fairly.

Those RM 15 could not help me anyway, given everything else that had been taken from me. Of the proceeds from the forced sale of my building, that is, of the sale price, which was downright ludicrous, I never saw a penny. In spite of everything, about RM 5,000 would have remained, even after all costs had been deducted; this sum was confiscated by the state as a 'Jewish levy'. The brutality of the Nazi regime was so extensive that I was not even allowed to keep my gold watch (a memento from my father) because I had honestly but stupidly listed it among my assets. I was given a receipt for the value of the watch. Whether the money (only the value of the gold in the watch) was ever sent to me, I do not know.

However, I shouldn't complain about this, given that a former colleague who lost both legs in the Great War and who received a military pension told me that he had filed a request with the Reich minister for economic affairs to leave him his gold watch in view of his war injury. His request was denied.

# ERNST BELLAK

## Manuscript 175 (16)

*Born in 1895 in Vienna; draper; arrested on 27 May 1938 and deported to Dachau, then transferred to Buchenwald on 23 September, released on 20 February 1939; emigrated in April 1939 to San Francisco, via Italy, India and Shanghai.*

Of the approximately 20,000 Jews incarcerated in November, a few hundred were given prisoners' clothing and put in the general camp. However, the majority were released after 1–3 months' imprisonment. The release procedure was this: before roll-call, the block elder gave the man to be released a little note telling him to go to a specific room immediately after roll-call. They had to run to the prescribed place. People often thought that having such a note in hand meant that they were certain to be released but sometimes they were only taken for questioning.

Many relatives of the detained men had engaged a Weimar notary to seek their release. He came to the camp two or three times a week and had a small office there where one could speak with him undisturbed. I know that this notary often succeeded in getting Jews with large amounts of capital out of the camp. I too was ordered to speak to him a couple of times and was able to do so unhindered. Thus I could convey my wishes to my nearest relatives through him. In my opinion, this notary must have acquired great wealth through his intervention on behalf of the prisoners because he saw about 200 people a week in his office and every conversation with them cost the relatives a pretty penny.

On 21 February 1939, I was once again handed a note ordering me to go to an area where about 50 men were already standing. Of these, 27 were to be released. An SS man read out the names of those concerned. We had to give our date of birth accurately because, we were told, many men had the same name and special precautions had to be taken not to release the wrong man. After personal data had been checked, we were taken to one side in order to be taken to the doctor. The doctor was a former lawyer from Berlin, also a prisoner.

We were then examined by him. First we were weighed. Then we were looked over to see if we bore visible signs of having suffered any serious injuries as a result of our stay in the camp. If a man had lost too much weight, which could be determined from the notes made upon our arrival, or if he had received serious physical injuries in the camp, then his release was put off for an indefinite period of time. Each examination took about two to three minutes. If a man was finally designated for release, then he was once again taken to the barber. There his beard was shaved off, and his head was also shaved for the last time, so that the outside world would know that he had been a concentration camp inmate. This took place around 9.00 a.m. At 1.00 p.m., we had to be at the personal effects room.

I then hurried to my former workplace in order to tell my comrades my good news. Each one had a special wish for me to communicate to his relatives in the outside world. I had to memorize the addresses very carefully because we were not allowed to take written things out of the camp. Then I said goodbye to my comrades. Most of us had tears in our eyes. Almost all their faces expressed hopelessness, and I tried to comfort them!

In particular, I said farewell to a lawyer from Vienna with whom I had formed a close friendship. We had often poured our hearts out to each other. Frequently, we had been full of despair, believing we would never be able to survive our time in the camp. We talked together about everything that tormented us, things we could share with no one else. In one of these depressions, we had decided to commit suicide together. We had set the end of the year 1939 as the date for carrying out our plan. Now I was being released, and this gave my friend new hope of coming out alive. I had to promise him to visit his relatives as soon as I arrived in Vienna and urge them to do everything they could to shorten his imprisonment. With tears in our eyes, we separated from each other.

I found myself in a kind of dream; I could not grasp the idea that the time for my release had come. I went into the barracks. My few possessions – my bread bag, a warm jacket, gloves and other small items – I left for my comrades, along with a little money. At 1.00 p.m., we gathered at the personal effects room.

175

Our names were read out once again. We were led in and made to take off all our clothes; we could only keep a handkerchief, but this, too, was searched very carefully. Then we were taken into a cellar storeroom where we were given back our civilian clothes, which were still in perfect condition. My underpants and socks, which were made of artificial silk, had become unwearable from remaining so long in storage. In exchange for these, I was given woollen trousers and good socks. People who needed a hat or other items of clothing could also borrow them. Various prisoners who had heard that we were being released came to see us, but we were not allowed to speak to anyone.

At 2.00 p.m., we were taken in our civilian clothing back to the muster ground, and from there to a large hall in which the SS worked on censuring correspondence. We received, in the form of pushes and shoves, our last mementos of camp. Our names were now called out for the umpteenth time. We were summoned one by one to a small room where the valuables that had been taken away from us were redeemed, right down to the last item, against a receipt. We were paid the amount of money in our accounts. As we were being led out through the hall again, an SS man was standing by the door with a collection box, where we were required to make contributions for the Winter Aid programme. Everyone had to pay 5 marks but I was able to use a dispute between the SS man in question and a prisoner to sneak out of the hall unnoticed.

We all had to line up in front of the building. We saw someone stick his head out of the window, but paid no attention to this. We all already envisaged ourselves in yearned-for freedom. Then all at once the window was thrown wide open, and in it appeared the figure of the camp commandant, whom we now recognized. His angry voice reached our ears: 'You Jewish pigs: you're still camp inmates, even if you're in civilian clothes. Why do you have your hats on? Why aren't you standing up straight?'

The SS men lined us up in rows of four, and we had to stand to attention in front of the commandant's windows for over three hours.

At this point a terrible icy rain was falling, and at any moment we were in danger of collapsing, but the idea of our impending release kept us going. After three and a half hours, the SS guards on duty led us into a large barracks. Here we were received by a Gestapo official. A piece of paper was shoved in front of us for our signature. We didn't have time to read it, but we knew that by signing it we were forgoing any claim to compensation by the Reich. After we signed, the official delivered a short speech:

'Now that you are going home, I would like to remind you that nothing that happened in camp may be discussed at home. Should you be asked about it, tell people that they can go to a camp at any time and find out about it for themselves. But if you do say anything about the camp, then you'll be put into camp a second time. And what a second time in the camp means, you probably already know. The arm of the Gestapo even reaches into other countries; if it should ever occur to you to talk abroad, you may not be arrested, but your family will certainly pay for it. When you get out of the camp, try to work and support your family. There is work for everyone in the Reich who has the necessary will to work.'

We received all kinds of other good advice in the same vein. We were asked whether we had a mark so that we could pay for the bus trip from the camp to Weimar. We were taken, under two-man guard, to a bus that was standing ready. We went as far as the tunnel of which we still had such terrible memories. This tunnel separated us from the outside world by a gate and it was reserved for us. There were three ladies from the Weimar Jewish Committee who gave us coffee and cakes. The SS man ordered us to clean up our clothing, which had been badly soiled by the icy rain. The ladies provided us with cleaning materials. At the gate, a few women looked in, hoping to find among us the husbands or sons for whom they had been vainly waiting for weeks.

Many people came up to us and inquired about their relatives. We knew that a few of them were no longer alive, but we didn't have the heart to transmit this sad news to them. At 8.00 p.m., the Frankfurt–Leipzig–Berlin night train arrived.[1] We were taken to a carriage specially reserved for us. A young lady from the Leipzig Jewish Committee travelled with us and on the way she told us what we had to do when later on we were questioned by the Gestapo. We had already been told in the camp that we had to report to the Gestapo after our arrival in Vienna.

In Leipzig, we had to change trains. We were led by a lady from the Committee to a small room reserved for us, where various people from the Leipzig Committee were waiting. There we were given something to eat, which we could pay for according to our means. We were put on the train to Vienna and were once again assigned a separate carriage. We could order everything from the dining car, but we were not allowed to go to it ourselves. The Viennese waiter serving us was particularly friendly because he knew we were former concentration camp inmates. On the way, the railway personnel also changed. And this was how we arrived in Passau.

An Austrian official in a brand-new German uniform came into our carriage. When he saw us, he said, after making sure that no one was nearby: 'You're from the concentration camp, I know, and you've been through a lot, but don't worry, the regime won't last in Austria.'

After a long and difficult journey, we arrived at about 9.00 a.m. in Vienna.

My parents, whom I had informed via a telegram sent from Weimar through the Jewish Committee, had come with my sister to meet me at the railway station. I was upset by how bad they looked. I now had to go immediately to the Gestapo.

En route, we had been told that we had to deliver our camp certificates to the Gestapo. In order to have proof that might later be of use to me, I went immediately to a photographer and had my certificate of release photocopied and then to a notary in order to have the copy certified. I then went to the Gestapo, where I had to stand until 3.00 p.m. with my face turned to the wall, like all the others, before being taken to the official assigned to my case. This official was not as unfriendly as one might have expected. He asked a few questions about the camp, to which I kept replying that I was not allowed to talk about it. He told me that he was a Gestapo official and that it was my duty to tell him everything he asked. I told him he could do with me as he wished, but I could not answer his questions about the camp.

He poked around in the files, pulled out my case and told me that I had been released as a result of an error. He said that I still had no passport, whereupon I replied that my passport was already prepared and only awaited my personal signature. He declared himself satisfied with this explanation, but added that he would give me four weeks to leave the Reich. I asked for an extension of this period, and he granted me six weeks; but if by then I was not gone, I would have to request another extension, and he could not tell me in advance whether such a request would be approved. I had to report to my local police headquarters three times a week, starting that day. I asked him if I might first report the following day, and again he agreed.

Finally, he asked me if I knew why I had been in the camp. Since I replied that I did not, he rummaged through the files again and read me a statement I was supposed to have made: 'All Germans are swine' – and it was for this statement that I had been put into camp. I said that I had never made such a statement, but he told me that it was in the files and so it must be true. My concentration camp certificate was taken from me, whereupon I was released.

# —Part III—

## Before Emigration

# MARTIN FREUDENHEIM

## Manuscript 243 (68)

*Born in 1875 in Berlin; lawyer; married; emigrated to Palestine in 1939.*

During the night of 9–10 November 1938, synagogues all over Germany were burned down and all [Jewish] shops were destroyed in an action that was carefully organized in every detail. On 10 November, I walked through the streets and saw the destruction and the revolting inscriptions written in red, as if in blood. Foreign correspondents have reported sufficiently on this. The concentration camps at Oranienburg, Buchenwald and Dachau were overflowing with Jews. Many of my acquaintances had been arrested and endured terrible abuse and cold. They had had to promise not to talk about events in the camp after their release, but we nonetheless gathered enough from the hints provided by the anxious, nervous men who returned with shaven heads. Almost without exception, they praised the humane attitude of the political prisoners who supervised them. In contrast, many SS men must have been brutal slave drivers.

Some of the Jews I knew had been warned in time and avoided arrest by not staying in their apartments nor sleeping there – people were usually arrested between 3.00 and 5.00 a.m. They camped out with families who had nothing to fear because there were no men in the house. Some of them also avoided arrest through bribery or were quickly released by the same means. I was not arrested, perhaps because I was already too old or perhaps also because I was not healthy, or because I had not been denounced. I knew no one at all in Nazi organizations. But the latter had very precise information about every Jew and political opponent.

181

People were gripped by extreme nervousness and anxiety. I too jumped with fright whenever the doorbell rang at an unexpected time of the morning. In many people, a bitterness and hatred had emerged that took almost pathological forms. I did not hate anyone. For years, I had struggled against feelings of hatred in myself. Like a prayer, I had repeated over and over to myself: no hatred, hatred strikes inwards. No thoughts of revenge: patience, patience, patience. That was my kind of religious discipline. It helped me. Of course I hate certain characteristics, including some of my own, I hate institutions and attitudes, but I do not hate people. I believe in redemptive justice in this world, in Emerson's 'compensation'. And I live in the conviction that the time will come when, as Benjamin Franklin said, men will eventually stop acting like wolves, and human creatures will begin to understand what humanity really is.

When my uneasiness became overwhelming and revulsion stirred within me, I took refuge in books: Schopenhauer, Nietzsche, my special friend Lichtenberg, Kierkegaard, Emerson, Pascal, Tolstoy and Dostoevsky, and Goethe, always Goethe. I read randomly, depending on my mood, and I always became calmer and found inner release.

One morning, I had some business near Potsdamer Platz. I felt tired, and wanted a coffee. I went into a well-known confectioner's in which I had previously spent many an hour but found instead the warning: 'Jews not welcome.' After crossing Potsdamer Platz, I saw the same sign on the Fürstenhof and on all the revolving doors of the adjacent Aschinger. I was worn out, nervous and thirsty. Then I noticed disgust rising in me and that I was in danger of losing control of myself and doing something stupid. It was then that I decided to emigrate as soon as I could to Palestine where my nieces and nephews already lived and to which my wife, a fervent Zionist, had always been attracted.

# ALICE BÄRWALD

## Manuscript 137 (15)

*Born in Berlin in 1883; in 1906 married the timber merchant Ludwig Bärwald from Nakel [Naklo] in the province of Posen [Poznan]; in 1921, the couple moved with their three children to the free city of Danzig, where after 1933 there were anti-Semitic denunciations and harassments similar to those in the Reich; on 17 August 1939, they emigrated to the USA via England.*

In the autumn of 1938, we received disturbing news from Germany that the synagogues were burning. We were paralysed with fear. After the murder of Herr vom Rath, we knew that terrible things were in store for Jews. But the madness that took hold could never have been predicted. I had two married nephews in Königsberg [now Kaliningrad] whom I was worried about. The next day I received a card from their wives asking us to come to visit them while their husbands were away, so that we three women could talk in peace. I immediately understood that their husbands had been arrested and went there.

Not in one's wildest imagination could one have pictured the city. The main shopping streets were covered with glass and bits of paper; the windows of all the Jewish shops had been broken. People were going about their business quietly; some perhaps were ashamed. The synagogue had been burned down. The adjoining orphanage had later been set on fire and the little children driven out of the building on a cold November night. A 12-year-old boy pulled a 3-year-old girl out of bed and ran with her through the streets to the home of an uncle. The man woke from a deep sleep, thinking he heard children calling, and looked out to see the children clad only in their nightshirts.

Every apartment in Königsberg that was owned by Jews had been demolished. It should be mentioned that the brownshirts all arrived

183

at these apartments drunk. Had they been sober, they would not have been moved to commit these atrocious deeds. They were all carrying the same tools to break mirrors, glass and porcelain to bits. The next day, I visited an old lady in whose home nothing had been left intact. The brown-shirt had come in, sat down on a chair and put the hammer in her hand. Under his supervision, she herself had had to destroy all her own very valuable property. That was one of the cruellest and most perverse incidents. The fact that all these women, young and old, endured it is testimony to their silent heroism.

It had taken my two nieces days to find out where their husbands were. The younger of the two brothers had had the good fortune to be put, along with 150 other men, in the local prison, where there were trained officials and a standard procedure. The elder brother, however, was interned in a fire brigade training school in the suburb of Megethen, along with a couple of hundred other men. In the suits they had been wearing when they were arrested, they had to cart stones and do the heaviest agricultural labour, so that in a few days their clothes were in tatters. While I was there, a card came from my nephew for his wife. He asked for a pillow, a blanket and something to smoke. It was permitted, he said, to deliver these things on certain days.

I drove out there with my niece. All the women had had similar news, and so there were about a hundred of them who had come to see their husbands. Some of the women were still beautifully and fashionably dressed, loaded with packages and wearing very concerned looks on their faces. The training school was far outside the city, in a very isolated place. The firemen looked on with interest from the windows as the long line of silent women approached. We then had to line up in pairs outside the door, and each woman was allowed to speak with her husband for two minutes, under supervision.

In advance, I had rehearsed with my niece every word that she should say to her husband in order to buck up his courage and his resistance. We had cabled relatives in the USA to ask for an affidavit and had already heard that it was on the way. She was able to tell him this happy news. After he had signed a document saying that he was emigrating and intended to give up his business, he was allowed to go by car under guard to make arrangements in the city. The cost of the car journey was 30 marks which he had to pay himself.

A few months later, when they were both free, I returned to discuss their emigration with them. Then my nephew told me about what had happened in the camp. The day was occupied with regular work, the firemen had acted properly, and in some cases even generously.

But every afternoon SS men came from the city and made them run and sing with them. There were about 250 inmates in the camp, including the rabbi of the Königsberg community. The rabbi was ordered to sing sacred songs which the entire crowd then had to repeat in accordance with their tormentors' instructions. For hours, they had to repeat the refrain: 'Who wants to shit on the German people? We Jews.' Most of what they had to say was so disgusting that I cannot write it down here.

Later on, when all arrangements had been made, my nephews had, under supervision, to pack up the things that they were allowed to take with them on emigrating. One gratifying incident did occur during the packing: usually silver was confiscated, but at that time objects for religious use were still allowed and could be taken. My older nephew had put his particularly fine silver on a table, on one side of which were the pieces that he was allowed to pack up and on the other side the pieces that had to be given up. The official began his work, sent my nephew out to get a few signatures, and when he came back, all the silver was packed up and the crates officially sealed. I often heard of similar cases in which officials acted in the noblest way and thereby critically endangered themselves and their families.

On the other hand, mad rampages were continuing in the small east Prussian border towns. Some of my relatives lived there in a town of 3,000 inhabitants; I don't want to give its name, because I am not sure whether these people have yet succeeded in getting out of Germany. The family had lived there for generations. Themselves wealthy factory owners, they were highly respected and friends of the landowners and nobility in the surrounding area. In this small town, at the same time that the synagogues were burned in Königsberg, all the [Jewish] men were arrested and deported. Only weeks later were their whereabouts discovered. In addition, this small town as far as I know was the only one in Germany to enjoy the sad notoriety of having also arrested women. Among the fourteen women in this small Jewish community, there was also a niece of mine and her mother-in-law. They were all taken to the police lock-up, lined up in pairs and led through the town while forced to chant in unison: 'We betrayed Germany.' The mob ran after them and shouted to the policemen: 'Beat them to death. Why are you still feeding them?' The women are said to have endured it all in silence and without complaining. When they were released after two days in jail, my relatives immediately travelled to Berlin, where I met them and heard what had happened.

Two lovely boys of theirs have been at school abroad for the past five years. These children's English teacher, who came to know and like the whole family very well, had arranged permission for them to emigrate to New Zealand. I hope they have succeeded in reaching their goal.

All of East Prussia tried to outdo the Nazi thugs in the rest of Germany. The first thing they did here was to demolish the Jewish cemeteries. In the Königsberg cemetery, the mortuary recently built by Professor Erich Mendelsohn, a masterpiece of modern architecture, was reduced to ruins and the gravestones and monuments overturned. Taking vengeance even on the dead is typical of the German resolve.

I had only been back in Danzig a few days, still completely shattered by the events in Königsberg, when one morning our rabbi appeared at our home and told us that during the night the synagogue in Langfuhr [Wrzeszcz] had been destroyed and the one in Zoppot [Sopot] burned to the ground. Then it became clear to me for the first time that the 'Free City of Danzig' was no longer for us. I had never felt it so starkly.

# SIEGFRIED WOLFF

## Manuscript 232 (245)

*Born in 1888 in Gnesen [Gniezno]; paediatrician; moved in 1920 to
Eisenach, where he founded a children's clinic; emigrated to Holland
on 27 August 1939; murdered in Auschwitz in October 1944.*

### 9 November 1938

The man who is mistaken makes up in vehemence
For what he lacks in truth and strength.

Goethe [*Tasso*, IV, 4]

Herr vom Rath had died. I do not want to go into all the rumours
regarding his death, and so on. To me personally it just seemed very
strange that a young Jew bearing a weapon was allowed access to a
high German official, whereas I, an elderly doctor, had to account for
myself in detail to the doorman when I once went to visit an old
friend of my family's at the American embassy.

In any case, early in the morning, bright red posters had been
pasted on all the buildings and apartments in which Jews lived. These
posters read: 'Jews get out! How long are you going to go on abusing
our hospitality!' Hospitality – that's what they called it! The whole
day passed in nervous unease. In the morning, when I arrived at the
bank where I got on very well with everyone, including the Nazi
officials, and was even friends with some of them, one of them said
to me, half-joking, half-ironic: 'Well, you're still alive. Today you're
all going to be made a head shorter. Why don't you get out of here?'
That was the so-called 'seething kettle' of the people's indignation –
people who knew exactly what was going to happen.

187

In the afternoon, the wife of our regimental commander was in our home for a full two hours; but she, too, was more uneasy than I had ever seen her. And in the evening we were visited by two elderly Aryan ladies who always stood loyally by us. They left about eleven o'clock. Columns of men were marching through the streets, and there were lots of people walking about. On the nearby market square, enormous loudspeakers had been set up, which were broadcasting the celebratory procession to the Feldherrn-Halle in Munich. We heard the names of the fallen spookily intoned. We heard braying speeches. It was all so eerie. Finally, they all sang together: 'We come to pray before the God of the Righteous'.[1]

It was about 12.30 a.m. I was happy and hoped that peace and quiet would now finally return. Far from it! Hardly had the song ended before the sound of shattering windows in homes and shops was heard. The sound was so horrible that I shall never forget it. From time to time, orders were shouted, whistles shrilled, cars roared by. 'Woe to us if they are let loose.' This all continued through the night until early morning. What had actually happened, I didn't yet know.

At 8.00 a.m. on Thursday, 10 November, my mother's housekeeper came in, pale and upset, and told us that all over the city Jewish shops had been demolished; people from the Hitler Youth were standing around as guards. At 9.30, the daughter of a Jewish lawyer friend of ours came and reported that during the night the synagogue had burned down, all the apartments belonging to Jews had been demolished, and all the men arrested, and that women, young and old, had also been taken away. Some of the women had come back, she said, and some of the very elderly. Her father had been told that he should have a good look at his home; he would never see it again. In most people's apartments, not even a drinking glass had been left intact. They were surprised that I was still there.

We thought it was a local problem, and so my mother urged me to go away. I had in any case intended to go to a class in Berlin that day, and I had a railway pass that allowed me to travel back and forth between E[isenach] and Berlin and get out at any station. Since our affidavits had come into the consulate three days before, we decided that I would immediately go to see my friend N., who was in charge of all the community's affairs in Leipzig and was also an advisor for emigrants, and discuss with him what had to be done; my mother was to follow in the afternoon.

As I came out into the street, there was an SS man standing in front of the door, who greeted me with 'Good morning, Herr Doctor.'

People in the streets were pale and upset and thought I was a ghost when they saw me. In front of the railway station, a police constable, standing all alone in the middle of the wide lobby, also saluted me. And even the station policeman, a disagreeable SS man, greeted me. Finally, the train came, and I started for L[eipzig].

There I drove past the burning synagogue, in front of which the Torah rolls were lying and being trampled upon – it's surprising that none of the people were reminded of Belshazzar!! – past the Jewish community's office, in front of which books lay burning, and finally to my friend's home. Only then did I realize what was going on. At his place, fifteen young men and women were completing preparations for Palestine. They had been chased onto the street, had had everything they owned stolen and burnt, and now had only the clothes on their backs. Then the building had been set ablaze. The doorman had been told that if anyone asked, he should say the Jews had done it themselves.

My friend, who often had to deal with the Gestapo and was highly respected and appreciated by them, enjoying their full trust because they needed him to help with emigration, had visited the officials that very morning and asked that at least passports and emigration documents be protected. And they were protected a little. He himself was at home, but terrible reports kept coming in. Women kept calling whose husbands had been arrested and whose apartments had been destroyed; desperate women and children were continually arriving. But, despite all the grief and misery, they behaved with dignity. And it has to be said that during this time, when they were defenceless and at the mercy of a horde of robbers and murderers armed to the teeth, the Jews conducted themselves in a brave, dignified and civilized way. I do not know whether Aryans would have shown such self-control in a similar situation.

The Jewish hospital was under guard, so that no one could hide there, and the rabbis and teachers had been taken away. One report followed another. In the evening, we heard that in a nearby forest, where a home for very young people had been established that trained them for emigration to Palestine, two children – children! – had been beaten to death; a rabbi had been requested. Foreign Jews drove there to get the rest of them.

> Nothing is holy any longer, loosened
> Are all ties of righteousness,
> The good gives room to bad,
> And all vices freely rule.

189

Dangerous it is to wake the lion,
Ruinous is the tiger's tooth,
But the most terrible of all the terrors,
That is the man when crazed.
Woe to those, who lend to the eternally blind
Enlightenment's heavenly torch!
It does not shine for him, it only can ignite
And puts to ashes towns and lands.
                    Schiller, 'Das Lied von der Glocke'

Towards evening my good, brave mother came; she had collected and put all the most important documents and my most important work and notes into a small suitcase. She wasn't concerned about money or jewellery – she just wanted to save and protect my work! Nothing had happened at our home. Had 'my children' protected me? I was the only person in E. who was not put in a camp, was not arrested, the only one whose apartment was not touched.

On Friday, my friend went back to the Gestapo, where he was told that he should go home and 'behave properly'. The arrests, destruction and arson went on. And in the evening the newspaper said that Jews had set fire to various department stores and shops. The degree to which everything had been carefully planned was illustrated, for instance, by the fact that a shop was completely burned out, but the storeroom above it, used by a factory that made celluloid which is particularly explosive, remained undamaged.

The following afternoon, men with revolvers herded a number of elderly people into a small river, where they had to stand for hours in the icy water, threatened with the revolvers, to the delight of the mob. Most of the public turned away in revulsion and some of them openly expressed their disgust and were thereupon arrested. It is significant that many, many people mocked the so-called Führer, as one often heard on the train. Thus Baron v. B. always said, instead of Gauleiter Saukel: Sauleiter Gaukel.

Most people were also very happy to tell Jews how they felt, since they did not dare to express their views even in the most intimate family setting. I knew many children who intimidated their parents by threatening to report what they had said. In Russia, a monument was erected to just such a young informer who got his own family into trouble.

No one knew what would happen to the Jews who were arrested; we only knew that they would first be put into the nice concentration camps. How many died there, how many succumbed to mistreatment, will probably never be discovered. However, I know for certain that one man from E. got pneumonia and, when he became delirious with fever, was simply beaten to death.

On Sunday evening, my mother went home; it had been announced that Jews had to hand in all weapons. So my mother took my father's old officer's dagger, which he had kept proudly all his life, to the police.

On Sunday morning, my friend was arrested – only for questioning, they said – and, since a cousin and I were in his home, we were also immediately taken along. The officials were absolutely proper and polite. We were taken to police headquarters, where I was instantly yelled at by a Hitler lout because I had kept my hat on in the corridor. Then the three of us were made to sit on a bench. A Hitler Youth member in an SS uniform – he could not have been more than seventeen – planted himself in front of us and asked my friend what he had in his briefcase. When he said pyjamas and a blanket, the man grinned scornfully and said: 'You won't be sleeping tonight.'

When I was asked my name and did not immediately stand up, I was, of course, called the most miserable, degenerate sort of person – that is, not a person, but rather a Jew – and thrown out. But I still had within me part of that power which always wills the Bad, and always works the Good. I ran into an elderly official, who took me to his office and questioned me in a very friendly way. I said my name was S. W., and he wrote it down at the top of a big form. When in the course of the interrogation he learned that I was a doctor, he said that the title 'Dr' should be put before my name, and from then on he addressed me only as 'Herr Doctor'.

He asked whether I could immediately return to E., and I replied that I would do that without delay if he ordered me to do so. He said it was not for him to order anything but, since I had things to do in connection with my emigration to the USA, he advised me to travel to Berlin the following day in order to speed things up. Finally, he said in a friendly way that he could see that I had a serious heart problem and could hardly breathe – of course, he was really suggesting that to me – and he wanted to accompany me to the door of the building, so that I could leave without difficulty. And he did so. Thus, after ten minutes I was free again – I simply cannot describe the feeling! Three thoughts prevailed: gratitude to God for saving me, an infinite happiness that my mother had been spared these worries, and concern for my friend, who, however, returned home two days later, while my cousin was held for two months.

The next morning, I travelled to Berlin, where I was unable to achieve anything at any of the consulates, and spent four weeks with an aunt and step-grandmother, where I was treated very well and gradually recovered. One day, I met the parents of a Baroness von L., whom I had known when I was a child and whose own child I had treated for life-threatening diseases at the home of the grandparents. They threw their arms around my neck, sobbing, because in E. the rumour had been going round that I had committed suicide, and they were glad that this was not true. They immediately called the baroness in order to tell her the good news that I was still alive.

The police in E. had also heard about my suicide and came to investigate, to my mother's horror. These officials, whose children I had often treated and who were very well disposed towards me, were genuinely delighted that I was still alive, and one of them told my mother that he had never believed I could do something that would cause her such grief. At this time, many, many others showed a genuine concern with my fate, visited my mother, helped her with grocery shopping, which was made difficult for Jews, and telephoned and wrote to her. W. v. M. wrote that she had wept for days before she knew that I was safe.

However, I was especially gratified by the leading National Socialist of E., namely Dr G., about whom I have spoken on several occasions. On 10 or 11 November, he asked my former chauffeur, who now drove a taxi, what had happened to me. When he heard that I had gone away, he said: 'Well, thank God; I had feared the worst. But now I'm glad. What has just happened is a disgrace to Germany. Tell Dr W. that while we were political opponents, and have argued, we will never get another doctor as capable. Give Dr W., my old opponent, my warmest greetings, and tell him that I wish him the best for the future.' That was chivalrous enmity.

It is well known that the public, both the upper and lower classes, the poor and the rich, was greatly embittered by these uncivilized outrages, and that people strongly denied that they had wanted any of this, and that they recognized what madness it was to round up every Jew and then destroy things of enormous value and make them valueless. However, no one drew the only obvious and effective conclusion: that they should leave the party in their millions.

Weeks later, I came home from Berlin and met my old acquaintances, patients and friends who had returned from the concentration camp. They all had bad colds and an indefinable block, as if they were being constantly persecuted and harassed. It was a long time before they returned to their old selves. For months, they had to continue to report to the police every day.

But now it was clear that we had to leave the fatherland, which was no longer a fatherland, or even a hospitable country. Germany had sunk from being a country of the highest degree of culture to one of brutality, to a level even lower than the start of civilization. For 'the first steps to civilization are taken when strangers are guaranteed hospitality', Virchow says, and he is certainly right. But what does this hospitality look like now?

# MARGARETE NEFF[1]

## Manuscript 93 (205)

*Born in 1892 in Vienna; actress; performed in Berlin, Meiningen and*
*Weimar; returned to Vienna in 1935; emigrated to the USA in 1939;*
*died in New York in 1984.*

On 10 November 1938 the long-planned pogrom took place. At 7.30 a.m.,
the same policeman who had visited us after the German invasion
returned to our apartment and ordered Alfred[2] to wait for him with
his identity papers at the door of the building in half an hour. So now
what I had foreseen for so long had finally happened. Alfred was
arrested. At 8 a.m., we were standing in front of the building. The
whole area was closely watched by policemen. Men between eighteen
and sixty were being taken out of all the buildings and driven like a
herd of cattle to the nearest police station.

When Alfred did not return after two hours, I and a few other
women from the neighbourhood walked to the police station. From
inside the building, we could look out of a window onto a courtyard,
in which a barracks stood; the overcoats of the arrested men hung
over a fence. I saw Alfred's coat, so he must still have been there.
That was in itself good, but my stomach tightened and I felt that the
old, worn-out coat at that moment was not an ordinary piece of
clothing; it was something that had belonged to a person and had
been taken away just as arbitrarily as he himself had been, defenceless
and mistreated. The police officer could not or was not allowed to
give us any more detailed information; he told us to ask again around
4 p.m.

While I was waiting in the hall to the stairway, a group of about
thirty men was taken downstairs. I looked at each of them, Alfred
was not among them. They all stared straight ahead, as if dazed. I

could have screamed! What was happening was madness. Madmen had been let loose on humanity! I decided to go at 3 p.m. to a lawyer's office and ask him what I could do to get Alfred released. A young woman in the neighbouring apartment building, whose husband had also been imprisoned, asked me to take her with me. At 2 p.m., I went to her apartment to pick her up. She had changed her mind. First, I should go with her to the police again. I agreed, but I wanted first to go home in order to put on an old overcoat.

At that moment, from the window I saw an elegant car stop in front of our building; six SA men jumped out and rushed into the building. I knew what would happen. I left my coat with the fur collar with the young woman because I did not dare to appear so well-dressed on the street, and borrowed an old, shabby coat from her; she was much smaller than I, and the sleeves reached only as far as the upper half of my forearms; I had no gloves, and it was cold. When I was outside, I heard a terrible crashing and clattering coming from our building; the destruction had begun. I raced along an indirect route to the nearest taxi stand. When I arrived at the lawyer's, our cook had already called, weeping; the apartment had been demolished. The lawyer could not tell me what to do; he suggested that I ask a high-ranking leader of the party in parliament for help; it wouldn't be of much use, he said, but I should try anyway.

I ran to the parliament building; the guards stood at the ramp as motionless as stone. I walked into the hall; at a long table sat SS men who handed me a questionnaire which I had to fill out in intricate detail before I could be granted permission to enter the offices. I no longer remember what the particular headings were; I know only that on the piece of paper I wrote: 'At the instigation of Frau Emmy Göring.' I was directed to an office where an official interviewed me. On the wall, immediately visible for every visitor, there hung, framed and under glass, a motto that derided all those who merely pretended to be fanatical Nazis; it was very well known that these people had not always thought that way; they had been seen through and they would receive their just deserts. The official spoke on the telephone with the man that I wanted to see. It was too late, he said; I should come back the next day.

Then it occurred to me that Felix Steinböck, an actor with the Vienna Burgtheater [National Theatre] and a good friend of Emmy Göring's, might be able to intercede with her on Alfred's behalf. I did not want to turn to her directly myself to spare her any unpleasantness. I drove to his place. He received me, and seemed at first shocked by my strange appearance; he obviously could not understand what the excited person in the peculiar get-up wanted from him. When I introduced myself to him as a colleague and explained everything, he expressed genuine sympathy for me, but could not help me. He told me that Emmy Göring had already intervened in so many such cases that she could no longer do anything for my husband; she had to be very careful in order not to put herself at risk.

My brother-in-law happened to be in Vienna; as a Yugoslavian, he had moved with his family to Zagreb in September, and my sister-in-law had taken their mother there in late October. I went to see my brother-in-law at the Yugoslavian consulate in the late evening before his departure for Zagreb; by that time, I was hardly able to stand up. Here, too, I got no help. I spent the night in my stepmother's home in the city centre. I did not feel safe going back to my apartment, because the SA men had threatened my cook: 'The Jew had better not dare come back, otherwise something will happen to her!'

The next morning, I went back to the parliament; after waiting for three hours, I was admitted. A man in civilian clothing received me and spoke to me as a gentleman would usually speak to a lady. He had a fine face and, despite a marked reserve, he was sympathetic. He wanted me to tell him what I had seen and experienced in the last 24 hours. 'Is that really so?' he asked, after I had reported very briefly what had happened to me personally. I sat across from him and gulped nervously; I was so afraid that my husband would be sent to Dachau or Buchenwald. If only this man could at least prevent that! I waited for him to say something. He sat there motionless, his dark eyes staring straight ahead; I involuntarily held my breath. It had become eerily quiet. He took a deep breath and quickly expelled it again; I have never seen such disgust, such aversion on a person's face. 'That is dreadful,' he said. Then he promised me to do everything he could to prevent my husband from being sent away. He dictated to a secretary a few lines for me that indicated that I could see him at any time. He advised me, despite the threat, to go to my apartment and immediately telephone him if any of the men showed up again.

My apartment was literally a heap of ruins. The panes in the cabinets in the living room had been broken, and everything we had had in the way of porcelain and glass lay in countless shards on the floor. I could not even get into Alfred's study; books lay torn and trampled in a pile on the floor, lamps were smashed, desk drawers ripped out, their contents torn to shreds, the wood partly broken. Shards of glass were strewn everywhere here as well, and my gramophone records, which I had collected over time in Weimar, approximately a hundred of them, were completely shattered. Pictures had been violently torn out of their frames; the men had trampled on my oil portrait with their boots after they had asked the cook whom it represented. Finally, they had ripped the double-door off its hinges and thrown it into the middle of the pile of rubble. A red book lay on top; I climbed over the ruins and picked it up – it was my *Odyssey*; the cover had partly come off and the pages were crumpled, but otherwise the book had remained intact.

In the bedrooms, all the mirrors had been broken, and in the bathroom too nothing breakable had been spared. However, it is noteworthy that they stole nothing but watches and glasses. One hour after the rampage, a few Gestapo officials had come and noted with satisfaction that the boys had done a good job. But it is remarkable that it took them no more than ten minutes. They had justified themselves to the cook by saying: 'We are the people's wrath.' A 76-year-old man who lived on the first floor was also punched in the face by the 'people's wrath' so hard that he collapsed, bleeding profusely.

On that 10 November, we had been abruptly woken from a deeply troubled sleep and cast into the abyss of a hellish nightmare from which we could no longer hope to escape by merciful waking. The terrible thing had happened; torment and agony made the blood freeze in our veins, wore down our reason and made our hearts pound to the point of bursting. Under the dark, starless sky, sirens howled, windowless vans roared through the turbulent streets, one after another, another, another, still another, and women stood in dense ranks in front of a former hotel and wept, pleaded, begged, were driven away and came back and were driven away again. They walked up and down the streets and stood for hours in front of this or that convent, school or stable and waited until they were dispersed again. And blinded by tears, they ran on to the next door that was also closed to them.

After seven eternities came a card on which had been scribbled in a shaky hand: 'I'm in the convent school at Kenyongasse 2, I'm all right.' Then we suddenly heard: Tonight, they're all coming home – and many did come home, but many did not. Then again: He was released on 17 November, so why isn't he home? – We'll look into it. – We are really very sorry, he has disappeared without a trace. We knew what that meant.

People ran about from morning until night. They ran in terror in order to get at least a little ahead of the game. And fear ran with them, ran ahead of them and ran behind them; the lacerated air screamed from their whiplashes, they gasped for breath, spittle

197

puddled in their mouths like water and saltpetre, their eyes starting out of their sockets, and then – suddenly they were in the 'assassins' den'.

I had been advised to go to see a lawyer, Dr Jerabek. He was a very influential attorney in the party; he had defended the murderer of the former chancellor, Engelbert Dollfuss. An elderly, white-haired man opened the door of the law office. 'Please may I speak with Dr Jerabek?'

'Yes, but you'll have to wait, Miss. Sit down here by the stove! It will be a long time. There are many people here.' The old man looked like a vain, worn-out comic actor. The room was crowded. I waited. I heard telephone conversations: 'The Weghuber file, please – no, not yet – yes, please, Herr colleague – unfortunately not – we are not allowed to represent them. No, I've already told you, entirely out of the question, no, we cannot represent Jews.'

The old comedian repeatedly brushed against my shoulder. 'Take your coat off; see here, someone like you can take off her coat. Are you Aryan? Your husband's a Jew? Oh, dear! Now just wait.' We all sat there in Dr Jerabek's assassins' den, he who once defended the criminals who cut a man down and let him bleed to death.

Finally, after endless waiting, I succeeded in speaking to Dr Jerabek's colleague in the office. He looked and acted like an Austrian aristocrat. He took down all the information and promised me he would do everything he could to find out where my husband was being held and if possible to get him released. He became especially friendly when he heard that my husband was also a lawyer. When I asked him whether I should pay a retainer and if so, how much, he took both my hands and said: 'The wife of one of my colleagues should not ask such a thing, ever.'

I spent every night in a different place. I was just a bundle of nerves. It was said that Alfred had been released, but he did not come home. I now wrote a letter directly to Emmy Göring. I had booked a cabin on the United States Line for the voyage to New York on 28 December 1938. I telegraphed the Gestapo and all the offices indicated to me to state that everything was ready for our departure because it was said that prisoners would then be released sooner. Nothing helped. With the greatest effort, I had dug the most important documents out of the pile of ruins in my apartment. A man who had earlier worked in a business run by friends of ours agreed to help me; he took charge of the documents and a little money because they were not safe at my apartment. He put himself at my disposal at any time; he was perplexed by the misfortune into which his Nazis had cast us.

He himself was a long-time member of the party, and he was dreadfully ashamed.

At last, I succeeded in discovering where Alfred was; he was in the police prison in Vienna. Thank God! I couldn't have been happier if I'd learned that he was on a pleasure trip to the Riviera. He had not been deported, and I had heard that in the police prison people were treated decently. However, on 13 November, a man had called me who had been detained for two days with my husband in a riding school. I met him; the SS had treated him so badly that he could hardly walk. Alfred and the others had had to stand up all during the first night, for twenty-four hours they got nothing at all to eat, not a single drop of water; they had to watch as other men were beaten with iron bars; they had to endure the cruellest, most inhumane treatment. One night, the police volunteered to take over the guard, after they had already been on duty all day. They did so to save the innocent men from the murderous SS.

When I learned where Alfred was, I made up a package with warm underwear, soap, a toothbrush, a pair of shoes and a few biscuits and chocolate bars. Women with packages were standing in long lines in front of the police prison. Finally, we were allowed to go in and deliver our treats. The policemen treated us decently and even allowed us to deliver chocolate, though this was actually forbidden. I was also allowed to send in RM 10 by post. Ten marks for Alfred J., Police Prison, Vienna IX, cell no. 95 – cell no. 95! The childhood friend with whom I had played and to whom I had been married for two years had been sitting in a prison cell since 17 November! And I was happy about that! What had happened to us during the short period of eight months! Every criminal had the right to defend himself and to be heard; he had the right to humane treatment, even if his guilt was proven. But us?

On 26 November 1938, when I returned to my stepmother's apartment after hours in law offices and government offices, her two maids were waiting for me, already joyful and excited: 'Herr Doctor has just called – he is home again.' I telephoned home and told him: 'I'm coming, I'm coming right away.' I could hardly hear his answer: 'Yes – yes . . . ,' then his voice broke off. 'I'm coming!' I shouted again. Then I ran down the stairs, jumped into a taxi and promised the driver a royal tip if he drove like the devil. On the way, I had him stop at a fishmonger's and bought the biggest trout he had, despite my haste, despite the fact that I couldn't wait to get home.

The car stopped. In a moment I was at the door to the apartment, in another I was in the hall; in the middle of the hall stood a man, a helpless-looking creature in a dirty suit, with his shirt collar unbuttoned, motionless, as if he could never again move from the place where he was standing. His face was puffy and his expression so disturbed and absent that I probably would have walked by him without recognizing him if I had met him on the street. I said: 'Come on. Let's go into the living room.' He looked at me with the same helpless, uncomprehending gaze. I put my arm around him and led him into the living room, which was still in a dismal state. I pulled up a chair for him, but he remained standing, and I pushed him down, carefully holding him by the hand and shoulder; he immediately got up again, his glassy eyes staring straight ahead. I drew his poor face to mine and held his head in both my hands; I felt his breath in my ear, a toneless whisper: 'Those are people' – and a sob.

I took him into the bedroom and undressed him. His feet and legs were dreadfully swollen. He took a bath, then I laid him in bed and told him to sleep; but he couldn't. He was overcome by a complete apathy and a just-as-unnatural vivacity. He had to talk. When I brought him the trout, he thanked me and said that it was much too fine for him, and behaved like a supplicant who is ashamed and is afraid that he will ultimately be a burden after all. But he ate and gradually grew calmer. He spoke without interruption, but no longer in such feverish haste. Towards evening, his mother's maids came along with three other cooks from the neighbourhood to wish him well, and they all wept for joy.

A few days later, we had confirmation that Emmy Göring had intervened on our behalf. We received the following letter:

Berlin W8, 29 November 1938
Chief of Staff
of Minister-President General Field Marshal Göring
Ministerial Director State Councillor Dr Gritzbach

J. No. 8774/38

In response to your letter of 23 November 1938 addressed to Frau Göring, I most respectfully inform you that in consideration of the intention to emigrate I have forwarded your petition to the Head of the Security Police.

per pro

Dr. Joachimi m. p.

On the morning of 5 December 1938, the maid announced that a gentleman wanted to speak to me. In the hall stood a fresh-faced man I did not know. He was excessively friendly and acted as if we had already met. He told me his name, which sounded like Rivoli; I knew no one by that name. I took him into the living room to see Alfred, because I thought he might at some time have had business with him as a lawyer. But he too had never seen the man before. The man went on talking to me, telling me that he came from Zagreb. Now I thought I'd found a clue; he might be an acquaintance of my brother-in-law in Zagreb who had come to convey his greetings.

I asked him to sit down and offered him a cigarette. He began to smoke and then looked at me, half confiding, half challenging, and asked: 'Do you really not recognize Rivoli?' This was getting embarrassing; I didn't know, was he Rivoli? I was certain I had never seen him before and that he was mistaken, but with exaggerated politeness and in order to put an end to the uncomfortable situation, I said: 'My brother-in-law always talks about so many people that it's possible he mentioned this name at some time, but –' Here my guest interrupted me: 'So now I've got you. You know him,' and, with a sleazy grin, he added: 'I'm from the Gestapo.'

My poor husband's face was ashen. My heart was hammering like crazy, and at the same time I'd gone ice cold. I looked at his gloating face and asked: 'And what do you want?'

'You know Rivoli!'

'I have told you from the outset that I do not know him.'

'But you yourself have just admitted it. You said that you had heard the name from your brother-in-law! Here, look at the paper.'

With these words he showed me a piece of paper on which, under a few names unknown to me, stood my name and that of my brother-in-law. 'What does this have to do with me?' I asked.

'Don't play-act with me!' he screamed. 'You telephoned Rivoli on Friday night.' –

'I never spoke once on the telephone on Friday evening.'

'You did.'

'That is not true.'

'You said: "You damned scoundrel, I'm going to denounce you!"'

I was scared to death; what had happened here? The grinning agent prattled on:

'Don't deny it. You spoke with me on the telephone.' I tried to smile: 'You must know that you did not speak with me.'

'You talked with Rivoli on the telephone.'

'I give you my word that I have never spoken with him on the telephone and that I do not know him.'

'I don't need your word. You have to report to the Gestapo this afternoon at 3 p.m., in the Hotel Metropole, Room 305. There you will tell the truth.'

'I will tell the truth, just as I have told it to you now.'

'You'll speak differently to the Gestapo.'

'I won't say anything different there from what I have already said here,' I replied as he continued to grin at me, 'or will the Gestapo perhaps force me to say something that is not true?'

He suddenly changed his tactics and spoke to me kindly: 'Your husband was imprisoned. Didn't you ask Rivoli to try to get him released?'

'I asked a whole series of people to intervene on my husband's behalf; that is allowed, and if you wish, I will give you the names of the persons involved, but I have never heard of a Rivoli except from you.'

For a while, he continued to quibble. Then he looked around the room as if he wanted to undertake a search. He grabbed a letter from a woman friend in Hamburg that had arrived shortly before, and eagerly read it through. 'Why are you getting a letter from Hamburg?' To this idiotic question, I had no answer.

'Who is this from?'

'My friend.'

'Is she Aryan?'

'Yes.' He wrote down her address and hissed: 'We'll look into her, too.' Then he took a letter I had just begun from the typewriter, read the insignificant lines and threw it angrily on the table. Finally, he triumphantly seized an address book and leafed through it; we had bought it the day before and it was still entirely empty. Furious and like a bad actor, he trumpeted: 'I see that I have come too soon; I should have come an hour later!' He gave me a summons for the Gestapo and then did the last thing one would have expected from such a diabolical idiot: he turned to my husband and said: 'It might be a long time before this woman comes back. But you don't have to worry about her.' Then he left.

The agent was gone, but that did not make us feel any more comfortable. Alfred and I stood alone in the living room, artificially calm; we were trying to think. I decided to go and see my protector in the parliament building; Alfred went to see a colleague to ask his advice. At the parliament building, I had to wait. I sat on a bench in the corridor along with four or five other women; sighs, barely repressed tears, a halting conversation. These were Aryan women whose husbands or sons were in concentration camps; most of them were being persecuted because they were suspected of being monarchists or loyal followers of the Dollfuss-Schuschnigg regime. The wife of the former minister of war and chancellor Vaugoin sat next to me.

After waiting for a while, I was called in. I told my protector briefly what had just happened. He could not help me and only offered this advice: 'Never say: "I don't know" or "I can't remember." That makes a bad impression.' I drove home. Alfred also had no solace to offer me. The cook brought in the noonday meal, and I managed to get a little of it down. I put on warm underwear because I assumed that I would be arrested. I told Alfred: 'If they try to force you to say something false while I'm gone, don't do it, I'm sticking to the truth.' He silently embraced me. I pushed him away and then started walking.

I went into the Hotel Metropole, the Gestapo's local headquarters, handed over the summons and climbed the stairs to the third floor. Door after door in a long corridor. Along the wall, a broken wooden chair. I joined a few people with frightened faces who were shuffling back and forth. We stopped for a moment to catch our breath; we were as out of breath as if we had run up a mountain. As we passed one another, a woman scrutinized me; at our next fleeting meeting I murmured with almost closed lips: 'Rivoli?' – 'Yes,' she replied. The third time we stopped without drawing attention to ourselves. The woman also did not know why she had been summoned.

We continued walking up and down. I was so exhausted that I wanted to sit on the chair. The woman warned me against doing so. 'Stand up,' she said, 'an old woman sat down there earlier, and an official came and scolded her dreadfully.' We kept walking. For hours. From time to time, one of the many doors opened, and an official came out and went into another room. At the end of this corridor was a stairway; you could see from the third floor down to the ground floor; if you stared down long enough, you felt drawn towards it. I kept walking. If only we were allowed to sit down for a few minutes! I began to understand how it happened that people could admit guilt for something they had never done. I began to understand, and my torment had lasted only a few hours.

At long last, I was called in to an official. He was a kind-looking young man, and he politely asked me to sit down. He questioned me. After I had assured him that I really did not know Rivoli, he said: 'I believe you; you are telling the truth.' Then he asked me if perhaps I had relatives in Zagreb who might have asked Rivoli to do something to get my husband released. A light bulb went on in my head:

that was possible, of course, but they had not told me about it. The official explained what this was all about. This Rivoli was a swindler who had taken advantage of the situation and had told the arrested men's relatives that he could get their men released and would procure an entry visa for Yugoslavia for them. This swindler had been caught and criminal proceedings begun against him. He had in fact obtained my address, as I learned much later, from my brother-in-law in Zagreb.

The door opened, and the agent who had been at our apartment that morning came into the room. 'The matter is completely cleared up,' the friendly official said, looking indignantly at the agent, 'this lady really doesn't know Rivoli.'

'You didn't see the glance the couple exchanged when I mentioned him,' the spy insisted slyly; then he left. I answered a few more questions. The official made a record of our conversation, which I had to sign. He was about to let me go when the agent came back again. The young official said to him rather sharply: 'The case is closed.'

'We'll just see if a Jew or Jewess ever once tells the truth,' was the idiot's jeering answer. The young official bowed to me as I went out.

We were working furiously to procure all the documents necessary for our emigration. Our emigration tax and the Jewish property levy, as it was called, were paid by the end of December 1938, so that nothing stood in the way of getting our passports. We hoped to be able to leave in the first half of January 1939. We waited day after day to be notified that we could pick up our passports in the former Rothschild Palace;[3] the central office for the emigration of non-Aryans and Jews was housed there. In front of the palace, where day and night people waited in long lines, the most desolate scenes were played out. Either people were insulted in the rudest terms or they were driven away after they had stood there all night and waited; those were the SA's and the SS's favourite amusements.

No one was allowed to enter the building without a summons; therefore, it was impossible to deal personally with one's own urgent affairs and to get information about the current status of one's application. Thus, one was forced to resort to asking the help of people who apparently had access to the files at all times, thanks to their connections. We asked three people, one after the other, to look into our case. They all insisted that everything was in order, that the passports were ready, and that we would certainly receive the summons to pick them up the next day. The 'next day' stretched into endless weeks.

On 15 January 1939, my husband was requested, in an excessively polite telephone call, to come to the Gestapo office in the Hotel Metropole that afternoon, bringing with him all the documents that could provide proof of his efforts to emigrate. There he was first received by an old Austrian official who checked the documents. Suddenly a very young north German came out of the adjoining room and bellowed in a threatening tone: 'Your wife lied to General Field Marshal Göring. She promised in her petition addressed to Frau Emmy Göring that you would emigrate on 28 December 1938; how is it that you are still here?' My husband replied that, as shown by the documents he had produced, he had done everything in his power to emigrate; however, until that day he had still not been able to get hold of the passports. The official answered: 'That doesn't concern me; I will give you both one more deadline: 15 February 1939. If you have not left by then, you and your wife will be sent to Dachau.' My husband asked for a written confirmation of the 15 February 1939 deadline, so that he could show it to the passport office and thereby speed up the process. The official refused his request, and also refused his request that the passport office be officially informed of the deadline. Saying 'It's your responsibility to get the passports for emigration,' he left the room.

In this vexing time, another amusing interlude occurred. My husband had a small collection of autographs that he wanted to take with him. To this end, he had to have it assessed by an expert and get permission from the National Library in Vienna to take it out of the country. So he went there with his collection. At the entrance gate he found a sign: 'Jews strictly forbidden to enter.' Despite this friendly invitation, he went into the building. He was received politely: the director took a personal interest in the collection and discussed the various items with my husband, and examined them down to the last one. Then he said: 'You may take everything with you except for that manuscript: that we absolutely must have.'

My husband had feared that the director wanted to keep a Beethoven letter but to his enormous astonishment the director was demanding the manuscript of a poem by Heinrich Heine from his 'Deutschland' cycle, on the grounds that the library did not possess a single manuscript of Heine's. When my husband remarked that manuscripts by Jewish authors had probably been removed from the library, the director replied: 'How can you think such a thing, Herr Doctor?!' My husband offered him the Heine as a gift. Thereupon the director, visibly embarrassed, asked: 'But Herr Doctor, certainly you are not a non-Aryan?' When my husband replied that he was, the director said that in that case he was sorry, but he could not accept the gift. He would have to purchase the manuscript, but first he had to inquire into its value to be sure that he set a fair price. A few days later he informed him that he was again very sorry, but because of the library's present financial condition he could offer him no more than RM 8 (!). Smiling, my husband declared that he accepted. This large payment could not be paid in cash because for that the education ministry's approval would have to be sought. My husband has still not received the money.

As 15 February 1939 neared and we still had not received our passports, I succeeded, with the help of a lady who had excellent connections with the Vienna Society of Friends,[4] in gaining access to Herr Gildemeester. He was the head of the organization named after him,[5] whose goal was to help non-Aryans persecuted by the Nazis to emigrate. The Gildemeester organization worked in cooperation with the Gestapo. Herr Gildemeester, a Dutchman, had long been helping people persecuted for political reasons. Thus he had helped the Nazis at the time when they were still illegal and now he was acting on behalf of those who were being persecuted by the Nazis. The organization was run along grandiose lines, and Gildemeester himself received no one personally, but a recommendation from the Quakers opened a door for me that was closed to everyone else.

I entered a large, almost empty room; in one corner stood a desk, and on the wall hung a large picture of Adolf Hitler, framed with evergreen. A gaunt gentleman rose from the chair behind the desk and bowed as I came in. I presented my case. Without speaking or moving, but paying close attention, Herr Gildemeester listened to my report. Then he rang a bell and instructed the man who came to look into the status of the case and to let him know the result. He shook my hand; his hand felt like wax, strangely smooth, cool and lifeless. From the moment I felt this hand in mine, I no longer quite knew what his face looked like.

Twenty-four hours later, it was determined that my husband's passport was ready but mine was not; that was the reason for the endless delay. After another 36 hours, my passport was also ready, thanks to Herr Gildemeester's intervention, and we were both able to pick up our passports the following day. Recently, a curious custom had been introduced: people were shown their completed passports, but these were handed over only in exchange for a further payment in cash, the amount depending on the whim of the Gestapo official involved, but often being as much as several thousand marks. It was practically impossible to fight this extortion. We were prepared for it, and so my husband had taken along all the documents as proof that he no longer had any cash and that therefore the tax office had even allowed him to pay off all his taxes by leaving behind effects that could not be sold.

These arguments, which we immediately introduced, caught the official off guard, and so we were not subjected to the usual extortion. In the meantime, the deadline for emigration, 15 February 1939, had come, and we had to apply for an extension; this was granted until 15 March 1939.

On 8 March 1939, at 2.30 p.m., our train left Vienna's Westbahnhof and headed for Zurich via Salzburg and Buchs. We sat alone in our second-class compartment; since 1 March, Jews had been forbidden to use the dining and sleeping cars.

We arrived in Zurich at 6.30 a.m. on 9 March; it was very dark, with snow flurries and thunder and lightning. The porter greeted us in good Swiss German: 'We are going to have a war; first, there is a snowstorm and, second, we have a National Exhibition this summer. When we have a National Exhibition in Zurich, there is always a war; it was the same in 1914.'

# FRITZ RODECK

## Manuscript 76a (188)

*Born in 1890 in Vienna; journalist; emigrated on 22 December 1938,
first to England, then to the USA; his account was written in January
1939, immediately after Rodeck's arrival in England and six months
before the Harvard competition.*[1]

### Vienna, 10 November 1938

A date that I shall never forget. A few days earlier, a young Polish
Jew by the name of Grynszpan had shot and badly wounded third
secretary Ernst vom Rath at the German embassy in Paris. It was
immediately clear to the greater part of the Jewish population of
Austria that this act by an irresponsible young man, a fanatic, which
they deplored and condemned, would have grave consequences for
German Jews. Immediately after the attack, a hate campaign began
in the newspapers and on the radio that went far beyond any previous one.

It was presented as a proven fact that, just as in the case of David
Frankfurter (who had shot the leader of the Swiss National Socialists,
Wilhelm Gustloff),[2] this act was masterminded by an international
Jewish conspiracy, for which all Jews had to bear responsibility – as
if a conspiracy against a legation secretary, that is, a very junior dip-
lomatic officer, could have had any political meaning or purpose. The
attack was represented as an attempt to provoke international ten-
sions and thereby to poison the improved atmosphere after the
Munich Four-Power Agreement. It was with these and similar claims
that Herr Goebbels's propaganda machine sought to stir up hostility
to Jews among the population.

On the evening of 9 November, the death of legation secretary vom Rath was reported on the radio.

It may be true that in Nazi circles this produced indignation and desire for revenge. But a storm of indignation broke out – timed like a grenade – in 150 German cities at precisely midnight, so that there can be no possibility of it having been spontaneous. In October, most Viennese Jews already knew that some major action against Jews would take place in the near future. The death of the aforementioned embassy official offered the external occasion and at the same time the necessary pretext. Whatever the case, the indignation was incited by the leading Nazi authorities, and the whole operation was ordered, directed and organized from above because in a Nazi state there are no spontaneous demonstrations. No Nazi would dare to undertake any kind of political action without an express order or at least without previous assurance that it would be silently tolerated.

On the morning of 10 November, a strange uneasiness prevailed in the city. Nazi officials hurried from one shop to another, people gathered in front of Jewish shops, and on the windows of many other shops, especially those of grocers, signs were put up: 'Nothing sold to Jews.' Jewish shops were hurriedly locked up. The sirens of the fire engines roaring through the streets were sounded continuously.

First reports came in: in the 12th district, the shutters of closed Jewish shops had been broken open, the shops looted and set on fire. Immediately afterwards, an acquaintance of mine who lived in the 2nd district turned up at my apartment and asked permission to stay there. In the 2nd district, a regular pogrom was underway; apartments and business establishments were being demolished and looted, and the residents of the apartments mistreated and arrested; the synagogue in Leopoldgasse had been set on fire, and the great synagogue in Tempelgasse was burning. He had fled and did not feel it was safe to go home.

On the basis of my own experience, observation and research, I believe I am able to provide, if not perhaps a fully complete, at least an absolutely characteristic picture of the events of 10 November. The methods used by the Nazis in the individual districts differed considerably. Evidently, the idea was to produce the impression that this was not an organized pogrom but a spontaneous outburst. However, totally reliable sources informed me that the Nazis, who were expressly forbidden to wear their uniforms, were ordered in the individual local group leadership offices (the local Nazi or SA organizations were always responsible for only a few streets), where residents' card files were kept, to enter the individual apartments of Jews

209

in the area in groups of three to five men and, after completing their work there, to return, report and receive new orders. The booty was also to be deposited in these local group offices or, in special cases, unloaded from lorries, for example, pianos, home furnishings, shoes and other items taken from looted shops.

In the 2nd and 20th districts (where most of the Jewish population of Vienna lives, especially the more indigent), and also in the 21st district, the order was given to demolish Jewish homes. The Nazis rang doorbells, asked once again, as a precaution, whether the occupants were Jewish and then immediately pushed their way inside. The furniture was overturned, hacked up and broken; glass panes, mirrors and crockery smashed, clothes and carpets cut to ribbons, duvets slit and their feathers shaken out of the windows, cupboards forced open, suitcases cut open, and in many cases furnishings thrown out of the windows into the street. Several people told me that sometimes the Jews who were in the apartments were also thrown out of the windows onto the street. I have no details regarding this, but know only that a number of Jews who had apparently been injured in this way were later treated in hospital. Then women with shopping bags frequently appeared in the demolished homes, crying 'We need things for our hungry children,' taking with them whatever still looked in some way usable. It also happened that the same homes were attacked by Nazis several times in the course of this day, and each time their inhabitants were badly abused.

In the 1st district, fewer homes were destroyed and looted. But in one apartment inhabited by Jews near the Stadtpark, five Nazis broke in and started beating up the 17-year-old son; when his mother saw this she collapsed. Thereupon the Nazis withdrew but came back a short time later and took the young man with them. Three days later, the family was informed that they could pick up his ashes. A 21-year-old Jew met the same fate.

In the 4th district, three Nazis broke into the apartment of an elderly man, a Jew who had fought in the war and held high office, and questioned him harshly about weapons and Communist writings. He put his sabre and two military revolvers on the table. Then one of the Nazis asked: 'Where is your weapons permit?', then took one of the revolvers and pointed it at the Jew. The latter replied: 'I was an Austrian officer during the war, and need no weapons permit. But if you intend to shoot, you'll have to take the safety catch off the revolver!' This impressed the Nazis, and, as the man's wife also threw a screaming fit, they left without arresting him or touching anything.

In the 6th, 7th and several other districts, the operation played out this way: three to five Nazis burst into a Jew's home, first ripping out the telephone, then asking for money, savings account passbooks and jewellery. The sums voluntarily produced were later returned, but money and so on found during a later search was ultimately confiscated, and in addition the owners had to expect 'unpleasant-ness' as well. As a rule, the people were so intimidated that they handed over all they had. The Nazis were as little inclined to justify themselves as they were to provide a receipt.

In individual instances – when business people were involved whose Nazi inspectors intervened to ensure that the salaries of workers or employees would be paid – the confiscated money was later given back. This clearly shows that in general the Nazis did not steal sums of money for their own use, and that therefore this was not a so-called illegal operation. The 'confiscated' sums of money, savings account passbooks and so on were deposited with the local group leadership and later transferred to higher Nazi command centres (e.g., district offices).

However, many a Nazi also took the opportunity to steal things for his own use. I know of a case in which an unemployed, penniless Nazi suddenly started running around after 10 November with a stuffed briefcase and soon after sold a 'confiscated' typewriter to the nearest dealer, where the following day the owners recognized their property and bought it back on an instalment plan. Gauleiter Bürckel[3] later sent twelve of these thieves to a concentration camp. But it can be assumed that the number of those who stole for their own use was much, much higher.

Moreover, Jews from individual buildings – always with only the clothes they were wearing – were herded into a single apartment. The other Jewish apartments were locked up, sealed, and their owners only given back the keys weeks later. Many of them found their apartments looted and even completely cleaned out, even though they had been 'officially sealed by the Party', and six weeks later some were still waiting for their apartments and the keys to their apart-ments to be returned.

In a state school in the 12th district, between nine and ten o'clock on the morning of 10 November, the pupils were urged by their teachers to destroy Jewish shops. The teachers told their pupils very precisely which shops were to be demolished.

Particularly genteel methods were used by the Nazis in Hietzing, Vienna's 13th district, which consists chiefly of villas for the wealthy. Here a group of Nazis came across a lawyer in a villa which had several Jewish tenants. They had the lawyer show them his money and jewellery, but took nothing; instead, they forced him to sign a statement to the effect that they had taken nothing away with them. With this statement in hand, they went away and completely looted the apartments of all the other Jewish inhabitants in the same building.

One Nazi patrol took a wealthy Jewish factory owner, along with his whole family and all his jewellery, valuables and cash, to one of the hastily set up prison camps. There he and his family were herded, with a whole series of other prisoners, into the courtyard and made to line up in the form of a square. SA and SS men loaded their weapons, pointed them at the terrified people and gave orders and acted as though they were going to shoot them. Then they lowered their guns and repeated this exciting game a few more times. They obviously thought making their victims fear for their lives was great sport.

Eventually, the Nazis had had enough and gave the factory owner back his cash and valuables – but not without a few of the smaller valuables sticking to their fingers – and let him and his family go. As a precaution, they had him sign a written statement regarding the restitution of his valuables. On the evening of the same day, another Nazi group showed up at his apartment, took away his money and valuables again – they had in their hands his statement saying the latter had been returned to him. Similar methods were used in several other cases. Savings account passbooks carrying significant sums and cash were confiscated from a former state official, and on the evening of the same day other Nazi thugs carried off all his silverware.

The 16th and 17th districts suffered looting and devastation in the main, whereas in the 18th and 19th districts arrests were especially numerous.

In other districts not expressly mentioned here, the pogroms were pursued in similar vein, with only slight variations in detail.

## Mass arrests

Everywhere in Vienna, on the streets, in the railway stations, in residences, many thousands of Jews were arrested on 10 November. Even men who had lined up in front of consulates to procure visas were arrested in large numbers. In one case, the consul saved people threatened with arrest by quickly opening the consulate's gates and letting people come into the building.

The Jews who lined up by the hundreds in front of the Jewish religious community building (partly to seek support, partly for emigration purposes) were led into the building by the Nazis in a conspicuously courteous way. There the Nazis suddenly fell on the people and beat them in the most inhumane way. One of those mistreated is said to have died of his injuries right there and then. Finally, most of the mistreated Jews were taken away and put into improvised prisons.

As for the number of those arrested, which I would estimate to be about 10,000–12,000, it is significant that there was hardly a Jewish family in Vienna that did not have at least one member arrested. In Vienna, Jewish men between the ages of 18 and 50 were literally decimated after 10 November.

The arrested men were for the most part taken to schools, convents, barracks and so on that had been set up as temporary prisons, and in many cases they were abused there most brutally. In some of these prisons, they received nothing to eat for days, or had to stand all night long with their arms raised; anyone who let his arms sink down was beaten half to death by the Nazi guards. In others, people were driven up and down the stairs for hours by Nazis wielding steel bars or rubber batons, and a few were thrown down the stairs, where they remained lying with fractured skulls. In the meantime, the prisoners were constantly made to line up with their faces to the wall and threatened with death. Or individuals were called out, taken into another room and there beaten so badly that those who had remained behind heard their screams of pain echoing through all the rooms.

The available toilets were obviously not sufficient for the large number of prisoners, so that people had to queue. The Nazis amused themselves, laughing loudly, by driving away those who had reached the front, making them start again at the back of the queue. I was told about other practical jokes of this kind.

The police had nothing to do with all this. The guards were under strict orders not to get involved and to ignore these things.

There were also some prisons in which the prisoners were treated better. In a few of these, the prisoners had been allowed to keep their money, and they could have food and tobacco brought in. Some were even urged to do so by individual Nazi guards, because they received a significant share – an arrangement that satisfied both sides. In general, prisoners saw it as salvation when they were later transferred from the Nazi prisons to police arrest, where they were treated decently and in accordance with the rules.

Things were worst in the Nazi prison that had been set up in a convent in the 7th district, in Kenyongasse,[4] in close proximity to the

213

Westbahnhof. Admittedly, the treatment was not equally atrocious in all the rooms. Day and night, green police wagons or lorries drove up, bringing prisoners in and taking others away. All around, shop owners complained about the inmates' screaming and wailing as they were driven out of or into the vehicles with kicks and blows. Whether in fact – as was said – seven Jews were killed in this prison, I was not able to determine.

Prisoners from other prisons were brought to Kenyongasse and some of them were then transported to the concentration camp near Dachau. Whether a prisoner was sent to the concentration camp or not, released or held in custody in a police prison depended partly on chance. People were sometimes chosen arbitrarily or by number, sometimes on the basis of lists prepared in advance.

Investigation was carried out in such a way that each prisoner was questioned by a whole series of interrogators, one from the point of view of 'racial defilement', another with regard to political activity or communism, still another with regard to alleged offences. Finally, the results of the separate interrogations were summarized in a report by a superior officer who then decided what would be done with each individual prisoner, generally either release or the concentration camp. Of the 10,000–12,000 men arrested, several thousand were probably sent to Dachau.[5]

All the people released from Nazi prisons, and particularly from the concentration camps, were conspicuously silent. Among Viennese Jews, it was considered good form not to ask those who had got out of one of these hell-holes about their experiences. However, the appearance of these people, their mental state and physical health, spoke eloquently for them. There were individuals among them who began to weep, to scream or to tremble when the bell in a clock tower rang. Also, the injuries with which many of them came home bore mute but unmistakable witness to what had happened to them.

For these reasons, there was little to be learned regarding the fate of the people taken to Dachau or Buchenwald concentration camps. One or two weeks afterwards, nearly identical postcards were received from those who after 10 November had been transported to Dachau. They wrote that they were healthy and that they could be permitted 12 marks or sometimes even 15 marks per week. They gave as their address: 'Protective Custody Jew [name]' followed by a number, usually low, and seldom over 20; I do not know whether it referred to a part of the concentration camp or the number of a company. A message from the camp headquarters was printed on each card, informing the recipient that each prisoner could write letters twice a month and receive them twice a month, but they must not exceed a certain length, that money could be sent to him, but no packages, since all articles he might need were available in the camp in exchange for money. Finally, that petitions for release addressed to the camp headquarters were completely futile.

Furthermore, we heard that in addition to the Jewish groups in Dachau, there were also groups of monarchists, communists and social democrats, Jehovah's Witnesses (a sect fiercely persecuted by the Nazis) and others consisting of various cadres of political prisoners; that the labour there was not equally hard for all; that those who worked harder also got more to eat. The layout of Dachau concentration camp was supposed to be such that escape was quite hopeless.

Mortality in the concentration camp seemed to be quite high. In a case known to me, a very polite police officer appeared at the home of a prisoner's relatives, expressed his regret and informed them as gently as possible that Dr N. had recently died in Dachau and that the urn with his ashes could now be collected. In other cases, the relatives were informed simply by postcard.

The worst reports about Dachau concerned the punishments commonly dealt out there, which were divided into four rankings. From what I have heard, the first level was detention, the second 'tethering'. This punishment, which was also practised, if only seldom, in the old Austro-Hungarian army, consisted of tying the offender's hands behind his back with a rope and then attaching the other end of it to a pole so high up that the tethered man had to stand leaning slightly forward on his tiptoes with his back against the pole. The fourth and most severe level of punishment in Dachau was the 'Bunker', that is, being locked up in a tiny, totally dark cell, and given only bread and water. A knife and a rope were put in the cell beforehand. The psychological calculation, that the mental depression caused by this incarceration and the preceding treatment ought to lead the prisoner to commit suicide, seems to have proven correct in numerous cases. Many prisoners must have done the Nazis the favour of themselves carrying out the death sentence imposed on them.

By the end of 1938, there were few Jews left in Vienna who had not themselves been in a concentration camp or who had one or more relatives or friends who had been in one. If a Jew was released from Dachau, as a rule a deadline was set for him to leave the country. This deadline was usually so short, however, that it did not allow enough time to acquire a residence permit somewhere abroad or to complete the tedious passport and emigration formalities involved. If the Jew had not left the country before the deadline, he faced imprisonment in a concentration camp again, with the friendly notification that he would not emerge from it a second time.

However, the deadlines were often not respected by the Nazis themselves, and people were taken back to Dachau before the allotted period had run out. Therein lies one of the main reasons for the countless attempts made by Jews to cross the German border illegally and reach another country without papers, since they far preferred a possible internment abroad to the horror of Dachau. In individual cases, people who were politically insignificant were released from the concentration camp if in the meantime their relatives had obtained permission to enter any foreign country.

This explains the fact that thousands of Jews of both sexes tried to get tickets for travel to Shanghai (most of them by sacrificing the last of their possessions), which were relatively easy to obtain. That living conditions in Shanghai were exceptionally unfavourable and offered Jews no way of making a living was scarcely considered because people hoped to use it only as a stopover en route to another country. To what extent this hope was fulfilled is demonstrated by the sad reports of the number and situation of the emigrants living there.

The number of Jewish people who died as a result of 10 November in Vienna alone has been estimated to be eighty. But Dr Goebbels – and following his example, all his lackeys in the German press – spoke only of 'a few broken window panes' and 'a Polish Jew killed in Munich who was himself to blame for his death because of his provocative behaviour'. Was the propaganda minister really so ill-informed regarding events in the German Reich, or did he believe that by denying facts he knew to be true he could make them go away? There is no third possibility.

In any case, it was Dr Goebbels who, at 4 p.m. on 10 November, had it proclaimed on the radio (after calling out all off-duty firemen and emergency technicians) that all further individual measures taken against Jews were to stop immediately, and announced 'legal sanctions'.

When I told this to my Nazi jailer during an inspection visit to my apartment, he ingenuously replied: 'Yes, all further measures, but the ones already underway will be continued and carried out to the end.'

## Burning synagogues

The strongest proof that the Vienna pogroms of 10 November, the so-called 'outburst of the people's wrath', were organized in accord-

216

ance with a plan is provided by the destruction and burning down of all the Jewish houses of worship in Vienna (with a single exception). There were more than twenty large synagogues in Vienna, not to mention the far more numerous smaller ones. The destruction was the work of a few hours; the rapidity with which it was carried out here was downright astonishing.

Of all the synagogues, only one was not burned down, the one in the 1st district, in the Seitenstettengasse, which is not a free-standing building but rather built into the office building of the religious community in such a way that burning it down would also have set fire to a very large block of buildings. But even though it was not burned, the inside of this synagogue (one of the oldest in Vienna) offered, as I myself later saw, a depressing sight: benches hacked up, smashed chandeliers, etc. In the case of each of these synagogue burnings, the fire brigade was called in, but not to put out the fire; instead, they stood about doing nothing and were there merely to prevent the fire from spreading to neighbouring buildings.

In the 19th district, the Nazis forced their Jewish prisoners themselves to destroy the local synagogue, using pickaxes and shovels. I know a Jewish woman who saw from the street her husband helping to demolish this synagogue and observed how those who injured their hands doing this unfamiliar work had them bandaged and were then forced to continue working. Here, the Nazis played still another practical joke. A few days before 10 November, a slight earthquake had been felt in Vienna, but did no great damage. In front of the ruins of the synagogue, the Nazis now erected a large sign that read: 'Destroyed by the terrible earthquake in November', so that, in the event of someone taking photographs, the sign would have to be visible in the picture.

Several of the destroyed synagogues saw the Nazis come back later on and search the ruins for the silver and semi-precious stones with which the covers of the Torah scrolls are usually ornamented.

In the Central Cemetery, both the old and the large new ceremonial halls, in which funeral ceremonies were held, were destroyed by fire. When I later visited the cemetery, all the windows in these halls were nailed up so tightly with straw mats that one could not see inside, and in the new hall all the entrances were also blocked off at a considerable distance. But I nonetheless managed to make my way to one of the doors. Smoke-blackened walls, charred doors, windows that had broken because of the heat, shards of glass on the floors,

217

marble debris, roof gutters melted by the heat – this very striking picture is firmly imprinted in my mind.

## Innsbruck, 10 November

On 10 November, the Nazis may have done more material damage in many German cities, but in no other city did they rampage more ferociously than in Innsbruck, the capital of the Tyrol. Only a few Jews lived there, and, as is usual in a small city, they were all known. Here the Nazis put directly into practice their basic principle 'Death to the Jews!' and their song, 'When Jewish blood spurts from the knife, then things are going well again', and organized, from 3 a.m. to 5 a.m., a 'Night of Long Knives'.

During the night, Nazis rang the doorbell of a businessman named Willy Bauer, who lived in a villa[6] also occupied by another Jewish family. He went out to see what had happened. His wife heard a loud cry in the hall, and when she rushed out, her husband was lying in a pool of blood on the floor. He had been stabbed several times but was still alive. His wife tried to call a doctor – the telephone had been destroyed. She tried to go out into the street to get help – the house was surrounded by SS men in uniform, who did not allow her to pass through. She ran up to the first floor to ask the owner of the house, who was also a Jew, for help. The door was open, and the apartment half-demolished, and the owner lay dead on the floor.

Another Jew in Innsbruck who had earlier been highly respected, a retired official of the Austrian National Railroad, Richard Berger, the leader of the Innsbruck Zionists, was woken during the night and told to dress warmly, because he had to come along.[7]

The next day Berger's body was found in an alleyway with several bayonet wounds. His brother-in-law, whose name was Adler, was also so badly beaten that he died in hospital of his injuries shortly afterwards.

An old Jewish couple, the husband 72 years old and the wife not much younger, were pulled out of bed and thrown into the Inn river. Both drowned.[8]

In the case of an elderly Jewish woman who had long been crippled and could not move from her bed, the Nazis broke in and hit her on the head with all the crockery they found in the apartment, with the result that she suffered concussion.

The number of the dead in Innsbruck ran to seventeen. 'Only broken window panes', right, Herr Goebbels?

## . . . and the Aryans?

We must now ask what the people of Vienna, the large number of people with halfway normal ideas of law and decency, said about the events of 10 November. On the basis of personal experience, I can say that broad strata of the Viennese population, and especially the better and more educated groups, were upset and enraged. I have spoken with people from all occupations and social classes, with workers, businessmen and intellectuals, Nazi supporters and Nazi opponents: I have not found a single person who approved of these events but many who were filled with the deepest revulsion.

The Nazis of my acquaintance spoke of 'abuses' committed by irresponsible groups, but insisted that Jews had to be held responsible for the murder of the legation secretary vom Rath, etc. However, others condemned the events of 10 November without reservation. There was a whole series of Aryans who hid their Jewish friends, or at least their valuables, in their own homes, even though they were thereby risking their own skins. I was also told about National Socialists who after 10 November got up the courage to leave the party.

After I had been robbed of everything and stripped of all my assets, a large number of Aryan acquaintances made what amounted to condolence visits to me, brought me gifts, offered me money and helped me in every conceivable way. They were all ashamed and deeply depressed, and one got the impression that they had a guilty conscience and feared the power of a higher justice, as certain individuals quite openly said. There were Aryan women who said, weeping: 'We are not to blame for this! Forgive us!'

These people saved, as much as that was still possible, the honour of the German people. I have never generalized, and for me it is a true satisfaction to be able to testify that even in National Socialist Greater Germany there are still decent people; there are still good human beings.

### 'Atonement measures'

As usual, the 'illegal' pogrom was followed by a legal one in the form of regulations issued by the government of the Reich or its individual ministers. First, Jews had to have their demolished shops restored or repaired. Many of them had insurance covering glass breakage, fire and other kinds of damage. The insurance payments that now fell due were declared to be forfeited to the Reich. Before a certain

219

deadline, every Jewish business had to have a sign with Hebrew letters as large as the German ones, even though all Jewish businesses, with the exception of those under provisional management or being Aryanized, had to remain closed. Wages, salaries and severance indemnities to Aryan employees and workers also had to continue to be paid, along of course with taxes and levies.

Above all, however, an 'atonement contribution' of one billion marks was demanded of all Jews in the German Reich. Within one year, every Jew who had assets of more than 5,000 marks, which he was already obligated by the law of 28 April 1938 to declare, had to contribute 20 per cent of his assets in four instalments to this 'atonement contribution', without any special notice of this obligation. The first instalment was to be paid by 15 December 1938 to the tax office responsible for receiving it. In case this 20 per cent turned out to be insufficient to bring in a billion marks, an increase in the percentage to be paid by individual Jews was foreseen.

To justify these measures, fantastic figures regarding the wealth of Jews in Germany and Austria were reported in the press and on the radio. According to these reports, Jews' assets in Germany and Austria amounted to eight billion marks, so that per capita each Jew had several times the average amount held by individual Germans. Whether these figures were correct, I don't know. On the basis of a closer examination of the facts, I consider them highly improbable. But even if they were correct, then since March 1938, through confiscations, theft, extortion, 'provisional managers', forced liquidation and expropriation of businesses without compensation, non-payment of Jewish accounts receivable, nullification of every legal [gap in the text] of Jews, special or excessive taxes, fees and levies, and other measures of various kinds, the Nazis had already appropriated the greater part of this sum before 10 November 1938.

The 'atonement contribution', with its proviso that the percentage might be raised, was nothing less than a barely disguised confiscation of all assets still held by Jews. After 10 November, this theft, which had been planned and legally prepared long in advance, was legalized with an alacrity and with a remarkable juridical ingenuity that is as admirable from a legal standpoint as it is despicable from a moral one.

All securities still in Jewish possession had to be deposited with banks. Access to them was possible, however, only with the permission of the Asset Transfer Office. Assets held by Jews in banks and savings accounts could no longer be withdrawn; instead, each account holder had access to a maximum sum of 400 marks per month.

Whether in the meantime the amount of this payment has been changed, I do not know.

And then, 'in the realm of cultural life', Jews were banned from entering theatres, cinemas, museums, art exhibitions or any public place since 'a German cannot be expected to sit next to a Jew.' I had not been in any of these places since March 1938 because, even though I have long been a friend and connoisseur of German culture, I no longer had any desire to enjoy the company of Nazis in what they called German culture. The prohibition on Jews borrowing books from lending libraries, along with the closing of the few Jewish newspapers that were still being published in the German Reich, completed the exclusion of Jews from cultural life. The granting of permission to establish Jewish cultural institutions, which Dr Goebbels publicly announced with great aplomb, was, in view of the confiscation of all the funds necessary to support such institutions, no more than empty words intended to deceive people abroad.

Since Jewish sports clubs had been dissolved and Jews expelled from all other sports clubs, they had long since been in practice excluded from frequenting sports grounds, public swimming pools and the like. Now there was also a legal prohibition in these areas.

A regulation applicable throughout the Reich gave local authorities the power to prohibit Jews from being in certain streets and squares and also from leaving their residences during specific times. In Vienna, this prohibition was put into practice for the first time in December, on the day of 'National Solidarity' (one of the days on which funds for the Winter Aid programme were collected).

In addition, Jews were legally forbidden to purchase land and buildings or, insofar as they already owned such land or buildings, to mortgage or otherwise dispose of them. Similarly, Jews were forbidden to buy, sell, pawn or otherwise dispose of gold, silver, precious stones, jewellery, antiques or other valuables, except in certain public redemption centres whose establishment was planned, one of which had already been set up in Berlin in December 1938. According to the provisions of this law, a Jew was also not allowed to give away a house or piece of jewellery belonging to him because even a gift was a so-called 'free disposal in the meaning of this law'. In practice, this meant that Jews who still had buildings, plots of land, jewellery, precious stones and the like could not do anything with them, but had to wait until they were taken away from them by some new law, or, in what amounts to more or less the same thing, such property was 'bought' from them at an officially dictated price or perhaps exchanged for a government bond.

As far as residences are concerned, a new law paved the way for the confiscation of all residential buildings in Jewish possession. Starting on a specific date, which in December 1938 had still not been set because of the lack of regulations for implementing it, Jews in Germany would no longer be allowed to own either buildings or plots.

The number of Jews driven out of their homes in Vienna can be estimated at 30,000–40,000, some of whom are no longer allowed to return. The Jewish religious community therefore sent all Jews who formerly owned residences a circular asking them to make available or put up for rent any rooms they could possibly do without, since otherwise obligatory billeting would have to be instituted.

When the Nazis declared that in future Jews would be allowed to live only in buildings owned by Jews and Germans allowed to live only in buildings owned by Aryans, in order to understand this trick we have to keep in mind that many Jews who owned buildings had either already had them taken away from them or would soon have them taken away in accordance with new laws, whereas the remaining Jewish buildings were managed by National Socialist property managers who did not, of course, accept any Jewish tenants. Thus as far as the housing question was concerned, Jews still living in Germany were threatened with a catastrophe of unimaginable proportions.

If a Jew who was emigrating wanted to take jewellery with him, every piece of this jewellery had to be assessed (that is, put on a published list) by an assessor approved by the authorities; now, only assessments made by assessors employed by the Dorotheum (the public pawn office operated by the state and the city of Vienna) were accepted. The values assessed had recently been sharply increased. I know of one case in which the same pieces of jewellery were assessed at a rate 30 per cent higher than that determined by another assessor at the Dorotheum on the preceding day.

Then an export permit had to be submitted to the currency exchange office. If the estimated value of the jewellery was less than 200 marks, as a rule, no export fee had to be paid. If the value was more than 200 marks, a fee of 50–100 per cent was usually charged, not only on the amount exceeding 200 marks, but on the whole amount. But this rule was not binding. The amount of the fee was left in each case to the official's own discretion. I would like to add here that the officials at the currency exchange office were the most unpleasant and stubborn Nazi officials I ever had to deal with.

Finally, on 1 January 1939, a new currency regulation entered into force, according to which an emigrating Jew was now only allowed

222

to take objects necessary for his personal use, and other objects – such as furniture – only with special permission from the currency exchange office. Whether taking useful objects other than purely personal ones would be subject to payment of an export fee was not known at the time I departed. In any case, for all objects sent to a Jewish emigrant after his departure, even if they were of little value, special permission had to be obtained from the currency exchange office.

In this respect as well, a confiscation of Jewish property was not only possible in practice, but obviously actually intended.

## The Jewish situation at the beginning of 1939

The events of November 1938 and the ensuing 'atonement laws' resulted in practice in the complete exclusion of Jews from economic life.

From 1 January 1939, no Jewish business could continue to exist in Germany. All Jewish businesses, large or small, were either transferred to Aryan ownership or closed for ever. Only a few export firms that are already in the course of Aryanization and that the Nazis do not want to close down because they are useful for exports are still temporarily in Jewish possession.

There are no longer any Jewish businessmen or tradesmen in Germany and Austria, but neither are there any Jewish commercial employees, lawyers, doctors or dentists (except for about eighty in Vienna, who are called medical or dental attendants (*Krankenbehandler* or *Zahnbehandler*) – they have to put a blue sign on their doors and are only allowed to treat Jews), no Jewish veterinarians, bank officers, bankers or stockbrokers, and, of course, no Jewish state or community officials, no Jewish architects or building contractors, no Jewish journalists, engineers, professors or teachers (except for those in the few remaining Jewish schools), no building superintendents, insurance men, agents, sales representatives or travelling salesmen, no film or theatre actors, no theatre directors, cinema owners or film distributors, no Jewish workers and, of course, no Jewish farmers.

In view of what is an almost complete exclusion of Jews from economic life, one must ask: how and on what do Jews actually live?

Every Jew who still has money in a bank or savings account can withdraw a modest amount each month. By working with a Nazi expert, those who still have furniture or other household items can sell them, though at very low prices. Retired bank officials over 65 years old receive their monthly pensions – though drastically reduced;

the pensions of younger retired bank officials were cancelled, and they receive instead 18 months' salary, which they now consume, just as individual sales employees are consuming their severance indemnities. Jews who retired as government officials still receive their pensions, though these have been greatly reduced.

In 1938, unemployed Jews, whose numbers have naturally greatly increased, still received, as did unemployed Aryans, unemployment benefits of 9–14 marks per week – depending on whether they had wives and children to support or not. But in December the tramway tickets that up to that point all unemployed workers had received to allow them to report for supervision and to pick up their unemployment payments were withdrawn, the ominous 'J' (Jew) was stamped on their unemployment cards, and finally they were separated from unemployed Aryans for purposes of supervision and no longer allowed to enter the general unemployment offices. After these measures, it is likely that they will be deprived of unemployment benefits on some pretext or other.

Individual Jews who still have residences can earn a little money by letting rooms, so long as the tenants still have money to pay the rent. Jews in Vienna are already frequently living five or ten to a room. Men, women and children, all jammed in together. And there are still Jews who are paid a small amount of money by other, elderly or ill Jews to stand in line for them at the various offices. Finally, the officials of the Jewish religious community still receive their salaries, as do teachers in Jewish schools and leaders of retraining courses.

But all these categories put together constitute only a dwindling minority. At the beginning of 1939, most Jews, at least in Vienna, are living by begging or, to put it less crudely, on support provided by the Jewish religious community, which is itself supported by funds from abroad. I believe that the number of those who receive meal tickets, that is, one meal a day, is at least 25,000. But just as many may also be receiving nothing, even though they need this one meal a day as much as anyone else. Still others are supported by relatives and friends. It is not unusual for a Jew who still has a little money or still receives his salary to be supporting and maintaining ten or twelve others who are destitute.

Under these circumstances, the number of deaths and especially of suicides is very high. The religious community's funeral department has not been so busy since the Anschluss, and a very large proportion of the burials have been pauper's burials, that is, burials of people whose relatives could not pay the burial fees. Statistics on the number of deaths, and especially of suicides, have never been published, but it can be assumed that among Viennese Jews the number of suicides must have become greater than, or at least as great as, that of deaths from natural causes.

Hitler knew very well what he was doing when he changed the 'social welfare' for Jews and why he is having barracks built near Gänserndorf, Lower Austria – and by Jewish prisoners, to boot.[9]

The situation is such that I really can't say which Jews should be helped first in any rescue operation conducted from outside Germany. To be sure, on the one hand children, and on the other elderly and ill people (in Vienna there is only one Jewish hospital and one Jewish retirement home, both of them incredibly overfull and flooded with applications) need help the most. But men aged between 18 and 50 are exposed to the greatest danger. None of them is certain that he will not be summoned to the Gestapo one day and never return home again, that he will not one day be arrested on the street or pulled out of bed, that some reason will not be found to send him to a concentration camp.

Just as at the beginning of Nazi rule, when Jewish men and women had to go 'washing', scrubbing floors, cleaning Nazi barracks and toilets, shining boots or washing cars, a new tendency to use Jews as helots, as slaves, has emerged. They are arrested in the streets and used during scrap metal collection to carry the metal and load it onto lorries, or to shovel snow after a snowfall. Men who shovelled snow all day long were even rewarded: a sausage and bread at noon and the same in the evening.

In these circumstances, the situation of children is particularly miserable, and the most dreadful thing about it is the complete lack of hope in their lives. They have only one advantage over the adults, and that is that they have not yet been imprisoned or sent to concentration camps. However, I also know of cases in which 16- and 17-year-old boys who were in school together were arrested for 'communist activities' and thrown in prison. The Nazi's mental cruelty, especially in its propaganda and the press, is directed as much against children as against adults and the elderly. In the stands where the *Stürmer* is displayed, I saw pictures of Jewish babies: pretty children who looked just the way babies of white races generally look. Over the pictures was the headline: 'Future criminals'.

In late 1938, with few exceptions, Jewish children enjoyed neither schooling nor any kind of education, neither intellectual nor physical training. They could not engage in any sport or enter an educational institution, a swimming pool, a theatre or a cinema. When in the summer Jewish boys tried to swim in the Danube, at a place entirely outside the city, they were attacked, beaten and driven away. Special Nazi patrols patrolled the banks of the Danube for that purpose. For similar reasons, excursions and hikes were completely impossible. Parents were frequently afraid to allow their children to be in the street alone at all.

I can cite a few typical examples of the mood prevalent among Jewish children in Vienna. Two children from a very good family begged their parents finally to emigrate; the 11-year-old son wanted to go to a country where he could go swimming whenever he felt like it, and his 8-year-old sister wanted to live in a country where she could go to Schönbrunn every day. Schönbrunn is a former imperial palace with a large park and a zoo that had been accessible to everyone. The child, who lived close to Schönbrunn, cried every time she walked by it, and could not understand why she was suddenly no longer allowed to go into this park.

Another very precocious 12-year-old boy frequently had thoughts of suicide and repeatedly said to his mother: 'Mummy, if we are really so bad and no other country wants to take us in, it would be better to make an end of it now and turn on the gas.' A small boy of five whose father had hanged himself at the beginning of Nazi rule was so traumatized that he couldn't look a stranger in the face and even when addressed in the friendliest way immediately hid behind his mother's skirts.

The psychological state of Jewry in Vienna is even more dreadful than their material situation. Early in the morning, newspapers with large anti-Semitic headlines are on view everywhere on newspaper stands and in tobacco shops. In bookshops, the wildest hate pamphlets against Jews are displayed, frequently laid open at particular pictures or pages, in order to make it possible for passers-by to read them, even if they are not interested in buying them. Anti-Semitic posters are everywhere; pictures of Hitler and other Nazi bigwigs everywhere. But the worst thing is Dr Goebbels's hate speeches on the radio. Before every news broadcast, usually focused on some attack on Jews and foreign statesmen allegedly in the service of Jews (Roosevelt, La Guardia, Dr Benesch, Winston Churchill, Eden, Duff Cooper, et al.), an anti-Semitic quotation is trumpeted as a kind of introduction: 'Voltaire said about the Jews – Napoleon, Goethe, Seneca said about the Jews . . .' These quotations were often not only incomplete, distorted and taken out of context, but also sometimes simply incorrect. Even the Jewish writer Karl Emil Franzos was quoted. On days when one of the Nazi bigwigs gave a speech, anti-Jewish agitation always achieved a new high point. Even convinced

Nazi supporters were, they repeatedly openly admitted, disgusted by this kind of radio propaganda.

This campaigning against completely defenceless people who have done nothing wrong (anyone who had was already in prison) and who can be reproached for nothing other than their heritage is being carried on with unprecedented obstinacy. I never understood why during the World War the English Admiral Beatty once described the Germans as 'despicable beasts' – but now I understand it. In the hate campaigns against Jews, we see the 'blond beast' (an expression that Nietzsche coined for the Germans of his time, whom he knew very well) venting his bloodlust without restraint. When the Nazis repeatedly declare that 'The Jewish question will be resolved for Germany only when the last Jew has left German soil,' by that they don't mean emigration; they mean 'Juda verrecke', not 'Juda verreise' ['Death to Jews', not 'Emigrate, Jews!']. But even then they will continue to incite hatred towards Jews. When there are no more Jews left in Germany, then it will be against Jews in Czechoslovakia, Poland, Russia, America, Palestine or Guyana. For Nazis, anti-Semitism is not only an article of faith, part of their so-called world view; for them, persecuting Jews has long also been a tried and true means of pursuing their domestic and foreign policies.

# FRITZ GOLDBERG[1]

## Manuscript 245 (89)

*Born in 1898 in Stettin; grew up in Alsace-Lorraine, had lived in Berlin since 1920; married, two children; from 1929 to 1936, advisor in a stage and theatre publishing house; emigrated to New York via London in 1939.*

Thus my preparations for emigration were gradually coming to a close, becoming increasingly difficult as new restrictions were introduced on a daily basis. But before it was my turn, before I got my visa for America, I still had to live through that infamous 10 November, which sealed the fate of the Jews in Germany.

During the night of 9–10 November, an organized operation was carried out throughout Germany in which the synagogues were destroyed and all Jewish shops were looted and vandalized. Repeatedly, mobs also broke into private residences which they transformed into heaps of rubble. Everyone was talking about the events of that night, and anyone who had a shred of decency was indignant and disassociated himself from them or simply refused to believe them. An elderly gentleman who, to judge by his appearance, was probably a retired high official, stood before the ruins of a burnt-out temple. And while he stared at the remains of the walls, I heard him say to his neighbour: 'Many things may happen – but you can't tell me that there are Germans who would attack holy places!'

In my apartment, a small group of fearful people gathered, and we listened again and again to the account of someone who had been an eyewitness to the outrages committed that night. Suddenly the bell rang in the corridor. Two policemen pushed their way in and told me I was under arrest, without giving any reason or presenting a warrant for my arrest. They gave me no time to say goodbye to my family, let alone make any arrangements.

228

On the way to the police station, I discovered that these two officers were representatives of two basic German types. The older one
incarnated Germany before Hitler's accession to power. He was
polite, proper, clearly taken aback by the recent events; he even tried
to calm me down by speaking to me. The other, younger, was a real
National Socialist – already shameless in his tone, without the slightest sensitivity. He knew that my arrest had absolutely nothing to do
with me personally, and still he acted as though he had succeeded in
capturing a long-sought felon.

With me and after me, hundreds of fellow sufferers came into the
courtyard of the police headquarters, and among them I saw many
a familiar face. We were divided up into groups and had to stand
there bare-headed and silent – for hours, and still without the slightest
idea what they had in mind to do with us. Then lorries drove up,
into which we were loaded like animals, while the mob jeered at us.
And soon we guessed what awaited us: the concentration camp.

I do not wish to describe in detail the time that I spent there. The
conditions are well known, and enough reports have reached other
countries. Like many others, I had not thought it possible that all the
things that people said about these camps could be true. Today I
know that it is all true and that the reports even fall far short of the
reality. I came to see the basest instincts in people. I saw how dehu-
manized guards and supervisors humiliated, cursed, abused and
badgered their defenceless victims to death. Eighteen-year-old boys
revelled in tormenting their prisoners, including a number of men in
their sixties and seventies.

How many were unable to endure this hunger, this hardship, this
psychological and physical torture! I counted sixty dead in the first
three weeks and observed the death of an elderly colleague of mine
that I knew well, who had been denied medical care and who was
simply allowed to die miserably. The number of victims would have
been greater still had fellow prisoners not stepped in as paramedics
and sometimes secretly cleaned and bandaged the wounds that the
cold, or the hobnailed boots and clubs, the knives and rifle butts of
the Hitler mobs had inflicted on us and to which we were exposed
without protection. What happened in these camps is beyond all
human imagination.

During this time, my wife was working day and night to get me
released. It took forever before she even found out where I was. She
approached all the authorities and everyone who she thought might
be able to help. Among them was the National Socialist writer who
had invited me to the premiere of his play and in the meantime had

risen to a high rank. He too had lost his moral courage. He no longer dared to give his name on the telephone, and spoke only in a whisper. Moreover, he could offer no more help than anyone else. Everything bounced off the walls and iron gates of the state police.

The invitation sent to me by the American consulate in Berlin was the document that saved me. My wife proved to the authorities that I could leave the Reich within a very short time, and so I was finally released. I returned home feverish and covered with lice, with a suppurating wound on my foot and a ceaselessly bleeding injury to my hand. My little daughter didn't recognize me because my head had been shaved as prisoners' heads were.

In the few weeks I was away, the world had changed again. There was no longer any Jewish life. There was only a frightened and persecuted group of people who were no longer permitted to hold religious services; there was no restaurant, public square, hospital or place of amusement they could go to, and all their possessions had been stolen or destroyed. The fact that they had lost money, jewellery, silver, paintings and all other valuables hardly interested anyone any more.

The Aryan neighbours on our street, who had all known me for years, gave me an almost hearty welcome. The postman, the grocer, the chemist all expressed their sympathy. Even our concierge, the most insolent and cantankerous woman in the neighbourhood, told me with tears in her eyes that she didn't want any part in this thing. I visited the widows of my camp companions, saw the children who had lost their fathers, the mothers who had lost their sons in the most horrible way – and that was far, far worse.

Some of the most testing and stressful days were yet to come. The American consul refused to issue a visa for me and my family because the documentation was still insufficient. The deadline the authorities had set for my departure from Germany was approaching, and I knew what awaited me if I did not make it. But at the last moment salvation came: friends who lived in London had obtained a transit visa for me for England. I had to depart right away, leaving my wife and children behind – I didn't see them again for six months – and my mother and brother, who are still living under the heel of the German rulers; and at the price of losing the few things to which I was still attached: my library and all my manuscripts, articles, letters, notes and collections.

But I was a man again; I was free, I had returned to life. I was saved!

# HARRY KAUFMAN

## Manuscript 105 (108)

*Born in 1912 in Westphalia, childhood spent in Essen; later worked there in the shoe business; married; emigrated to the USA at the end of 1938.*

Then came the pogrom in November 1938, which fundamentally changed the whole situation for the Jews, which was already bad enough.

The action taken against Jews was triggered, according to the Nazis, [by] the shooting of the legation secretary vom Rath in Paris. This act, which was carried out by a Jewish adolescent, was laid at the door of 'world Jewry', which in this case resulted in the enraged German people demolishing, looting and setting most of the Jewish synagogues, community buildings, business buildings and restaurants on fire. That was what was reported in the Nazi press, which called the event an act 'of the seething soul of the people'.

This seething soul of the people looked like this: following a precise programme, SA and SS men in civilian clothing went from building to building with axes and crowbars, petrol and matches. How little truth there is in the Nazi account can be seen by the fact that not a single synagogue in the whole German Reich was spared destruction. If in fact no order had come down from above, in at least one or two places there would have been no pogrom, which moreover started everywhere at the same time. Here I want to describe what I myself saw and experienced and what I was told shortly afterwards.

Very early on the morning of Thursday, 10 November, we received a visit from an Aryan man to whom we had sold a few pieces of furniture because we were liquidating our household. When I asked him why he had come so early and for what reason, he answered: 'I

231

only wanted to see if my furniture is still intact.' In response to my astounded question, he then told me that all Jewish shops in the city were being demolished and that the synagogues and the youth centre belonging to the religious community were in flames.

Thereupon I drove into the city as fast as I could and took a short walk through the various main streets. I saw that all the Jewish shops had indeed been demolished and looted. Synagogues and the youth centre were burning brightly, and the fire brigade was protecting only the surrounding buildings from the danger of the fire spreading, whereas nothing was being done to put out the fires.

After I had returned home, my mother came and told us that all Jewish men were being arrested. She had been at the neighbour's when the police arrested two of her cousins and took them off to prison. As I was leaving the apartment shortly thereafter, I saw police officers go into a building not far away in which several Jewish families lived and soon afterwards come out again with three men I knew. Since I had been told to come to the American consulate in Stuttgart a few days later in order to pick up my entry visa, I was very anxious to remain free.

For that reason, I left Essen a few hours later with my wife and travelled to a nearby city where I spent the night at the home of a cousin who is unmarried – and was thus not endangered by the round-up. Late that night, my brother and father-in-law arrived unannounced. My brother was about to be arrested and had saved himself by jumping over the balcony as the police officers were trying to break down the door. Here I want to add that my brother later spent six weeks in hiding with an uncle and never went outside. Only in that way was he able to escape closer acquaintance with a concentration camp. Almost all our male friends, acquaintances and relatives aged between 15 and 70, and sometimes older, were arrested, though later on the elderly and sick were released again, while the rest of the unfortunate men were taken away to various concentration camps.

My wife and I succeeded in reaching Frankfurt unharmed, where fate in the form of arrest caught up with us as well. However, after we had proven that we were on our way to Stuttgart in order to emigrate, we were released after a short time and allowed to leave. Nonetheless, we were arrested a second time in the same city when we tried to continue our trip to Stuttgart. This time as well, we were allowed to go after waiting for an hour and having our papers examined. So that we would not be arrested again on our way from the police station to the train, a policewoman accompanied us. Along the way she said: 'Keep your chins up, it will be all right; we officials are just doing our duty.' She said goodbye in a very friendly way and wished us good luck.

In Stuttgart, we received our visas but, after hours of waiting and such terrible experiences, we were not in a condition to travel home that evening. The next morning, despite my visa, I was taken from my bed at 6.30 to the prison. There I had to remain until 4 p.m., after which I was told that I had to leave Germany within three weeks. My wife, who had done everything she could to get me released, was sent from one office to another without success. At the American consulate, she was told that this was the first case they had heard of in which people with valid emigration papers had been arrested.

In the prison itself, hundreds of Jews were brought in every hour, and questioned in the afternoon by Gestapo officials. They were badly treated, shouted at and threatened. Only a very few were allowed to leave the prison again. In my cell, which was actually designed for only two persons and into which more than 35 men had been packed like sardines, there were mainly older men, some of them in very poor health.

Here I should like to repeat a few of the stories I heard told by these men and which I, after all that I had personally experienced and seen, regard as true. A man from Trier, 55 years old, had all his papers for emigration to the USA ready and was planning to begin his voyage three days later on an English ship. On the night of the pogrom, he was taken out of the house, terribly beaten, and all his papers, including his passport and boat ticket, were torn up and burned. After he had been released in Trier, he immediately travelled to Stuttgart in order to get copies of his papers. On his arrival at the railway station, he was arrested by the police and taken to prison.

A man from Dortmund who is married to an American also had all his papers destroyed on the night of the pogrom and he had been beaten with rubber truncheons. On arriving in Stuttgart, he had the worst black eye I have ever seen. On his body – in the cell he briefly opened his shirt – there was not a single area that was not black and blue. A man from Stuttgart had had his arm broken and for three days he had been denied access to a doctor. The arm had become infected and was as thick as his thigh. Only then was he allowed to see a doctor. In addition, there was a 70-year-old man in the cell who was almost blind, and another of almost the same age who had serious heart problems and continually suffered heart attacks, in my opinion because of the bad air, the oppressive heat and stress.

233

On the following day my wife and I left Stuttgart, after we had received from the Gestapo a statement to the effect that 'The Jew H.K. has been released from protective custody in Stuttgart because he plans to emigrate soon.'

This statement was supposed to serve as proof, in the event of my being arrested again, that my papers had been checked and that I was legally at liberty. The next day, I presented this statement to the Gestapo in Essen, as I had been told to do in Stuttgart. The official there said that I should leave Germany as soon as I could because the Gestapo might otherwise change its mind and put me in a concentration camp too. I left Germany that same evening, after my wife had obtained for me the necessary 50 marks (about 20 dollars). Saying farewell to my mother was difficult; I was the second of her sons who was leaving her behind. I was not able to say goodbye to my brother, who was hiding in another city.

At the German border, I was thoroughly searched by two ticket inspectors, while two SS officers checked my papers. They went through my little suitcase, which contained nothing but essential items; they opened my shirt and searched my naked body for hidden money or other valuables. I was allowed to take with me my gold watch, which I had received from my company as an anniversary gift, but the chain attached to it was taken away from me on the ground that it was not part of the watch. The officials informed me that the chain would be sent to my wife, who had stayed behind to complete all the remaining tasks. Here, I want to add that my wife did in fact get the chain back as she was passing through Emmerich about six days later, after she had shown the officials the certificate proving that she had permission to take all the things with her.

In order to take our personal things with us – a very few pieces of furniture and a few pieces of jewellery – we had initially been asked to pay 4,000 marks (about 1,600 dollars). However, after my wife had made several visits to the currency exchange office in Düsseldorf, the fee she had to pay was reduced to 1,500 marks (600 dollars).

The official was dreadfully arrogant and on my wife's first visit he had her literally thrown out after she had told him that she could not pay the sum he demanded. Later, he told my wife that so far as he was concerned, we could take all the things with us without paying anything. But he was an official and it was his job to take the money and if he were to let us go without paying, his superiors would have his head.

When I was first in Zevenaar, the railway station on the Dutch side of the border, I really didn't know what I should do. The Dutch official laughed when he saw how agitated I was. A German lady who was sitting in the next compartment and who had overheard my conversation with the German official said: 'You've lost your gold chain but at least you got out.' I could only agree heartily and in Emmerich, where I had to change trains, I wrote a card to Essen, in order to inform my wife that I had crossed the border.

Later, I heard that we had in fact been lucky. Another Jewish man who was travelling on the same ship to America had been stripped at the German border station of all his valuables and money except for two dollars, even though he also had a certificate proving that he could take the things and the money with him and had paid all the fees. In my opinion – in this case SS men were involved – these people put these valuables and this money in their own pockets, since they calculated that any Jew would be glad to get out of Germany, even if he had to sacrifice everything he had. In any case, he would not have time to file a complaint, and thus I know of no case in which Jews complained about their belongings and money being taken away from them.

Thus ended my life in Germany,[1] and I am not sorry that I left Germany in order to be able to live as a free man in a free country. America has given us a new homeland, and we hope to be able to show our gratitude to it.

# AFTERWORD: NAZI MADNESS

## Uta Gerhardt

### The sociologist Edward Y. Hartshorne
### and the Harvard Project

In January 1933, the journalist Edgar Ansel Mowrer, who had for a decade been the Berlin correspondent for the *Chicago Daily News*, published a remarkably accurate description of the break-up of the Weimar Republic. *Germany Puts the Clock Back*[1] showed how Reich Chancellor Franz von Papen's 'Prussian coup' (*Preussenschlag*) on 20 July 1932 destroyed social-democratic Prussia, the last bastion of the republic, and thereby paved the way for the National Socialist mass movement under 'The Leader'. Mowrer's book, whose publication got him expelled from Germany, was read not only by leading American politicians such as Henry Morgenthau, Jr, Franklin D. Roosevelt's future Secretary of the Treasury, but also by a recent graduate of Harvard College, Edward Y. Hartshorne. Hartshorne was a politically engaged student in the Department of Ethics and Sociology, who had been honoured by his university in December 1932 as one of the best students in his class.

Hartshorne's interest in Germany was kindled in August 1932 when, at the age of 20, he served as the leader of a group of American students participating in the Experiment in International Living, one of whose founders was a young doctor involved in the Mental Health Reform movement, Kenneth Appel, who also came from Philadelphia. In this private youth camp, students from France, Germany, Belgium, England and the USA met for discussions in a Swiss castle. They debated issues of international understanding and afterwards travelled through Germany for two weeks. After his return, Hartshorne reported in the *Philadelphia Inquirer*, at the time one of the

236

major daily newspapers in Pennsylvania: 'I feel the idea will spread because it provides each young man with an international viewpoint.' Just a year later, he held a much more critical view: such a camp might well establish some friendships among the participants, but 'we are neither blind to the realities of the contemporary world, nor so optimistic for the world of the future, that we allow ourselves to believe that pure *friendship*, unorganized and undirected, can effectively put an end to war.'

When in November 1932 he was offered an opportunity to participate in another European camp the following year, Hartshorne suggested that a female student, with whom he was bound by friendship and soon by deep love, also be invited: 'This girl is 19, daughter of one of America's leading historians of Germany and the World War, was twice in Europe as a child, mostly in France, and two years ago spent a winter at the Marquartstein School.... Her languages are therefore excellent.' Elsa Minot Fay studied at Radcliffe College – which is associated with Harvard – where she was the head of the Liberal Club and the International Club. In May 1934, Elsa and Edward Hartshorne married. In the summer of 1939, Elsa's father, the historian Sidney Fay, was one of the organizers of the prize competition 'My Life in Germany Before and After 30 January 1933', to which we owe the eyewitness accounts on the pogroms of November 1938 on which this book is based.

In the winter of 1933–4, Hartshorne was a doctoral student in the History of Social Thought graduate programme in the University of Chicago's Department of Anthropology and Sociology. In early 1935, the Social Science Research Council gave him a travel grant. He planned his PhD thesis on German universities under National Socialism and wished to gather the necessary facts on site. From July 1935 to February 1936, Hartshorne and his wife lived in Berlin, where they stayed for a time at the home of the historian Friedrich Meinecke in Dahlem. Meinecke, who was a friend of Sidney Fay's, helped Hartshorne find crucial documents in the Prussian State Library on the reforming of the academic sector under National Socialism. In February 1936, the couple travelled back to Chicago and Cambridge by way of London, where Hartshorne studied the information collected by the Academic Assistance Council about scholars driven out of Germany. In his PhD thesis, which appeared in book form in 1937 under the title *The German Universities and National Socialism* and is still considered a standard work, Hartshorne gave a comprehensive account of how the traditional German university had been destroyed and political conformity had been enforced over scholarship.[2]

237

On 31 December 1935, Hartshorne, who was on a skiing holiday in the Dolomites, wrote to the sociologist Talcott Parsons, who had been his mentor at Harvard.[3] He spoke about his plans for the future, which remained fluid, and his hesitation about embarking upon an academic career. His mailing address, 'American Express in Berlin, Unter den Linden 4', was followed by a postscript: 'Incidentally, part of the N. S. Revolution has been the cutting down of all the Lindens on it! (Subway)! At least the Communists have not been blamed for that un-German act.' After he returned to the USA, Hartshorne wrote up his observations of Germany. Under the title 'The German Intellectual of Today',[4] he described the increasing pressure put on people to change their views. Thus, for example, he wrote about Meinecke's son-in-law, a doctor, that he had partly given in to Nazi indoctrination: 'Much as this able man dislikes the harm done to medical training in Germany by faculty dismissals on "racial" grounds, . . . he too found an easy way to achieve peace of mind. After all, the eugenics program, especially sterilization of those unfit to propagate the race, is in the direction of progress.'

The 12-year-old son of a professor who had been transferred, against his will, to a provincial university lectured him about Jews: 'To an American, this same boy, very bright and very bold, would subscribe every bit to the main articles of Nazi creed. The Jews were *on the whole* bad Germans, although there had been exceptions; therefore just as a teacher must punish the whole class because of the uproar created by a few unidentifiable mischief-makers, so all the Jews had to be eliminated from Germany because of the crimes of some. . . . With the most scornful look imaginable this little fellow (part-Jewish himself, although perhaps he did not know) could put the American in his place with: "You are such a *mixed* people that you don't *have* any real patriotic feeling."'

It can be assumed that, during his stay in Germany, Hartshorne heard about concentration camps: among his papers there is, neatly typed up, the then-popular satirical song about the 'ten little rabble-rousers' who disappeared one after the other into a camp because they had criticized the regime (saying, for example, that the Hitler Youth boys were 'lousy brats') or did something forbidden (for example, listening to radio broadcasts from London) until finally the last of them ended up in Dachau – 'and there were ten of them together again'.

Hartshorne was hardly alone in taking a sociological interest in the events transpiring in Germany. From January to May 1937 a group of lecturers and graduate students in sociology, including Hartshorne,

238

Robert K. Merton, Robert Bierstedt, Edward Devereux and Kingsley Davis, met at Harvard's Adams House. In long and intensive discussions chaired by Parsons, who had studied in Heidelberg in the 1920s, these young Americans sought to understand the German dictatorship as a society where propaganda replaced public opinion and force ruled out voluntary commitment.[5]

In the course of 1938, Hartshorne wrote further articles on the German universities under the Nazi dictatorship.[6] He was becoming an ever more acute observer of the unprecedented menacing events taking place on the other side of the Atlantic. In tranquil Cambridge, Massachusetts, he met people driven out of Germany, who told him the story of their gruelling experiences and this made him all the more conscious of the repression in the Third Reich. He meticulously recorded what was reported to him and took extensive notes in his diary – a practice that he was to continue for the rest of his life.

When American newspapers reported on the pogroms of November 1938, many Harvard scholars were highly concerned about what had happened. Up to that point, Parsons had not yet publicly expressed his aversion to Nazi rule, but in his theoretical work he had left no doubt that Germany was in a state of anomie, a chaos involving coercion and persecution. Now he became more explicit: his verdict appeared on 23 November in the *Radcliffe News*. National Socialism, he wrote, was a regime like no other. It meant both the destruction of European intellectual culture and denial of Christian virtues unprecedented in European history. It threatened modern life itself. Persecution of the Jews was no accident, he stated. They symbolized the world destined for destruction. One had to realize, Parsons went on, how profound National Socialism's hatred for western culture and institutions is: 'This makes it necessarily a deadly enemy for us. We must oppose it with all our strength.'[7]

The November pogrom in Germany was probably the turning point in how Hartshorne as well as Parsons felt about getting involved in anti-Nazi activities. While sitting by the fireside one evening in January 1939, Hartshorne – who had just become a father – wrote feelingly in his diary about his concern for the people being persecuted in Germany: 'It's hard to think that people just like us over there are committing suicide. Emigration – suicide – ghetto. We can't put ourselves in that position. Life just wouldn't do it, we say. Yet we live.' It became clear to him that he could not simply pursue an academic career for himself; he wanted to give his life a higher meaning, to do something for others:

Perhaps we live to *feel* – to know, to work, to do, to help, to see God, to feel beauty + pathos. Perhaps that's it? Or perhaps we just work a little, strive to understand things a little, try to do a few big things, to help make others happy a little, to see the vision of eternal stillness now + then + to be aware of the value of things. – Add them all up. Does *that* give the answer?

## The context of the prize competition

It is no longer possible to determine precisely who, in the spring or early summer of 1939, had the idea of organizing a prize competition on the subject 'My Life Before and After January 30th, 1933'. But there was a well-known model to emulate. In June 1934, Theodore Abel, Professor of Sociology at Columbia University in New York, had been able to organize a prize competition in Germany. With the permission of the Ministry of Information and Propaganda, a competition with prizes whose total value was 400 marks was announced. The 'best personal life history of an adherent of the Hitler movement' was sought, and every German who had been a member or supporter of the NSDAP on 1 January 1933 was eligible to participate.

Altogether, 683 manuscripts varying in length from one handwritten page to eighty typed pages were submitted to the organizers. Abel evaluated about 600 of these autobiographies in order to inform American readers about the Nazi dictatorship by reference to the motives and views of party members. The result was a book published in 1938: *Why Hitler Came into Power*.[8]

When Hartshorne read this book, he must have been shocked by it. The persecution in Germany in 1938 had revealed a reality vastly different from the one suggested by the autobiographical accounts Abel had collected in 1934. Although Abel had tried not to depict Hitler's dictatorship too uncritically, before showing, by means of six concluding case studies, how someone could become a party member, he summed up what in his view was the foundation for Nazi rule: 'Various events simultaneously threatened the personal and social values of many individuals, resulting in discontent and attempts to find methods of collective action. The solution offered by Hitler's group appealed to many because the flexible ideology of that group embodied a large number of popular current views.'[9]

Abel's book consisted of three parts: a historical account, an analysis and the six case studies. The historical part included quotations not only from the autobiographical material but also from Hitler's

*Mein Kampf.* The analytical part did mention anti-Semitism, but only as the fourth and last point in the chapter entitled 'Ideology as a Factor'. Abel described anti-Semitism as 'a prevailing sentiment in Germany after the World War'.[10] He cited long passages from the autobiographies in order to show that many Germans had had unpleasant personal encounters with Jews, which in turn had heightened their prejudice. According to Abel, however, what was new about National Socialism was the allegation that 'the Jews were trying deliberately to degrade the morals of the German nation.'[11] Abel's *naïveté* was obvious and barely concealed by clichés. Thus he assured his readers that there had always been people in Germany who had protested against the discrimination and persecution to which Jews were subjected – for example, 'the great writer G. E. Lessing'. Without mentioning that there were concentration camps and the Nuremberg Laws that had been in effect since 1935, Abel wanted to explain to his readers 'why the main ingredients of the ideology – the idea of National Socialism, the principle of leadership, and the racial doctrine – exercised an appeal and therefore contributed to its growth'.[12]

Hartshorne published a review of Abel's book in the April issue of the *Journal of Social Philosophy*.[13] In it, he first praised Abel's successful account of the rise of the totalitarian Nazi movement to absolute power in the state, but launched two criticisms that were devastating. The playing-down of anti-Semitism in Abel's book might be explained, he granted, by the fact that the autobiographical accounts had been written for foreign readers: these National Socialists had depicted their regime for an American audience. Worse, however, in Hartshorne's view, without being aware of it, Abel had justified Nazi rule:

> The subliminal distortion of the book consists in the fact that it creates the impression that the Nazi movement was inevitable and its victory pre-programmed . . . The reader, if he does not want to succumb to the illusion of fatefulness, must continually keep in mind that this is not a history of post-war Germany but rather the history of a political movement written by those who made it and who were made by it.[14]

Methodologically, the Harvard prize competition was essentially based on the so-called Chicago School of Sociology.[15] Since the turn of the century, interviews, letters and other authentic materials dealing with social issues and disenfranchised groups had been collected in Chicago. From these emerged works such as the five-volume collection on the fate of Polish immigrants in Chicago[16] or a study of the life of 'hobos', the migrant workers who practically lived on the railways.[17] In the first half of the 1930s, a regular life-history method was developed on the basis of these studies.[18] Using autobiographical materials, larger empirical research projects could now report on the hardships of the present time – the most famous of these were a memorandum written for the Social Science Research Council on the difficulties faced by an average American family during the Great Depression[19] and a study of the effect of unemployment on men.[20]

Of the three organizers of the prize competition, Hartshorne was the only one who had already long had a scholarly interest in National Socialism. It may have been through him that his father-in-law, Sidney Fay, first realized the desperate situation of the Germans. Although as a historian Fay was very well acquainted with German history, he apparently began to examine National Socialism closely only when he became involved in organizing the prize competition. The same goes for the psychologist Gordon Allport (1897–1967). He had studied for a time in Berlin with the Gestalt psychologist Kurt Lewin, who had been able to flee to the USA in August 1933.

Allport's main work – *Personality: A Psychological Interpretation*[21] – was partly based on psychoanalysis, but its main thesis was that a person's current life-situation was a major influence on the development of his personality. In 1939, Allport was elected president of the American Psychological Association; in the same year, he founded, in the Department of Psychology at Harvard, a section for research into the psychological foundations of political action.[22] Until 1944, this section issued 'Worksheets on Morale', readable and instructive texts about propaganda and the roots of prejudice. Large philanthropic associations undertook to distribute these texts free to millions of Americans all over the country. Among the themes were 'Democratic vs. Totalitarian Morale in Groups', 'Points of Attack for anti-Nazi Propaganda' and 'The ABCs of Scapegoating'.

In Boston, in collaboration with the Massachusetts Committee on Public Safety, Allport organized a round-the-clock telephone service where callers could get information on rumours launched by German propaganda in the United States. Such rumours sought to fuel Americans' fear of a war and strengthen them in their indifference to the political events of the day. Finally, as the editor of the *Journal of Abnormal and Social Psychology*, in 1943 Allport made it possible for the first reports on the concentration camps to be published in a scholarly journal. In two long articles, the psychologists Bruno Bettelheim and Curt Bondy described the brutal reality of the concentration camps, the victims and their tormentors, which produced a shocked reaction everywhere in the USA.[23]

Sidney B. Fay (1876–1967) had studied at the Sorbonne and in Berlin and became well known in 1928, when he published a two-volume work on *The Origins of the World War*.[24] The book was debated nationwide, above all because of Fay's thesis that the First World War had not been started by Germany alone but had been the outcome of a configuration of two hostile power blocs, the Triple Entente and the Triple Alliance. Fay argued that a confrontation between these two power blocs finally became inevitable; those responsible for the war were not only in Berlin but also in Vienna, London, Paris and St Petersburg. In the 1930s, Fay published two shorter works on Germany – in 1937 a history of the rise of Prussia up to the end of the eighteenth century, and in 1939 a selection of writings on Germany by the poet Bayard Taylor, who had produced the first English translation of Goethe's *Faust* and died in 1878 in Berlin, where he was the accredited American State Minister. From the autumn of 1941 on, Sidney Fay kept a sharp eye on the current war situation and international problems in his role as editor of the journal *Current History*. In the journal's first issue, published three months before the United States entered the war, he anticipated not only the victory over Hitler's Germany but also the crucial question of the post-war order: 'Germany should not be dismembered.'[25] He concluded: 'Such a federal Germany (somewhat after the Weimar model of 1919, but avoiding some of the mistakes that are now evident), brought about by the Germans themselves, but not imposed by the victors, would probably be the best solution for Germany herself and for the future peace of Europe as a whole.'[26]

Hartshorne, the youngest of the three organizers of the prize competition, was the driving force among them. He wrote the German-language description of the prize competition and he also travelled to Europe to personally invite exiles to participate in the project. In 1939, Donald B. Watt, the executive director of the Experiment in International Living, had asked Hartshorne to accompany another group of Americans to Europe. Hartshorne's trip to France, the Netherlands and England at the end of August may have served this purpose, but he also used it to promote the prize competition. In any case, two years later his curriculum vitae notes for the year 1939: 'Visited refugee centers offices in Paris, Holland and London, August 21–September 2 in this connection.'[27]

Three weeks after the announcement of the prize competition in the *New York Times* and one day before Hartshorne's return to

243

America, Germany invaded Poland, and France and Great Britain declared war on Hitler. Four weeks later, after the conquest of Poland, the war at first seemed to be over; for England, it was for the time being a 'phoney war', but in the spring of 1940, and especially in the summer of 1941, the German attack on large parts of Europe posed a threat to the United States as well. But until December 1941, Americans continued to see the conflict as 'the European war'.

Between September 1939 and 1 April 1940, the deadline for submissions to the 'My Life Before and After January 30th, 1933' competition, more than 250 émigrés sent their life stories to Cambridge. In addition to Allport, Fay and Hartshorne, others took part in the evaluation of the texts, such as the cultural psychologist Edward Devereux and the psychology student Ernest (Ernst) Jandorf, who reported on his internment in Dachau (Jandorf died in 1944 while serving in the American army). Finally the prizes were awarded. The first prize was divided between Carl Paeschke, a Social Democrat and journalist from Upper Silesia, and Gertrude Wickerhauser Lederer (cf. pp. 110–14), each of whom received $250. The final report on the project, which Hartshorne mentions in a letter written in 1941, has unfortunately not been preserved.

The sole scholarly outcome of the prize competition, which sought to be a 'purely scientific collection of materials', was an article in the journal *Character and Personality*. The article,[28] which appeared in October 1941, was signed by Allport, Jandorf and the psychologist Jerome Bruner, a young scholar who in the summer of 1942 was named deputy director of the survey department in the newly created Office of War Information. The two Hartshornes – Elsa and Edward – were mentioned, along with five others, only in a footnote that also thanked the Committee on Research in Social Science at Harvard University for its generous financial support for this project.

The article examined ninety selected autobiographies submitted for the prize competition from the point of view of the psychology of personality. Five conclusions were drawn from the material:

1 The adults tended to brace themselves mentally in order not to feel defenceless when exposed to persecution.
2 When a persecuted person withstood the ordeals, this was a sure sign of a capacity, anchored in his personality, which made him able to master catastrophes in his social environment.
3 Only a very small number of participants in the prize competition ever seemed to have harboured sympathy for the Nazis; most of

them were still haunted by the fear that the regime instilled in its victims, and they suffered angst as émigrés.

4  That most of their friends had disappeared, plus the loss of their occupation and property, had caused extreme frustration in the afflicted, and many refugees seemed to have developed some kind of personality disorder; they either suffered from resignation, escaped into daydreams or had a strong yearning to belong, a feeling that sometimes resulted in their readiness to align themselves with, or submit readily to, any kind of repressive regime, or else cultivate powerless feelings of rage and/or some overwhelming need to punish.

5  Psychological conflicts in some SS and SA men that were reported in some of the autobiographies (for example, that a policeman secretly returned to the house in the evening after the search to bring back stolen property) suggest that at least a few convinced National Socialists had at least some guilt feelings. 'The obvious conclusion must be that these men suffered acutely from their activities with pangs of conscience and conflict. Whether a regime demanding from its adherents so schizoid an adjustment can survive is the fateful question before the world today.'[29]

## 'Nazi Madness' – The book project

In April 1941, Ernest Jandorf presented his own study.[30] In a manuscript of over a hundred pages, he analysed the material submitted for the prize competition using the life-history method and drawing on Abel's study, *Why Hitler Came Into Power*. He wanted to show that Nazi domination included all the 'domains of human existence and life-planning': 'It is not wild speculation to maintain that everyone who lived in Germany during these years, whether Christian or Jew, rich or poor, young or old, was decisively affected by the events.'[31] But then he added an astonishing qualification: 'Since we ourselves were unable to obtain Nazi life-histories, the prize competition from which our material is gathered yields only the story of the revolution as told by its victims, the refugees in Germany.'[32]

Hartshorne did not share the latter viewpoint. In December 1939, he presented a paper at the annual meeting of the American Sociological Society on 'Socio-psychological Effects of National Socialism as Revealed in Life-History Documents'.[33] He did not feel that the life stories taken from the prize competition were second-best as choice of empirical material. On the contrary, he had held a different viewpoint from the start – and may have shifted his understanding further towards the perspective of Parsons during the summer of 1940 when they worked together as sociology teachers at Harvard.

In August 1940, Parsons wrote a memorandum for the Council for Democracy, a group that supported Roosevelt's efforts to convince the nation of the necessity of intervening in the European war. Parsons made it clear in his memorandum how different American democracy was from National Socialism.[34] His memorandum listed five structural features of the latter: nationalism, socialism, anti-intellectualism, militarism and particularism (the Führer cult). The Führer cult was the most dangerous of these: 'There is considerable possibility that large elements of the population could be organized under the leadership principle in a way which could be deeply subversive to our structure of authority.'[35] Although there was discrimination of coloured people, Jews and immigrants from Latin America or the Slavic countries in the United States, Parsons said, only in a democratic country could equality of rights be achieved for all citizens one day.

In November 1940, Parsons became, on behalf of Harvard, the chair of the Committee on National Morale of American Defense, a loosely organized group of university professors who devoted their scholarship to the battle against National Socialism. Hartshorne became his deputy, and together they organized a lecture series in which German history since the Wilhelmine Empire was presented as the background of National Socialism.[36] Hartshorne now concerned himself with the question as to how Germans' longing for freedom could be reconciled sociologically with the Führer principle. He saw the dreamy certainty with which the Germans expected victory under National Socialism as a sign of the naive belief in the German 'master race', a late product of the anti-bourgeois spirit of the German *Jugendbewegung* (Youth Movement), which had been converted into aggressiveness in the songs of the Hitler Youth, who chanted: 'Today Germany belongs to us and tomorrow the world.'

In May 1941, Hartshorne's slim book, *German Youth and the Nazi Dream of Victory*, appeared in the series *America in a World at War*.[37] In the foreword, he wrote that he 'is now engaged in editing and interpreting more than 200 unpublished autobiographies by Germans, written during the last year, describing their lives as influenced by the Nazi Revolution'. At the time, he seems to have been the only one of the three organizers of the prize competition who was still working on the material. In his book on German youth, Hartshorne distinguished three generations of Germans which were each affected in its own way by the mysticism of the Nazi world view: the 'pre-war generation', the 'war generation' (within which Hartshorne distinguished between pacifists, internationalists and those whom the First World War had uprooted socially and radicalized politically, among them Nazi leaders such as Göring, Goebbels, Himmler and Hitler himself), and finally the 'post-war generation'. In different ways, the defeat in the First World War had become a turning point in the lives of these three generations, and this was reflected in the Harvard project autobiographies: 'The tragedy of the appeal of this mysticism to the youth of the post-war period was that it offered them a dreamy refuge from the pressing problems of the day.'[38]

Hartshorne was convinced that the ruling power in Germany was in the hands of a criminal clique. In the same year, he deepened this insight, which was in no way obvious to Americans, in two sociological articles. In 'Reactions to the Nazi Threat: A Study of Propaganda and Culture Conflict',[39] he analysed the ideological message in German propaganda. Although some ideological doctrines could be observed in most cultures, the dictatorship in Nazi Germany forced its *Weltanschauung* ruthlessly on its citizens, threatening danger to life and limb to those who refused to conform. According to Hartshorne, the 'strategy of terror'[40] overshadowed everyday life everywhere, if only through the fact that the 'Hitler salute' [*Hitlergruss*] was obligatory: 'Non-conformists, easily identified, are soon eliminated, while conformists in overt behaviour gradually find their minds and emotions "regimented" as well.'[41] But Hartshorne pointed out that it was not only in Germany that propaganda interfered with common sense. In the United States as well, Nazi propaganda tricked many people into condoning, even supporting, the Nazi regime, actively or passively, consciously or unconsciously. Sometimes, Hartshorne noted, even social scientists refused to admit how terrible the reality was in Germany when they downplayed the danger of, and involuntarily, maybe from fear, identified with the Nazi aggressor. Whom did Hartshorne have in mind?

The second article, written in 1941 – a fascinating study of the Germans' devotion to their charismatic leader[42] – remained unpublished. Hartshorne interpreted the 'Führer complex' psychologically, as an uncritical idealization, together with a blind obedience and passionate devotion to the Führer (*Kadavergehorsam* and *Führerschwärmerei*; Hartshorne used the German terms); they are two sides of the same thing, namely the quasi-religious belief emanating from insecurity and fear and that in turn was a reaction to the aggression that stemmed from an apparently hopeless situation. The charismatic spirit had a long history in Germany:

The deviation in the direction of charisma is characterized as being *echt deutsch*, a 'strong' Germany, true to the values of *Blut und Eisen* and of the mystical dream of German unity: *Deutschland über alles, ersehnte Einigkeit*. The personality stereotype of the soldier, the hero, the *Ritter*, the *Kämpfer*, the *Führer*. It is *Gemeinschaft*. In politics there is the leadership principle, totalitarianism, militarism. Loyalty, self-sacrifice, unthinking obedience take precedence over the 'western' values of decency, humanitarianism and 'fair play'.[43]

But Hartshorne was sure that the regime would not last for ever: subjection to the charismatic leader would end with a terrible awakening when the dominance of the Führer collapsed.

In the summer of 1941, the United States was still not involved in the war. Since November 1939, it had been supporting the British war effort, and in September 1940 general conscription had been introduced, American industry was being converted to military production, and since February 1941 the United States had also been financing Great Britain's battle against Germany through the Lend-Lease Agreement. Nonetheless, the isolationists, who wanted to keep America out of the war, were still a strong influence on the American public. Even after Germany's invasion of the Soviet Union, the America First movement, with its figurehead Charles Lindbergh, had millions of supporters.[44] In a three-part series published in July 1941 in the *Christian Science Monitor*, one of the largest daily newspapers in the country, Hartshorne accused America's isolationist forces of downplaying the danger of the Nazi regime at a time when large parts of Europe had already fallen under its yoke: 'Our civilizing influence can most effectively be best preserved by defeating the arch enemy of our civilization, not be stupidly waiting, ostrich-like, until the danger strikes at our heart.'[45]

Hartshorne stated that Germany had been the first victim of the National Socialists, followed by Austria, Czechoslovakia, Poland and many others. In America, Hartshorne suggested, many citizens felt that the Nazis were, after all, not so bad, and in any case posed no real threat to their nation. But Americans had to see the deadly danger, he warned, and they should not try to reassure themselves by belittling the threat. Germany's Jews had been a dramatic illustration: 'Amazing was the persistence with which the German Jews refused to take Hitler's threats at their face value. Five and a half years after he came to power, during which time the Jews had been disenfranchised, all but excluded from economic and cultural life and persecuted in numerous other ways, there were still so many Jews who

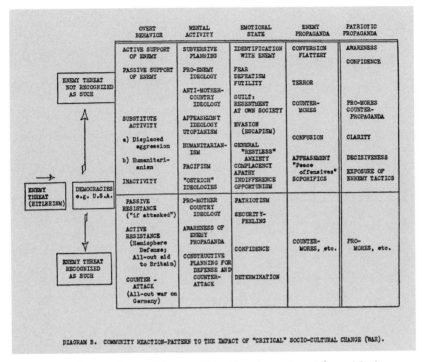

DIAGRAM B. COMMUNITY REACTION-PATTERN TO THE IMPACT OF "CRITICAL" SOCIO-CULTURAL CHANGE (WAR).

**Figure 3:** The caption to Diagram B in Hartshorne's article on Nazi propaganda shows how complicated the scenario was that had to be taken into account in the early 1940s when the average American in the community reacted to the threat of Hitlerism in his overt behaviour either by indifference or action, which could range from active attack to support of the enemy

had failed to emigrate that Hitler had to stage the ghastly pogrom of November 1938 as a final effort to overcome their psychic inertia!'[46]

In the early summer of 1941, it must have become clear to Hartshorne that he could use the materials collected in the framework of the prize competition in his battle against Americans' indifference. The earliest document preserved among Hartshorne's papers is a list in which he wrote down – in no discernible order – the names and numbers of the autobiographies that might prove useful. One of these lists was entitled 'Pogrom Study'. Another list contained references to passages in the texts; on the cover of the folder was written by hand: 'Record & Mss. Re: November Pogrom 1938 ... 82 Mss. Relevant ... Book I and #'s 1–197.' Mrs Wilson, clearly a capable

NAZI MADNESS: NOVEMBER 1938

By E. Y. Hartshorne and Collaborators

INTRODUCTION: A lesson from Nazi Germany for free men, told by participants and analyzed by experts.

PART I: <u>WHAT HAPPENED?</u>

Chapter I. THE WORLD REACTS

Newspaper accounts of the outbursts in Nazi Germany as reflected in press excerpts from leading papers of New York, London, Paris, Rome, Moscow, and Tokyo.

Chapter II. THE PEOPLE SUFFER

This chapter will show how the pogrom looked "from the inside". Here will be reproduced the first-hand stories of the victims, stories excerpted by the author from the more than 250 unpublished autobiographies in his possession. Certain stages in the development will be distinguished:

1. Expulsion of the Polish Jews in October 1938.
2. The murder of Von Rath early in November.
3. The destruction of household and commercial property belonging to Jews on November 11.
4. The burning of the synagogues.
5. The sequestering and fining of the Jewish population.
6. The arrest of all able-bodied Jews and their transportation to Concentration Camps.
7. The panic and pressure for emigration.

Chapter III. GERMANY EXPLAINS

Here excerpts from the leading German (Nazi) newspapers and legislative sources show the official myth by which the Nazi leaders sought to justify these outrages: namely, that they were only a "natural response of popular indignation" resulting from the murder of the German legation official Von Rath in Paris by a Polish Jew.

PART II: <u>WHY DID IT HAPPEN?</u>

Chapter IV. THE SYNTHETIC POGROM

A. <u>A persecution made to order: the alleged purpose.</u>
B. <u>The hidden purposes.</u>
C. <u>The effect.</u>

APPENDICES

A. <u>Description of the autobiographical materials.</u> These were collected by three members of the Harvard faculty (Gordon W. Allport, Sidney B. Fay, Edward Y. Hartshorne) less than a year after the November pogrom in response to a prize competition which they organized in 1939-40.

B. <u>The development of the anti-Semitic movement under the Nazi Government.</u>

**Figure 4:** The table of contents and outline of *Nazi Madness*, the book that Hartshorne was unable to complete, gives an overview of what he planned to convey to the American audience secretary in Harvard's sociology department who was proficient in German, was assigned to copy the selected passages.

The eyewitness accounts were the heart of the book that Hartshorne now planned to publish under the title *Nazi Madness: November 1938*. The outline for the book was preserved among his papers.

The book was intended to make Americans realize how serious the threat posed by National Socialism was and also to prepare them for war: 'A lesson from Nazi Germany for free men, told by participants and analysed by experts.'

In a letter written on 25 August 1941, Hartshorne offered the publisher, John Farrar of Farrar and Rinehart, which had published his book on German youth, two publication projects. One was a small study of about a hundred pages: 'Because of my deep concern over the unenlightened state of American public opinion with regard to Germany and its intentions, I have been searching for the right means of bringing home the necessary lessons to American readers in some brief publication. I could . . . include . . . evidences of the fundamental role of force and aggression in the Nazi system. I thought of a small book of about one hundred pages.'[47] The sketch that Hartshorne enclosed in his letter to Farrar has not been preserved among his papers. Three days later, Farrar replied: unfortunately, this project was not suitable for his publishing programme, but Viking Press, which published scholarly books for a general audience, might be interested. Farrar did not even mention the second project.

The selection of eyewitness accounts that Hartshorne described as 'probably unequalled in any other collection anywhere' may have been the collection taken from the material of the Harvard project. The manuscript, which bore the working title 'Nazi Madness: November 1938', was found among Hartshorne's papers and runs to about 500 pages. The outline calls for two parts or four chapters. Part I (chapters 1–3) was to be called: 'WHAT HAPPENED?'; Part II (chapter 4), 'WHY DID IT HAPPEN?' An appendix was to explain the prize competition, and a further appendix was to describe the dramatic increase in anti-Semitism in Germany since 1933.

Chapter 1 was to be based on the newspaper articles that had been published in New York, London, Paris, Rome, Moscow and Tokyo regarding the events of 9–10 November.[48] Forty-eight such articles, copied out by hand – not in Hartshorne's handwriting – were specially collected for the book. The horror was worldwide; in South Africa, the *Cape News* reported on 12 November 1938: 'Responsibility for the orgy of destruction & looting . . . lies directly on the Ministry of Propaganda, whose newspapers from the first used the

251

assassination in Paris to inflame the Germans' dangerous hatred of everything Jewish. The actual actors in this sordidly horrible business seem to have been the young people of the Nazi party.'[49]

Chapter 2 was to reproduce the eyewitness accounts. Using excerpts from the texts chosen by Hartshorne, seven levels of persecution, culminating in expulsion, were to be described. The accounts were supposed to range from the deportation of the Polish Jews in October 1938 to the murder of vom Rath and the destruction of Jewish property and the synagogues, and then to the transportation of people to concentration camps; at the end came forced flight and the panic of emigration.

For chapter 3, Hartshorne had prepared a collection of newspaper reports from National Socialist Germany. Thus the formerly liberal *Frankfurter Zeitung* wrote on 12 November 1938: 'The German people are an anti-Semitic people. They cannot stand it that the parasitical Jewish race continues to impugn their rights, nor would they be provoked by them any more as a nation.' To give an example of how that same newspaper had reported on the Nazis prior to their seizure of power, Hartshorne selected an article from the *Frankfurter Zeitung* for 3 April 1932 which stated: 'One thing we all know: we can judge a politician or statesman only by whether he has used successfully for the welfare of the nation the powers that he has been given. Herr Hitler can hardly say that about himself.' For Hartshorne, such juxtapositions made it clear how quickly and how radically the mood in Germany had shifted under the Nazis.

In Part II, Hartshorne tried to answer the question: 'WHY DID IT HAPPEN?' The subtitle 'The Synthetic Pogrom' indicated the direction this would take. No doubt Hartshorne wanted to argue – and the titles for the subsections confirm this hypothesis – that the pogroms of November 1938 were not spontaneous. Among the material in Hartshorne's papers is a memorandum prepared by an émigré German entitled: 'Are the November Pogroms spontaneous outbreaks of the wrath of the people, or have they been prepared long in advance? Analysed with special regard to the laws and administrative measures that preceded them.' The author was Fritz Abraham, a specialist in administrative law and a former government official who had presumably emigrated from Germany in the winter of 1938 or the spring of 1939.[50]

In fifteen paragraphs, with insightful examples and highly persuasive argumentation, Abraham discussed the single 'goal' of the November pogroms: the exclusion of Jews from all areas of life in Germany. The string of laws and administrative regulations issued throughout the year 1938 could only have this one explanation: the dates of anti-Jewish legislation were 6 February (highest tax rates for Jews), 26 April (registration of Jewish property), 6 July (cancellation of the right to run or own a business, retroactive to 1 January 1939), 22 July (obligatory identity card for Jews, with the additional name of Israel or Sara), 15 September (loss of licence for doctors and lawyers), to name but a few. Abraham stated:

> Even before November 1938, Jewish shops in Berlin were being defaced, and 'spontaneous' SA had lists giving them directions where to go . . . These lists were veritable proscription lists compiled in the autumn of 1938. A few officials tried to keep Jews they knew off the lists. I know of at least one such case with which I am familiar in every detail.

For Hartshorne, *Nazi Madness: November 1938*, the book for which the eyewitness accounts of the pogroms were to provide the core, was supposed to make Americans realize how dangerous the Nazis were. He hoped that the supporters of America First isolationism, who even in summer 1941 would not recognize Hitler as the enemy of civilization, would finally see how violence and infamy ruled in contemporary Germany.

In summer 1941, Hartshorne took leave from Harvard for the winter semester 1941–2. Harvard University and the Harvard-Radcliffe Bureau of International Research released him from teaching duties on full pay. He was to spend the semester working on the study, *Social and Psychological Aspects of National Socialism, as Revealed in Life-History Documents*. At the same time, however, in a letter of 10 July 1941, Hartshorne also applied for a position in the Office of the Coordinator of Information (COI) in Washington, the predecessor of the Office of Strategic Services (OSS) and the Office of War Information to be established the following year.

On 1 September 1941, instead of starting on his book, Hartshorne left Harvard and went to work for the government. As an expert in the Research and Analysis Branch of the COI, his job was to compile reports on the current war situation. He was one of a number of social scientists who used the extensive materials available in the Library of Congress to prepare research and analysis reports that are still regarded today as impressive works. Hartshorne went to Washington willingly and enthusiastically; he wanted to make his personal contribution to the battle against National Socialism. However, when he entered the COI, he had to agree that he could no longer publish his work under his own name as long as he worked for the government, a rule he had to obey. So he had to postpone all book plans until after the war.

When Hartshorne accepted the job in Washington, the fate of *Nazi Madness: November 1938* was sealed. The work for which he had been granted leave of absence from Harvard would never be written. Over the following years, the pile of manuscripts sat unattended in his study in Cambridge. In his diary entries, he occasionally asked himself when he might find the time to work on the book that he still planned to write.

Hartshorne continued to work with Talcott Parsons for American Defense Group, and at the end of 1941 they conceived the idea of writing a book entitled *German Social Structure and National Psychology*.[51] They sent a proposal to various publishers. But the project went nowhere, and in 1942 Parsons published his preparatory work in the form of three articles that appeared in sociological journals.[52]

## Re-education

As European dictatorships consolidated their hold on Europe – after Mussolini in Italy and Hitler in Germany, Franco had established himself in Spain – and as the situation on the European continent became increasingly threatening, a growing number of American scholars came to study totalitarianism. In 1939, the psychiatrist Edward A. Strecker, who worked with Kenneth Appel, among others, at the University of Pennsylvania, delivered a series of lectures in New York that was published the following year. *Beyond the Clinical Frontiers* was a plea for the application of the still young science of social psychiatry to the understanding of the totalitarian mass movements of the 1930s.[53]

In 1941, Richard Brickner, a New York neurologist and psychiatrist, began his study of the paranoid aspect of National Socialism.[54] His book *Is Germany Incurable?*[55] appeared in April 1943 and became a bestseller. For more than a year, it aroused intense interest throughout the country and brought the *Saturday Review of Books*, then a popular forum of public opinion, more letters from readers than any other subject. Brickner's thesis was that Germany as a nation – not every individual German – had long behaved like an 'individual who suffered from the most dangerous psychological disorder, paranoia'; were Germany a patient, the psychiatrist would diagnose paranoia: 'It is paranoia, as grim an ill as mind is heir to, the most difficult to treat, the only mental condition that frightens the psychiatrist himself – because, unless checked, it may end in murder. Murder is the logical denouement of its special outlook on the world.'[56]

Brickner had a solution to propose, which was based on psychiatry: re-education – a therapeutic pact between the doctor and what were the remaining clear (that is, sound) elements of the patient's personality – then the only means of healing paranoid delusions. 'If the Germany-group contains a sizable number of individuals, however unorganized and unaware of one another, whose emotional values are prevailingly non-paranoid, the outside world has a clear area at hand to work with and from in treating the Germany-group case.'[57]

Hartshorne was familiar with social psychiatry. His sister Emily Hartshorne Mudd (married to a molecular biologist), with whom he had planned a project on life-histories in the late 1930s, had established the Clinic for Marriage Counselling at the University of Pennsylvania, and she and her brother were both supporters of the Mental Health Movement, a strong current in psychiatry in the 1930s and 1940s, when people believed that mental hygiene could help solve psychiatric problems in everyday life. Mudd published her work in a scholarly journal in 1939, analysing one hundred life-histories under the perspective of mental hygiene.[58]

The title Hartshorne chose for his book project – *Nazi Madness: November 1938* – fitted perfectly into this scientific context. This book would continue to occupy him during the following years when he came to serve OWI at home and abroad and eventually transferred to the Psychological Warfare Division. As he mentions in his diary, he kept thinking about going back to his book after the war was over. After the victory over Germany, he wanted to collect further autobiographies – by Germans who had survived National Socialism, who had managed not to succumb to it: how did these people withstand the pressure, how had they been able to endure their fear?[59]

Nearly everything Hartshorne did between 1941 and 1946 could be summed up under the rubric 're-education'. First he worked at the COI as an expert on German propaganda and morale in Germany. Then he moved to the Research and Analysis Branch of the Office of Strategic Services (OSS), where he wrote, for example, a memorandum on the controversial issue of whether the regime might collapse as a result of the Allied bombing of German cities. In the OSS, he met German social scientists who had emigrated from Germany – Paul Baran, Felix Gilbert, Hajo Holborn, Herbert Marcuse, Franz Neumann and Hans Speier. In addition to analyses of the situation in Germany, this group of experts also produced, starting in 1944, shocking memoranda on the more than 1,600 concentration camps in Germany, amassing evidence that would be used by the International Military Court at the Major War Criminals trial in Nuremberg in 1945–6.

In spring 1943, Hartshorne became a lecturer in the Office of War Information. Since the summer of 1942, first in the USA, then in England as well, this office had been preparing officers for duty as future representatives of the military government in Germany. He lectured on the Nazi propaganda machine, the Gestapo, the concentration camps. For this purpose he also made use of a few of the eyewitness accounts about Buchenwald, Dachau and Sachsenhausen that were submitted for the prize competition.

In October 1943, Hartshorne joined the combat troops. He became an interrogator with the Psychological Warfare Division (PWD) in Algiers. After the German defeat in North Africa and in preparation for the Allied landing in Italy, German prisoners were to be questioned regarding the condition of the Wehrmacht. In November 1944, the transcripts of Hartshorne's interrogations of Prince Ludwig of Bavaria, two generals and a few members of the German Embassy in Rome were requested by Edward Stettinius, the acting Secretary of State in Washington.

In early summer 1944, Hartshorne met Klaus Mann in Rome. Both of them were at that time associated with the PWD, where they were working on the preparation of leaflets urging Wehrmacht soldiers to defect. On 21 May, Mann wrote in his diary: 'This morning here . . . Caserta – the incredible "Palazzo". PWD office there. Mr. Hartshorne.' On 3 August – still in Rome – he wrote: 'Evening at the home of Mrs. Leni Boccianti, with Hartshorne etc. Music on the terrace.' On 7 September, north of Florence: 'Letters to Robert Sherwood, Hartshorne, Col. McCulloch, Mielein.' And on 4 October, now back in Rome, Mann wrote once again to Hartshorne, who had been transferred in the meantime to London.[60]

During this period, both Mann and Hartshorne wrote texts in which they contrasted two German soldiers – one a supporter of the regime, the other not. Both drew on original sources; Hartshorne used the diaries of two soldiers that had been found in an abandoned German pillbox, while Mann compared the records of the interrogation of two Germans, their views of National Socialism, their concerns and fears, their relationship to the war and to civilian life.[61]

In July 1944, Hartshorne seems to have been one of the liaison officers between the German ambassador to the Vatican, Ernst von

Weizsäcker, and the Allies.[62] After the failure of the attempt to assassinate Hitler on 20 July, he was transferred to London, where he collaborated on the preparations for the re-education of occupied Germany. His team selected the films that Germans were to be shown immediately after the capitulation. In November of that year, Hartshorne returned to the United States, where he advised research groups that were preparing a comprehensive survey of the German population for the United States Strategic Bombing Survey (it was carried out between March and July 1945 and was intended to investigate the effect of the Allied bombing campaign on German morale and German industry).

New tasks awaited Hartshorne in Europe in January 1945: the Supreme Headquarters of the Allied Expeditionary Forces (SHAEF) assigned him to various duties, first in Paris, then near Frankfurt. Among other things, he led the denazification of the staff of the *Kölnische Zeitung* in Cologne.

In May 1945, Hartshorne moved to Marburg. He was now the officer in charge of the reopening of the universities in the American Zone. Marburg, where his cousin Charles Hartshorne had studied, quickly became a home for him for the rest of his life. Until autumn 1945, he travelled back and forth between Marburg, Frankfurt, Heidelberg, Erlangen and Würzburg in order to advance the denazification of the universities in these cities. In Marburg, where the procedure was first applied with remarkable success, the so-called University Planning Committee, consisting of members of the faculties who had not been Nazis, oversaw the reopening of the university. Hartshorne is remembered as an American with outstanding expertise, and without whom the new beginning for German universities would not have been so successful.

In January 1946 Hartshorne published – under the name of his father-in-law, Sidney Fay – in the American journal *Forum* an article on the difficulties of reconstructing the universities in post-war Germany. In May 1946, the *Weekly Information Bulletin*, published by the military government, printed his assessment of the reopening of the universities.[63] In it he wrote:

> Since the German university faculties have a tradition of self-government stretching back to the Middle Ages, it was hoped that out of the wreckage of defeat each university would be able to put forward a 'citizens' committee' of this sort capable of taking charge and not merely working under MG directives but of doing the job – our job – to all intents and purposes for us, and better than we could have done it ourselves.[64]

At the end, he endorsed the occupational policy based on helping rather than on punishing:

> In short, we must endeavour to create for these 'higher schools of democracy' whatever modicum of freedom is possible within a society burdened by defeat and military occupation. We must continue at the same time to be alert and be sure we know at all times what is going on; but above all we must not let our suspicions stand in the way of the genuine and generous effort to help them.

He concluded with a quotation from Werner Richter's book *Re-Educating Germany*, which had appeared in the United States in 1945: 'One cannot simultaneously enslave and educate for freedom.'[65]

On 17 June 1946, Hartshorne's wife Elsa arrived in Marburg with their three children, Robin, Marian and Caroline. Although Talcott Parsons kept urging him to return to Harvard and resume his academic career there as soon as possible, Hartshorne had decided to remain at least two to three years longer in Germany in order to do what he could to help with the rebuilding and democratic reform of the country. He was highly respected by both his superiors in the military government and by Germans who had to deal with him. He was known for his capacity to find workable solutions to difficult cases and tricky situations, dealing admirably with a wide range of problems.

On 1 August 1946, Hartshorne was named denazification officer for Bavaria, while at the same time retaining his sphere of influence in Marburg. Denazification had been so poorly carried out at the University of Munich that newspapers in the United States considered it a scandal. Something had to be done, and Hartshorne was asked to take on the job. In the first three weeks of August, he travelled regularly between Munich and Marburg. On 21 August, he set out with his wife on a trip through Munich to Alpach in Tyrol, where he participated in a conference on methodological problems in philosophy. On the way back, they made a brief stop in Munich and then on 28 August got on the motorway and headed for Erlangen, planning to continue on to Marburg the next day.

The Hartshornes and their driver were travelling in a small car owned by the military government. At about 10.30 p.m., their car was overtaken by a jeep, and then, because the jeep suddenly slowed down, they were forced to overtake it in turn. As they did so, Hartshorne was struck in the head by a bullet fired through the car window and was so seriously wounded that he immediately lost consciousness and died two days later in the military hospital in Nuremberg.[66]

Lucius D. Clay, the American deputy military governor, wrote a personal letter of condolence to Elsa Hartshorne: 'Dr Hartshorne's outstanding work covering many years must be acknowledged by our Government with deepest appreciation. . . . As Chief of Higher Education in Greater Hesse, he developed the new universities in truly democratic form and with sympathy and understanding. . . . The crowning work of his activity was the International Semester beginning today in Marburg. . . . He will be sadly missed. . . . Our sincerest condolences are with you in this trying period of your bereavement.'[67] The *New York Times* reported Hartshorne's death on 1 September, the day on which the International Military Court began its work in Nuremberg.[68] Willy Hartner, the first post-war rector of the Johann Wolfgang Goethe University in Frankfurt, wrote in the *Frankfurter Rundschau*: 'The history of the most difficult period in German university life will always be associated with the name of E. Y. Hartshorne. Our universities will always preserve a grateful memory of this man who was so deeply devoted to his task in the service of humanity.'[69]

Who would murder a man who had done so much to rebuild a democratic Germany? Who could want to kill this man who had fought National Socialism out of deep conviction? Perhaps the motive was to be sought precisely therein. The Counter Intelligence Corps (CIC), which was the military government's unit responsible for denazification, had begun in 1946 to smuggle high-ranking National Socialists to South America by way of a secret route that passed through the Vatican. One of these refugees was Klaus Barbie, the 'Butcher of Lyon', who was living in Marburg under the name Altmann. He was employed *pro forma* by the CIC in Munich. Hartshorne may have known about this. On the way to Alpach, he seems to have interrupted his journey in Zurich and flown secretly to Stockholm, in order to give his sister Emily Mudd documents regarding the so-called 'ratline'.

In a conversation in Cambridge in 1992, Emily Mudd told me the following story: At that time she was on her way to Moscow with her husband, who had been invited to give a talk before the American-Soviet Medical Society. During a stopover in Stockholm, she met her brother in the airport. He handed her a sealed envelope, which she took on to Moscow, as they had agreed. They had also agreed that she would deliver the reply on her way back. But in the Moscow lecture hall someone gave her a note: her brother was no longer alive.

259

Emily Mudd's story may be a clue to who was responsible for Hartshorne's death. He may have 'betrayed' the secret escape route to Latin America used by Nazis coming out of the Soviet Union. His death served the interests of those who would otherwise have been put on trial. Thus he may have been the last victim of the system that he had battled so passionately for years.

# NOTES

INTRODUCTION

1   From Harry Kaufman's account, cf. pp. 231–5.
2   Quoted from Saul Friedländer, *Nazi Germany and the Jews*, vol. 1, *The Years of Persecution 1933–1939*, New York, 1997, p. 268. Cf. Trude Maurer, 'Abschiebung und Attentat. Die Ausweisung der polnischen Juden und der Vorwand für die *Kristallnacht*.' In Walter H. Pehle, ed., *Der Judenpogrom 1938. Von der 'Reichskristallnacht' zum Völkermord*. Frankfurt am Main, 1988, pp. 52–73.
3   In the hearings preparatory to his show trial in 1942, Grynszpan referred to these rumours and implied that he had had a homosexual relationship with vom Rath; this spared him being judged by the People's Court. But he was killed anyway – probably in the same year, in Sachsenhausen concentration camp. On the details of Grynszpan's fate and the preparations for the trial, see Hans-Joachim Döscher, *'Reichskristallnacht'. Die Novemberpogrome 1938*. Munich, 2000, pp. 159–84.
4   Facsimile in Döscher, op. cit., p. 79.
5   Max Domarus, ed., *Hitler. Reden und Proklamationen 1932–1945*. Leonberg, 1988, vol. 2, p. 574 f.
6   Instructions to the press quoted from Peter Longerich, *'Davon haben wir nichts gewusst!' Die Deutschen und die Judenverfolgung 1933–1945*. Berlin, 2006, p. 124.
7   Ruth Andreas-Friedrich, *Der Schattenmann. Tagebuchaufzeichnungen 1938–1945*. Berlin, 1947, p. 28 f.
8   For the most detailed account, see Angela Hermann, 'Hitler und sein Stosstrupp in der "Reichskristallnacht".' In *Vierteljahrshefte*

*für Zeitgeschichte* 56(4) (October 2008), pp. 603-19; here, p. 606 f.

9 Hitler neither referred to the attack in his speech on the evening of 8 November in the Bürgerbräukeller nor spoke about it during the state funeral for Ernst vom Rath on 17 November in Düsseldorf. See 'Die Fiktion eines spontanen Ausbruchs des Volkszorns gebot Schweigen'; Friedländer, op. cit., p. 300.

10 Ian Kershaw, *Hitler*. London, 2008, p. 461.

11 *Die Tagebücher von Joseph Goebbels. Im Auftrag des Instituts für Zeitgeschichte und mit Unterstützung des Staatlichen Archivdienstes Rußlands*, ed. Elke Fröhlich. Munich, 1993 ff., part 1, vol. 6, p. 178, entry for 9 November 1938.

12 *Zum Judenproblem. Januar 1937.* Quoted from *Die jüdische Emigration aus Deutschland. 1933-1941. Die Geschichte einer Austreibung. Eine Ausstellung der Deutschen Bibliothek Frankfurt am Main, unter Mitwirkung des Leo Baeck Instituts.* New York and Frankfurt am Main, 1985, p. 216.

13 Goebbels, *Tagebücher*, part I, vol. 6, p. 180, entry for 10 November 1938.

14 Quoted from Döscher, op. cit., p. 133.

15 Quoted from *Die jüdische Emigration aus Deutschland*, op. cit., p. 71.

16 Ibid., p. 68.

17 Ibid., p. 69 f.

18 Goebbels, *Tagebücher*, part I, vol. 4, p. 429, entry for 30 November 1937.

19 Quoted from *Die jüdische Emigration aus Deutschland*, op. cit., p. 71 f.

20 Goebbels, *Tagebücher*, part I, vol. 6, p. 180, entry for 10 November 1938.

21 According to the Supreme Court of the Nazi Party, in a decision issued on 13 February regarding the question of how Goebbels's speech and the carrying out of the orders were to be understood. It was necessary to call upon the party's court in order to fabricate a state of emergency and thus spare the perpetrators a criminal proceeding. Quoted from *Der Prozess gegen die Hauptkriegsverbrecher vor dem Internationalen Militärgerichtshof (IMT), Nürnberg 1948*, vol. 32, pp. 20-9.

22 Ibid.

23 Quoted from Friedländer, op. cit., p. 292.

24 Kershaw, op. cit., p. 458. 'Disorder and uncontrolled violence and destruction were not the SS's style.'

25 Facsimile in Döscher, op. cit., pp. 95–7.
26 Dachau: 10,911 deliveries; Buchenwald: 9,845 deliveries; Sachsenhausen an estimated 6,000–10,000 deliveries.
27 Goebbels, *Tagebücher*, part I, vol. 6, p. 182, entry for 11 November 1938.
28 Ibid.
29 Instructions to the press quoted in Longerich, op. cit., p. 125.
30 Quoted from Avraham Barkai, ' "*Schicksalsjahr 1938*". Kontinuität und Verschärfung der wirtschaftlichen Ausplünderung der deutschen Juden.' In Pehle, op. cit., p. 99.
31 It is all the more astounding that the stenographic record has still not been published *in toto*. The literature cites the partial record presented to the International Military Court in Nuremberg: IMT, op. cit., vol. 28, p. 499 ff. Cf. Döscher, op. cit., p. 123 f., there pp. 133–44.
32 Domarus, op. cit., vol. 3, p. 1058.
33 Harry Kaufman, unpublished manuscript (Houghton Library, Harvard University, bMS Ger 91, File 108); extracts from memoirs in this volume, pp. 231–5.
34 Both concepts were formed in connection with Auschwitz, but can be directly applied to the November pogroms. A good overview of the state of the question in Longerich, op. cit., pp. 7–21.
35 Longerich, op. cit., p. 24.
36 Ibid., p. 133.
37 *November Pogrom 1938. Die Augenzeugenberichte der Wiener Library, London.* Ed. Von Ben Barkow, Raphael Gross and Michael Lenarz. Frankfurt am Main, 2008.
38 Moritz Berger, unpublished manuscript (Houghton Library, Harvard University, bMS Ger 91, File 24).
39 On the approach of the organizers, the scholarly preparations, and the evaluation of the materials, see the Afterword, p. 236 ff.
40 Cf. the Bibliography, p. 275 ff.
41 Cf. the Editor's Note, p. vii ff.

### HUGO MOSES

1 In the German Reich, on 27 and 28 October 1938, Friday and Saturday, 16,000 Polish Jews were taken into custody pending expulsion and transported to the Polish border.
2 Two lines from the poem, 'Hoffnung' ('Hope') by Emanuel Geibel, 1815–1884.

3  On 11 November 1938, education minister Rust instructed the rectors of German universities to immediately suspend Jewish students and deny them entry to the universities; the same decree prohibited Jewish children from attending German schools.

## SIEGFRIED MERECKI

1  28 September was a Wednesday.
2  In the original, this word is blacked out.
3  The Gestapo headquarters were at Hotel Metropole on Morzinplatz; Stefan Zweig's *Schachnovelle* made the Gestapo headquarters famous.

## RUDOLF BING

1  Maxtorgraben 25.
2  Karolinenstrasse 16.
3  Julius Streicher, the Gauleiter of Franconia and the editor of the anti-Semitic hate sheet *Der Stürmer*, had said in his speech on 10 November: 'But we know that there are also people among us who have sympathy for the Jews, people who are not worthy of living in this city, not worthy of belonging to this people of which you are a proud part.'
4  This probably refers to the White Book on the Shootings of 30 July, in which was discussed, among other matters, the homosexuality among leading party members, especially in the ranks of the SA and Hitler Youth.

## TONI LESSLER

1  The private Waldschule Grunewald, founded by Toni Lessler in 1930, was at the corner of Hagenstrasse and Kronbergerstrasse. All non-Jewish pupils had to leave the school at Christmas 1933; afterwards the school, which from then bore the name Private Jüdische Waldschule Grunewald, accepted children who had been forced to leave their 'German' schools and had at times more than 400 pupils.

264

## SOFONI HERZ

1  Dr Leopold Jehuda Rothschild, who was director of the Jewish orphanage in Dinslaken from 1913 to 1938, had begun evacuating children to Palestine in 1935 and in the summer of 1938 emigrated there himself.

## MARIE KAHLE

1  This refers to the Munich Agreement of 30 September 1938, in which Great Britain and France accepted the cession of the Sudetenland to Germany. In opposition circles in Germany, people had hoped that the western powers would remain firm despite the threat of war and thereby deal Hitler a painful defeat.

2  Margarete Philippson, the wife of Alfred Philippson, professor emeritus of Geography at the University of Bonn; both the Philippsons, along with their daughter Dora, were deported to Theresienstadt, but survived and died in Bonn in 1953.

3  Dr Eduard Aigner of Freiburg, on 12 January 1939.

4  Mark 5:34; Luke 8:48: 'Daughter, your faith has made you well; go in peace, and be healed of your disease.'

## KARL E. SCHWABE

1  At the Gehringshof near Fulda, the Brith Chaluzim Datiim (Bachad), the association of religious pioneers, had organized an agricultural school in the form of a kibbutz; there young people were made familiar with the basics of agrarian life in Palestine.

2  Monday was 14 November 1938.

3  An agricultural school near Güstrow that prepared students for life in Palestine (cf. note 1 above).

4  Karl Koch (1897–1945), Obersturmbannführer, named in 1936 commandant in Sachsenhausen, from July 1937 commandant at Buchenwald; dismissed in 1941 and put 'on probation' for corruption; assigned in 1942 to develop the Majdanek death camp; executed by the SS in Buchenwald on 5 April 1945 for corruption.

5   Carl Haensel (1889–1968), *Der Bankherr und die Genien der Liebe*, Frankfurt am Main, 1938.

### GERTRUD WICKERHAUSER LEDERER

1   Arthur Rödl (1898–1945); 1937–1940, the first commandant of the detention camp in Buchenwald.

### KARL ROSENTHAL

1   In the original text, a skull and crossbones was drawn here.
2   Probably Dr Alfred Glücksmann (1875–1960), from 1912 to 1924 mayor (*Oberbürgermeister*) of Guben.
3   Hermann Baranowski (1884–1940), in 1936 appointed Schutz-haftlagerführer [detention camp commandant] in Dachau, and then in Sachsenhausen, where he became commandant on 1 May 1938.

### GEORG ABRAHAM

1   This account was written in February 1940 in Camp Kitchener, a refugee camp near Richborough, Kent, that served as an intermediate station for several thousand Jews from Germany, Austria and Czechoslovakia on their way overseas. The camp was shut down in June 1940; the remaining Jews, about 8,000 of them, were considered by the British to be 'enemy aliens' and deported to internment camps in Australia and Canada. Nothing is known of Georg Abraham's later life; cf. also the biography of Sofoni Herz (pp. 72–81).

### HERTHA NATHORFF

1   Ferdinand v. Bredow (1884–1934), retired major general and long-time confidant of the Reich defence minister and chancellor Kurt von Schleicher, murdered by the Nazis during the so-called 'Röhm putsch' on 30 June 1934. Since 1930, he had lived in the same building as the Nathorffs: Spichernstrasse 15.
2   Bellevuestrasse 8, in the Tiergarten district.
3   That is, for having performed an illegal abortion.

## CARL HECHT

1 Correct spelling, *Rankestrasse*; from 1935 to 1945 this was the name of Emil-Claar-Strasse in Frankfurt's Westend district. From there, Carl Hecht had about a half-hour walk to his place of work in Windmühlstrasse.
2 Now Münchener Strasse.
3 Frankfurt's Jews were taken to the Festhalle from 10 to 12 November 1938 and sent from there to Buchenwald.
4 Karl Koch (cf. the note on p. 265), the son of a Darmstadt registrar, had been an office employee, a bank officer and an insurance company representative before 1933, when he began his career in the SS, in which he rose quickly.

## ERNST BELLAK

1 In the original, the 'Berlin-Leipzig-Frankfurt night train'.

## SIEGFRIED WOLFF

1 The so-called Netherlandish hymn of thanks from the seventeenth century, which Kaiser Wilhelm II had popularized, was commonly sung during mass rallies under the Third Reich.

## MARGARETE NEFF

1 The manuscript, which runs to 83 pages, was submitted to Harvard under the pseudonym Franziska Schubert.
2 In 1936, Margarete Neff had married the lawyer Dr Alfred Junck, a childhood friend. It was her second marriage.
3 Since August 1938, the Central Office for Jewish Emigration, headed by Adolf Eichmann, had been located in the former Rothschild Palace, Prinz-Eugen-Strasse 20–22.
4 The official name of the Quakers, who provided various kinds of help for Jews seeking to emigrate.
5 The Gildemeester organization was set up after the annexation of Austria in March 1938; it coordinated the emigration of wealthy Jews who were not members of the Jewish religious community. In order to acquire the necessary emigration papers,

they had to turn over all their property to the trusteeship of a bank and deduct 10 per cent for the Gildemeester Fund, which used this money to pay travel costs for destitute Jews.

### FRITZ RODECK

1 The editors have only had access to the copy of pp. 122–56 that Edward Hartshorne had had made, along with the title sheet and Rodeck's cover letter (Pontiac, Michigan, 18 March 1940). The text by Fritz Rodeck archived in the Houghton Library under no. 188 (156 pages) was evidently confused with manuscript no. 116 (Koganowski, 175 pages).

2 Cf. Introduction, p. 2.

3 The Gauleiter of Vienna was SS-Standartenführer Odilo Globocnik, who ever since the Anschluss had had actions carried out against the Jews. His rival in the Vienna Nazi leadership was Josef Bürkel, Reich Commissar for the Reunification of Austria with the Reich.

4 On the conditions in the former convent school in the Kenyongasse which served as a holding camp, cf. also the accounts by Siegfried Merecki (p. 36 ff.) and Margarete Neff (p. 104 ff.).

5 The number of Jews deported from Vienna to Dachau in connection with the 'November action' is estimated to be 3,700.

6 Gänsbacherstrasse 5. Wilhelm and Edith Bauer lived on the ground floor, Richard and Margarethe Graubart on the first floor; both men were murdered on the night of 9–10 November.

7 Richard Berger, chairman of the religious community, was the third victim of the two SS men, Hans Aichinger and Walter Hopfgartner. In the records of the SD's Tyrol sub-department concerning the actions of that night, we find: 'If Jews have suffered no damages through this action, that may be attributable to the fact that they were overlooked.'

8 From the SD report: 'The Popper couple were thrown into the Sill after their apartment was demolished, but were able to reach the bank. The husband is among the prisoners.' The Innsbruck report can be found at www.doew.at/frames.php?/thema/thema_alt/wuv/pogrom_2/tirol.html

9 In Gänserndorf, near Vienna, a so-called emigrant-retraining camp was erected in late 1938 in order to speed up the emigra-

tion of Jews to Palestine: in fact, it was probably a labour camp to keep unemployed Jews busy.

### FRITZ GOLDBERG

1 Submitted to the Harvard competition under the pseudonym John Hay.

### HARRY KAUFMAN

1 This expression is also found in other texts submitted to Harvard in 1940. It echoes the title of the prize competition announcement, 'My life in Germany before and after 1933', and reflects the definitive nature of the farewell.

### AFTERWORD

1 Edgar Ansel Mowrer, *Germany Puts the Clock Back*, New York, 1933. In the third edition of November 1933, the journalist Dorothy Thompson, who was a friend of Helmuth James, Count Moltke, reported in a brief foreword that, because of this book, Mowrer had been forced to resign as chairman of the Foreign Press Club in Berlin and to leave Germany.

2 Edward Yarnall Hartshorne, Jr, *The German Universities and National Socialism* (London: Allen & Unwin, 1937, Cambridge, Mass.: Harvard University Press, 1937). The book was reissued in 1981. The frontispiece in the original edition showed the leaders of the German universities in the year of the Olympics, 1936; young men marching in rows of five, their torsos naked.

3 Letter from Hartshorne to Talcott Parsons, Albergo Alpino Plancidos, 31 December 1935, Parsons papers, Harvard University Archives, HUG(FP) – 42.8.2, Box 2.

4 'The German Intellectual of Today', typescript, 15 pages.

5 The transcripts of the discussions, made by participants, are preserved in Parsons papers, HUG(FP) – 42.45.1, Box 1.

6 Hartshorne, 'Numerical Changes in the German Student Body', in *Nature* 142 (July 1938): 175–8; Hartshorne, 'The German Universities and the Government', in *Annals of the American*

*Academy of Social and Political Science*, vol. 200 (November 1938): 210–34.

7  Parsons, 'Nazis Destroy Learning, Challenge Religion', rpt. in Uta Gerhardt (ed.), *Talcott Parsons on National Socialism* (New York: Aldine de Gruyter, 1993), pp. 81–3.

8  Theodore Abel, *Why Hitler Came Into Power* (New York: Prentice Hall, 1938, rpt. Harvard University Press: Cambridge, Mass., and London, England, 1986). Interestingly, Abel omitted from his analysis the 43 submissions written by women.

9  Ibid., pp. 183–4.

10  Ibid., p. 156.

11  Ibid., p. 163.

12  Ibid., p. 165.

13  Review by E. Y. Hartshorne, Harvard University, of three books on National Socialism, including Theodore Abel, *Why Hitler Came Into Power*. The review began with the sentence: 'Totalitarian society is one of the unique features of the contemporary world.' *The Journal of Social Philosophy* (April 1939): 277–80.

14  Ibid., 279.

15  Martin Bulmer, *The Chicago School of Sociology: Institutionalization, Diversity, and the Rise of Sociological Research* (Chicago: The University of Chicago Press, 1984); Dennis Smith, *The Chicago School: A Liberal Critique of Capitalism* (New York: St Martin's Press, 1988).

16  William Isaac Thomas and Florian Znaniecki, *The Polish Peasant in Europe and America* (Chicago: The University of Chicago Press, 1918–20).

17  Nels Anderson, *The Hobo: The Sociology of the Homeless Man* (Chicago: The University of Chicago Press, 1923).

18  John Dollard, *Criteria for the Life-History Method* (New Haven: Yale University Press, 1935).

19  Samuel Stouffer and Paul F. Lazarsfeld, *Research Memorandum on the Family in the Depression* (New York: Social Science Research Council, 1937).

20  Edward Wight Bakke, *The Unemployed Man: A Social Study* (New York: E. P. Dutton & Co., 1940).

21  Gordon W. Allport, *Personality: A Psychological Interpretation* (New York: H. Holt & Co., 1937).

22  On Allport's political activity during the Second World War, see Uta Gerhardt, *Talcott Parsons – An Intellectual Biography* (New York: Cambridge University Press, 2002), pp. 144–6.

23 Bruno Bettelheim, 'Individual and Mass Behavior in Extreme Situations', in *Journal of Abnormal and Social Psychology* 38 (1943): 417–51; Curt Bondy, 'Problems of Internment Camps', in *Journal of Abnormal and Social Psychology* 38 (1943): 453–75.

24 Sidney B. Fay, *The Origins of the World War* (New York: Macmillan, 1928).

25 Sidney B. Fay, 'Germany Should Not Be Dismembered', in *Current History* 1(1) (September 1941): 12–15.

26 Ibid., 15.

27 In his curriculum vitae, we find for 10 July 1941: 'Initiated project to collect life histories from Germans and others who lived in Germany before and after January 30, 1933, in collaboration with G. W. Allport and S. B. Fay, and with the help of grants from three independent, anonymous sources. Visited refugee centres in Paris, Holland and London, August 21–September 2 in this connection.'

28 G. W. Allport, J. S. Bruner, and E. M. Jandorf, 'Personality under Social Catastrophe: Ninety Life-Histories of the Nazi Revolution', in *Character and Personality* 10 (1941): 1–22.

29 Ibid., 21.

30 Ernest M. Jandorf, *Some Socio-Psychological Effects of the National Socialist Revolution – As Revealed by Ninety German Life-Histories*, Harvard College, April 1941 (typescript), p. 1.

31 Ibid., p. 2.

32 Ibid., p. 3. I thank Detlef Garz for drawing my attention to this passage.

33 This information taken from *Curriculum Vitae*: Edward Yarnall Hartshorne; Cambridge, Mass., 10 July 1941, *Papers at Scientific Meetings*.

34 Parsons, 'Memorandum: The Development of Groups and Organizations Amenable to Use against American Institutions and Foreign Policy and Possible Measures of Prevention', rpt. in *Talcott Parsons on National Socialism*, pp. 101–30.

35 Ibid., p. 119.

36 The stenographic transcripts of the papers and discussions are available in the Parsons papers, HUG(FP) – 15.2, Box 3.

37 Hartshorne, *German Youth and the Nazi Dream of Victory* (New York: Farrar & Rinehart, 1941).

38 Ibid., p. 12.

39 Hartshorne, 'Reactions to the Nazi Threat: A Study of Propaganda and Culture Conflict', in *Public Opinion Quarterly* 5 (November 1941): 625–39.

40 Hartshorne used the same concept as Edmond Taylor, *The Strategy of Terror* (Boston: Houghton Mifflin, 1940). In this book, Taylor had investigated the way French fears were both fuelled and undermined by the German propaganda campaign after 1933.
41 Hartshorne, 'Reactions to the Nazi Threat', p. 630.
42 Hartshorne, 'Social Structure and Charisma: A Note on Romantic Love and the Fuehrer Complex', typescript, 48 pages.
43 Ibid., p. 43.
44 Wayne S. Cole, *America First: The Battle Against Intervention 1940–1941* (Madison: University of Wisconsin Press, 1953).
45 Hartshorne, 'Taking Apart the Isolationist Case', in *The Christian Science Monitor* (12, 19 and 26 July 1941); quotation taken from 19 July installment.
46 Ibid., 12 July 1941.
47 Edward Hartshorne to John Farrar, 25 August 1941.
48 Newspapers all over the world reported with horror the events of November 1938. Cf. Deborah E. Lipstadt, *Beyond Belief: The American Press and the Coming of the Holocaust 1933–1945* (New York: Free Press, 1986).
49 The materials taken from newspapers – handwritten excerpts from twelve different newspapers from all parts of the world – are in the *Nazi Madness: November 1938* bundle (the handwriting is not Hartshorne's).
50 In 1943, Abraham – born in 1880 – published a book on Germany's international relations and in 1947 a further work that was published by the Harvard Graduate School of Public Administration. I thank Robin Hartshorne for this reference.
51 The documents for this collaborative book are available in the Parsons papers, filed under HUG(FP) – 42.42, Box 1, 15.2, Box 10 and 15.2, Box 11.
52 Hartshorne's unpublished article, 'Social Structure and Charisma: A Note on Romantic Love and the Fuehrer Complex', may have been a chapter or a preparatory work for the book to be written with Parsons.
53 Edward A. Strecker, *Beyond the Clinical Frontiers: A Psychiatrist Views Crowd Behavior* (New York: Norton, 1940); see also Edward A. Strecker and Kenneth E. Appel, *Psychiatry in Modern Warfare* (New York: Macmillan, 1945).
54 Brickner worked in close collaboration with the cultural anthropologist Margaret Mead, with whom Parsons and Harts-

horne also discussed National Socialism in letters and at conferences between 1940 and 1944.

55  Richard Brickner, *Is Germany Incurable?* (Philadelphia: Lippincott, 1943).

56  Ibid., p. 30.

57  Ibid., p. 304.

58  In 1937, Emily Hartshorne Mudd wrote 'An Analysis of One Hundred Consecutive Cases in the Marriage Council of Philadelphia'. The manuscript is available University of Pennsylvania, Philadelphia, University Archives and Record Center, Mudd Family Papers, 1919–1980, signature UPT 50 M944, Box 1, FF 4. The article was published in *Mental Hygiene* 2(2) (April 1939): 198–217.

59  See the diary entries written in Paris in January and February 1945, when Hartshorne was giving lectures to officers of the future military government (the subjects included the judicial and educational systems in Germany and 'The German Character and Our Information Policy') and also supervising the PWD's interrogators.

60  For the diary entries: Klaus Mann, *Tagebücher 1944 bis 1949*, ed. Joachim Heimannsberg, Peter Laemmle and Wilfried F. Schoeller (Munich: Edition Spangenberg, 1991), pp. 29, 42, 47, 98.

61  In Klaus Mann, the reference is to 'Zwei Deutsche', in *Mit dem Blick nach Deutschland. Der Schriftsteller und das politische Engagement*, ed. and with an afterword by Michael Grunewald (Munich: Edition Spangenberg in the Ellerwald Verlag, 1985), pp. 114–16; there the addendum 'as yet unpublished, undated typescript produced in 1944' and the note that it was a radio talk prepared by Mann for the American Fifth Army on the Italian front. In Hartshorne, the reference is to the manuscript 'Introduction to Two Captured Diaries', Psychological Warfare Branch Ref. DOC/22, 3 p.

62  William Frend, 'Ein Beweis der tiefen Uneinigkeit. Ernst von Weizsäcker, die deutsche Botschaft und der englische Geheimdienst im Rom des Jahres 1944', in *Frankfurter Allgemeine Zeitung* (12 July 1997).

63  E. Y. Hartshorne, 'Reopening German Universities', in *Weekly Information Bulletin* 43 (27 May 1946): 5–9.

64  Ibid., 6.

65  Ibid., 8. Werner Richter had been a state secretary in the Prussian ministry of religion.

66  Strangely, in Harvard College's memorial book for the class of 1933, published in the 1950s, Hartshorne is said to have been 'killed in the war by a "sniper"' rather than assassinated.

67  Letter from Gen. Lucius D. Clay to Elsa Hartshorne, 2 September 1946.

68  'U. S. Official in Germany Dies of Bullet Wounds', in *New York Times* (Sunday, 1 September 1946), p. 24.

69  'Dr. Edward Y. Hartshorne – In memoriam', in *Frankfurter Rundschau* (3 September 1946), p. 4.

# BIBLIOGRAPHY

INDIVIDUAL PUBLICATIONS FROM THE HARVARD COLLECTION BMSGER 91

Bärwald, Alice (forthcoming) *Kulturbürgerin, Jüdin und Deutsche. Aberkennung in nationaler Unbestimmtheit. Portrait einer Emigrantin aus Danzig.* Ed. Wiebke Lohfeld and Detlef Garz.

Bing, Rudolf (1988) 'Mein Leben in Deutschland nach dem 30. Januar 1933', *Mitteilungen des Vereines zur Geschichte der Stadt Nürnberg* 75: 189–210.

Frankenthal, Käthe (1981) *Der dreifache Fluch: Jüdin, Intellektuelle, Sozialistin. Lebenserinnerungen einer Ärztin in Deutschland und im Exil.* Ed. Kathleen M. Pearl and Stephan Leibfried, Frankfurt am Main/New York.

Gebhard, Bruno (1976) *Im Strom und Gegenstrom. 1919–1937*, Wiesbaden.

Gyßling, Walter (2002) *Mein Leben in Deutschland vor und nach dem 30. Januar 1933. Der Anti-Nazi. Handbuch im Kampf gegen die NSDAP.* Ed. and introduction by Leonidas E. Hill, Bremen.

Hallgarten, Constanze (1956) *Als Pazifistin in Deutschland – biographische Skizze*, Stuttgart.

Hirschberg, Max (1998) *Jude und Demokrat. Erinnerungen eines Münchener Rechtsanwalts 1883–1939.* Prepared by Reinhard Weber, München.

Kahle, Marie (2003) *Was hätten Sie getan? Die Flucht der Familie Kahle aus Nazi-Deutschland. Paul Kahle: Die Universität Bonn vor und während der Nazi-Zeit (1923–1939).* Ed. John H. Kahle (?) and Wilhelm Bleek. 2nd expanded edn, Bonn (1st edn

1998; both texts first published privately in England, London 1945).

Katz, H. W. (1994) *No. 21 Castle Street, New York 1940* (published in German under the title: *Schlossgasse 21. In einer kleinen deutschen Stadt*, Weinheim).

Löwith, Karl (1986) *Mein Leben in Deutschland vor und nach 1933*. With a foreword by Reinhard Koselleck and an afterword by Ada Löwith, Stuttgart.

Nathorff, Hertha (1987) *Das Tagebuch der Hertha Nathorff. Aufzeichnungen 1933–1945*. Ed. and introduced by Wolfgang Benz, Munich.

Reuß, Friedrich Gustav Adolf (2001) *Dunkel war über Deutschland. Im Westenwar ein letzter Widerschein von Licht*. Ed. Ursula Blömer and Sylke Bartmann, Oldenburg.

Salzburg, Friedrich (2001) *Mein Leben in Dresden vor und nach dem 30. Januar 1933*. Prepared and introduced by Sabine Wenzel, Dresden.

Samuel, Arthur (1999/2000) 'Mein Leben in Deutschland vor und nach dem 30. Januar 1933', in *Bonner Geschichtsblätter* (vol. 49/50), pp. 399–457.

Vordtriede, Käthe (1999) *'Es gibt Zeiten, in denen man welkt.' Mein Leben in Deutschland vor und nach 1933*. Ed., with an afterword, by Detlef Garz, Lengwil.

Wysbar, Eva (2000) *'Hinaus aus Deutschland irgendwohin . . .' Mein Leben in Deutschland vor und nach 1933*. With forewords by Maria Wisbar Hansen and Tania Wisbar and an afterword by Detlef Garz, Lengwil.

SECONDARY LITERATURE (INCLUDING TITLES WITH EXTRACTS FROM THE HARVARD COLLECTION)

Allport, G. W., Bruner, J. S. and Jandorf, E. M. (1941) 'Personality under Social Catastrophe: Ninety Life-Histories of the Nazi Revolution', *Character and Personality* 10: 1–22.

Bartmann, Sylke (2006) *Flüchten oder Bleiben? Rekonstruktion biographischer Verläufe und Ressourcen von Emigranten im Nationalsozialismus*, Wiesbaden.

Bartmann, Sylke, Blömer, Ursula and Garz, Detlef (eds) (2003) *'Wir waren die Staatsjugend, aber der Staat war schwach.' Jüdische Kindheit und Jugend in Deutschland und Österreich zwischen*

*Kriegsende und nationalsozialistischer Herrschaft*, Oldenburg: Selbstverlag Universität Oldenburg.

Bartmann, Sylke and Garz, Detlef (1999/2000) 'Wir waren vogelfrei.' *Bonner Geschichtsblätter* 49/50: 457–90.

Becker, Eva D. (2000) 'Autobiographie im Exil', *Exil* 20(2): 15–27.

Blömer, Ursula (1997) 'Emigrantenbiographien. Biographische Untersuchungen zu Lebensverläufen deutschsprachiger Emigranten im Nationalsozialismus. Projektmitteilung.' *BIOS, Zeitschrift für Biographieforschung und Oral History* 1: 128–32.

Blömer, Ursula (2001) *'Im uebrigen wurde es still um mich'. Aberkennungsprozesse im nationalsozialistischen Deutschland*, Oldenburg.

Blömer, Ursula and Garz, Detlef (1998) ' "Es war ein langsames Getriebenwerden . . ." ' Biographieanalyse eines nichtjüdischen Emigranten.' *BIOS, Zeitschrift für Biographieforschung und Oral History*: 76–102.

Blömer, Ursula and Garz, Detlef (eds) (2000) *'Wir Kinder hatten ein herrliches Leben . . .' Jüdische Kindheit und Jugend im Kaiserreich 1871–1918*, Oldenburg.

Garz, Detlef (2005) ' "Mein Leben in Deutschland vor und nach dem 30. Januar 1933." Das wissenschaftliche Preisausschreiben der Harvard Universität und seine in die USA emigrierten Teilnehmerinnen und Teilnehmer aus dem deutschen Sprachraum,' in John M. Spalek, Konrad Feilchenfeldt and Sandra H. Hawrylchak (eds), *Deutschsprachige Exilliteratur seit 1933*. Vol. 3: USA. Munich, pp. 305–33.

Garz, Detlef (forthcoming) *Margarete Neff: 'Und, lieber Gott, lass mich eine Schauspielerin werden'* .

Garz, Detlef and Lee, Hyo-Seon (2003) 'Mein Leben in Deutschland vor und nach dem 30. Januar 1933', in Irmtraud Wojak and Susanne Meinl (eds), *Im Labyrinth der Schuld. Täter – Opfer – Ankläger. Zur Geschichte und Wirkung des Holocaust*. Ed. for the Fritz-Bauer-Institut. Yearbook 2003, Frankfurt am Main/New York, pp. 333–57.

Garz, Detlef, Blömer, Ursula and Kranke, Stefan (1996) ' "Mein Leben in Deutschland vor und nach dem 30. Januar 1933." Projektskizze', in Friedrich Busch (ed.), *Aspekte der Bildungsforschung in Oldenburg*, Oldenburg, pp. 175–89.

Gerhardt, Uta (2009) 'Ein Amerikaner der Stunde Null. Edward Y. Hartshorne und die Wiederanfänge 1945–1946', in Uta Gerhardt, *Soziologie im zwanzigsten Jahrhundert. Studien zu ihrer Geschichte in Deutschland*, Stuttgart, pp. 131–78.

Gerhardt, Uta (forthcoming) 'Idealtypen in der fallvergleichenden Forschung der historischen Biographieanalyse', in Gerd Jüttemann (ed.), *Komparative Kasuistik*, 2nd edn, Weinheim/Munich.

Hartshorne, Edward Y. (1941) *German Youth and the Nazi Dream of Victory*, New York.

Hartshorne, Edward Y. (1941) 'Reactions to the Nazi Threat: A Study of Propaganda and Culture Conflict.' *Public Opinion Quarterly* 5: 625–39.

Hill, Leonidas E. (1993) 'Walter Gyssling, the Centralverein and the Büro Wilhelmstrasse, 1929–1933,' *Leo Baeck Institute Yearbook*, vol. 38: 193–208.

Liebersohn, Harry and Schneider, Dorothee (2001) '*My Life in Germany Before and After January 30, 1933': A Guide to a Manuscript Collection at Houghton Library, Harvard University*. *Transactions of the American Philosophical Society*, vol. 91, pt 3, Philadelphia.

Limberg, Margarete and Rübsaat, Herbert (eds) (1990) *Sie durften nicht mehr Deutsche sein. Jüdischer Alltag in Deutschland 1933– 1938*, Frankfurt am Main.

Lixl-Purcell, Andreas (ed.) (1988) *Women of Exile: German-Jewish Autobiographies since 1933*, New York.

Lixl-Purcell, Andreas (ed.) (1992) *Erinnerungen jüdischer Frauen 1900–1990*, Leipzig.

Lohfeld, Wiebke (1998) *Es waren die dunkelsten Tage in meinem Leben. Krisenprozeß und moralische Entwicklung. Eine qualitative Biographieanalyse*, Frankfurt am Main.

Lohfeld, Wiebke (2003) *Im Dazwischen. Porträt der jüdischen und deutschen Ärztin Paula Tobias (1896–1970)*, Opladen.

Lohfeld, Wiebke (2007) 'Aberkennung und historisches Beispiel. Das Beispiel Alice Bärwald', *Zeitschrift für Qualitative Forschung* 8(2): 225–48.

Milton, Sibyl (1984) 'Women and the Holocaust: The Case of German and German-Jewish Women', in Renate Bridenthal, Atina Grossmann and Marion Kaplan (eds), *When Biology Becomes Destiny: Women in Weimar and Nazi Germany*, New York, pp. 297–302 and 317–22.

Quack, Sibylle (1995) *Zuflucht Amerika. Zur Sozialgeschichte der Emigration deutsch-jüdischer Frauen in den USA 1933–1945*, Bonn.

Richarz, Monika (ed.) (1982) *Jüdisches Leben in Deutschland*. Vol. 3: *Selbstzeugnisse zur Sozialgeschichte 1918–1945*, Stuttgart.

Schad, Martha (2001) *Frauen gegen Hitler. Schicksale im nationalsozialistischen München*, Munich.

Vordtriede, Käthe (1998) '*Mir ist es noch wie im Traum, dass mir diese abenteuerliche Flucht gelang . . .*' *Briefe nach 1933 aus Freiburg im Breisgau, Frauenfeld und New York an ihren Sohn Werner*, Lengwil.

Weissberg, Liliane (1998) 'Preisfragen zu einem Leben in Deutschland vor und nach 1933 – das Beispiel Karl Löwith.' *Exil* 18(2): 14–23.